Think life as a [illegible] life in and out of the classroom is [illegible] and think again! – *Theo Griff, Teach* [illegible] *s. Educational consultant, author and* [illegible]

Becoming a teacher is a privilege. Packed full of anecdotes from teachers that will make you smile, cringe and laugh aloud, this book is a must for anyone considering a career in teaching. Sarah Mullin's collection of generous, honest reflections from colleagues shows us why teaching is truly the best job in the world – *Professor Dame Alison Peacock, DBE, DL, DLitt Hon Fellow Queens' College, Cambridge, CEO of the Chartered College of Teaching, Visiting Professor of the University of Hertfordshire, Teach First trustee, author*

An entertaining yet highly educative book; one which so accurately captures the roller-coaster of emotions and experiences that colleagues encounter in the classroom. There is something to learn and reflect upon in each of the experiences shared. This book is pure genius and is a 'must read' for anyone interested in entering the wonderful and rewarding world of teaching. So, sit back and devour! – *Professor Michael Green, Associate Executive Director of People Development, Dartmoor Multi-Academy Trust, visiting professor, author*

Storytelling is such an important part of how we process our identities, explore our world, build relationships and create a sense of belonging. Stories humanise us and create shared understanding. As teachers, we use storytelling as a way to bring learning to life. This collection of stories from educators in the classroom, compiled during the global pandemic, creates a shared narrative of the teaching profession. With a range of voices and lived experiences sharing the highs, the lows and the a-ha moments of being a teacher, this book will have you nodding, laughing and weeping as you devour it. – *Hannah Wilson, Director of Diverse Educators @DiverseEd2020, former Executive Headteacher, resilience trainer, Co-founder of WomenEd, former Head of Secondary Education at the University of Buckingham*

This is the book which should be slipped quietly into the bag of every new teacher across the globe as a secret gift for them to discover and delight in. It is page after page of utter joy, warmth, encouragement and a thousand reminders of why working with children is the greatest privilege and the greatest fun. Packed with stories, anecdotes and words of wisdom from across the sector, this is a book which is sure to raise a smile, offer a friendly hand of collegiate reassurance and illuminate why teaching is the sparkling jewel in the crown of all the professions—even if that jewel is glued on messily onto a wonky cardboard crown in the school play. Another absolute triumph from Sarah Mullin, who has once again brought together the voices of teaching in beautiful and uplifting professional harmony—a massed choir of encouragement and positivity. – *Emma Turner FCCT, Research and CPD Lead Discovery Trust*

Sarah and her writing team have once again provided such a gift to the sector. In the demands of working in schools, we can easily be trapped into feeling we are alone in the challenges we face. In facing these challenges, some of the most powerful knowledge we can share is that of our stories. These stories can take all shapes and sizes: the funny ones, the poignant ones, the stories of success, and the stories sharing when it didn't quite go to plan. Every author in this book has provided a story that will be the hand on the shoulder of every teacher across the sector, offering kindness, celebration, reassurance, humour and resolve. – *Dr. Neil Gilbride BSc (Hons) MEd (Cantab) PGCE MBPsS FHEA PhD, Lecturer in Education, ACL for PGCE Secondary Education, PI: Getting Heads Together ERASMUS+ Project, University of Gloucestershire*

Chronicles from the Classroom: Great insights from practitioners; gruesome and glorious in equal measure. – *Mary Myatt, education writer, speaker and curator of Myatt & Co.*

This book is a gift to trainee teachers, new teachers, experienced teachers and retired teachers. Sarah, once again, has captured the essence of teaching, the ups and downs of days in the classroom from around the world. We hear of socks on radiators, fun in the playground, school trips, as well as challenges for teachers and how to remain positive when all seems lost. The pages are imbued with wisdom from powerful narratives that capture the wonder and joy of being a teacher and remind us that when things get tough, teachers get tougher! This is a must read for anyone in or joining the profession. – *Miriam Colum. Lecturer in Inclusive Education. School Placement Coordinator. Marino Institute of Eduction, Trinity College Dublin*

As always with Sarah this book is a powerful combination of hilarious anecdotes and profound truths about the power and often raw emotion of being a teacher. Stories help us make sense of the world and the important ways in which we connect with and have impact on others. This book is an uplifting example of teacher positivity at its best—just like its author! – *Professor Samantha Twiselton. Director of Sheffield Institute of Education (SIoE). Vice President of the Chartered College of Teaching*

A highly entertaining book which will make you laugh and cry simultaneously about life in a classroom. It also shows that you are not alone; the stories in this book show the good and tough times of being a teacher. If you are looking for a book to show you the wonderfully rewarding career that is teaching, then I'd highly recommend this one. – *Jonathan Coy NPQH FCCT, Founder of HeadteacherChat, Former Primary School Headteacher*

Chronicles from the Classroom is a delightful cornucopia of stories from the chalk face that will inspire, delight and motivate aspiring and existing teachers. As ever Sarah Mullin has curated this book with thoughtfulness and heart to reflect the joys, delight and occasional tribulations of teaching! – *Rae Snape. Headteacher and National Leader of Education. Author of the Primary Headteacher's Handbook*

There are many things in this book that will be useful to anyone starting their career as a teacher. I'm not thinking of the entertaining anecdotes—but I discovered that high absorbent green towels are the teacher's equivalent of the sports coach's magic sponge. Nor am I thinking of the many examples of advice and guidance gained from years of experience in the classroom—but they are legion, insightful and immensely helpful. No, I'm thinking of the extraordinary diversity in circumstance and challenge faced by the teachers who offered contributions to this volume, all of whom draw inspiration and energy from their sense of professionalism.

Of course, as one of them tells us, life as a teacher is interestingly more than 'crisp and polished professionalism', but also requires a sense of humour and perspective. Oh, and you know how everyone remembers at least one teacher from their time in school? Well, it turns out every teacher remembers at least one class—and often more—from their time in school!

A final note to keep in mind for the beginning teacher is that some of those consummate professionals you'll see, who seem to engage with their pupils with effortless skill, have been teaching for longer than you've been alive—so don't envy them, learn from them! – *Professor Tony Gallagher, Professor of Education at Queen's University, Belfast*

Like many of the contributors to this excellent book, becoming a teacher was something I aspired to from an early age. 'Playing' school with my sister and our friends, who were 'encouraged' to take the role of my 'class', was my absolutely favourite childhood game, and although it may not have been theirs, I convinced myself that I was teaching them some valuable lessons. When I entered the teaching profession as a very excited newly qualified teacher, I really did consider that I had made it and had achieved my ambition. I convinced myself that the stories from my classroom, which I shared with my friends and family, were as amusing, sad and thought provoking to them as they were to me. However, in reality I didn't quite have the right audience—it was in the company of other teachers where I realised that our shared experiences, good and bad, where we laughed and cried and moaned, was where our story telling had resonance. *Chronicles from the Classroom* replicates these shared experiences with huge success. All teachers, whether experienced or new to the profession, should be encouraged to read this book. - *Professor Lynne McKenna, Dean of the Faculty of Education and Society, University of Sunderland*

This book will enthral you and give you hope that what you are doing as a teacher is more than just teach. It makes one feel part of a community, with stories and reflections that point to some kind of solidarity that had probably been hitherto untapped in education publications. Indeed, the book stresses the humanity of the role and accessibly engages every reader who wants to seek a genuine (and sometimes humorous too) re-appraisal of what education is really about in the 'day-to-dayness' of practice

Lovely to have by your bed and dip in and out of it to re-connect with a pedagogy of love and hope—something so much more needed these days! - *Dr Karima Kadi-Hanifi, Director of Post-graduate Studies, Graduate School, Newman University*

Chronicles from the Classroom is a delight. Drawing on the experiences of teachers from across the educational continuum, it challenges, encourages, entertains and, above all, inspires. Story is at the heart of the human experience—and is at the heart of this book. We are brought into the daily lives of teachers and their students and helped to understand what it means to be part of a school community in a manner that is both relatable and uplifting. For those of us who have spent time in a classroom, there will be moments of recognition, and for those who have not had that chance, there may be moments of perhaps revelation and explanation. I can't recommend this book highly enough, and look forward to dipping into it in the coming months and years. – *Professor Joe O'Hara, Professor of Education, Dublin City University Institute of Education, Director Centre for Evaluation, Quality and Inspection (EQI), President European Educational Research Association (EERA)*

In her book *Chronicles from the Classroom: The treats, truths, trials and tribulations of working in education*, Sarah Mullin collates the words of wisdom and experiences from across the world of teaching, drawing on a range of voices from various contexts to explore both what it means to be a teacher and how we can improve.

From sharing inspirational moments, to reminding us of why teaching is such a beautiful profession, to exploring how teachers have developed and collaborated, to seeing what we can do when things go wrong, there is much to take away from this book.

Experienced teachers will nod, and sometimes laugh, along with stories of school trips and tales of students jumping out of the classroom windows (something many of us will have experienced), and those new to the profession will find guidance on securing a teaching role and tips which will help them to make the most of their time in the classroom. The stories within, some short and snappy, some reflecting in more depth, provide something for all, and this will be a text I am certain I will be dipping in and out of time and again, always finding something new to explore.

What is so important about this book is that it gives a platform to the voices of teachers. It reveals the reality of what they are doing day by day and how they have overcome challenges in order to do exactly what we know all teachers strive to do: be a little bit better all the time.

The tales within are woven together by Sarah's narrative, as she reflects on what each of the different chapters mean for teachers, and education as a whole, and opens up a window for us to look at the different experiences of teachers and really learn from them. – *Zoe Enser, Evidence Lead in Education (ELE) for Kent, author*

This book is 'unputdownable'! It is filled with entertaining, heart-warming, funny and true stories that illustrate the joys, highs and lows of the best job in the world. What a treat to read—but if you pick it up, be prepared to not put it down until it is finished! – *Dr Victoria Carr, Headteacher, TEDx speaker, British Army Reservist*

Entering teaching is a little like entering the cupboard to Narnia. A wonderland of delights and treats can await, but so can tricks and traps to trip you up. Sarah does it again, bringing together an array of stories and anecdotes from a variety of people in the profession. If you need a reminder as to why teaching is an incredible job, then read this book. If you want to laugh, nod and say 'No way! That happened to me!', then read this book. Regardless of how long you have been teaching for, this is a must read. – *Sam Strickland, Principal of The Duston School*

As we induct beginning teachers into the complexities of 'Teacherly Knowledge' (Shulman, 1987), we often struggle to convey the passion, commitment and humanity associated with this wonderful profession. This book does this with a range of voices, contexts and experiences painting a picture of the many highs and lows we experience when we embark on a teaching career. There is much in this collection of narratives to inspire and reassure all teachers, and most significantly to motivate future educators to take that first step into a classroom in order to make the difference we all hope to achieve through teaching and interacting with children and young people. Moreover, Sarah's ability to offer words of wisdom in between each of the many themes she has identified reassures us of the impact educators can and will have in schools, colleges, and even prisons and beyond as our students go on to shape their own futures. The book will be something for our new teachers to dip into throughout their professional journey: it offers reassurance, inspiration and joy. – *Amanda Brougham, Strategic Lead for Educational Partnerships, Birmingham City University*

This collection of stories edited by Sarah Mullin is a joyful celebration of every facet of teaching. Each anecdote and memory highlights the heart and soul of education and is why we are all so privileged to be a part of this profession, from trainee to teacher to school leader to lecturer in Initial Teacher Education. If you want to know why we teach, the answers will be found in this book. – *Dr Branwen Bingle, Head of Primary Initial Teacher Education at Newman University, Birmingham*

Teaching can be incredibly uplifting, hopeful, exhausting, inspiring, devastating, exciting and bellyachingly hilarious. Sarah's book captures this all, and so much more. Prepare for a treasure trove of honest, reflective and downright awe-inspiring stories and advice from a diverse range of educators that capture the absolute heart of being a teacher. My new go-to whenever I need a reminder of why this job is the absolute best in the world. What a privilege. Thank you, Sarah. – *Thahmina Begum, Headteacher*

As teachers we love a story—and every teacher is a teller of stories. You will find a whole raft of stories in this book to inspire, reassure and develop you as a teacher. From children jumping out of windows, to finding your style as a teacher, this book has so much humour, wisdom and comfort to offer to teachers at any stage of their career. – *Andrew Taylor, Mr T has been an NQT mentor for 11 years. He runs the popular Twitter page @MrTs_NQTs*

If there was ever a book that brought back all the rollercoaster moments of teaching, Sarah's *Chronicles From The Classroom* does just that! A wonderfully written book in which teachers share their honest reflections, expressing the highs and lows of a job that just keeps on giving. Grab a tea or coffee, sit back and immerse yourself in the wonder of a job in education: you will not be disappointed! – *Michael Chiles, Associate Assistant Principal, Chartered Geographer, author of the bestselling books 'The Craft of Assessment', 'The Feedback Pendulum', and 'The Sweet Spot'*

I'm not convinced one ever really 'becomes' a teacher—in reality, one is always in a state of 'becoming'—we're better teachers now than we were last year (and after the year we've had, we're better teachers in so many ways we could never have imagined!). Sarah Mullin's latest collection of stories, anecdotes and tales from the classroom demonstrates that process—of becoming—very well indeed. From the magic properties of paper towels, through to determined and (note that—determined AND caring, not determined but caring) antiracist work, through to giving ourselves permission to be human and to laugh at and with ourselves—this volume is excellent reading both for those just starting out in the profession and those of us who have trouble remembering a time we were not 'teachers'. For those just starting out—these stories and reflections will inspire you to keep going through those first, dauting and sometimes seemingly unending first few terms. For those of us who have been around … well, a bit longer, *Chronicles from the Classroom* reminds us why we do the job. Teachers are agents of change—and this volume proves just how important that change can be. – *Dr Janet Goodall, Associate Professor in Education at Swansea University*

When Sarah says 'Being a teacher means embarking on an exciting career with limitless opportunities', she's absolutely right. When I started, I had no idea that 40+ years later I would be doing what I do today. Others have very different opportunities and take very paths, and this is what this wonderful book shows. From Jeanne Rogers' story about being LGBT in the teaching profession, through Rochelle McFarlane's powerful messages about being a young black teacher (Representation really does matter!) to Margaret George playing with the 'F' word, Prof. Colin Richards' narrow escape and, of course, Annie Pendrey's magic paper towel (!), this

book is a joy to read. It is a compendium of what makes teaching magical and deserves to be in every teacher's goodie bag. As Sarah concludes and so many of us concur; 'Teaching really is the best job in the world!'
– Paul Garvey, Educational mentor

Chronicles from the Classroom

The treats, truths, trials and tribulations of working in education

Sarah Mullin

Word & Deed Publishing Incorporated
1860 Appleby Line, Suite #778
Burlington, Ontario, Canada, L7L 7H7

Chronicles from the Classroom

Copy-editing by Steve Viau, Pointed View Editing
Additional Editing by SJE Editing
Book design: Jim Bisakowski – www.bookdesign.ca

978-1-7773454-4-0

Word & Deed Publishing Incorporated
1860 Appleby Line, Suite #778
Burlington, Ontario, Canada, L7L 7H7
(Toll Free) 1-866-601-1213
Visit our website at
www.wordanddeedpublishing.com

Dedication

For all the children I have taught over the years. Thank you for the wonderful memories you have given me. You may have left my classroom, but you are often in my thoughts.

For all the contributors who have shared their stories for this collection of narratives. Thank you for helping me to create the book that I have always wanted to read.

For the family, friends and colleagues who have listened to me sharing my own chronicles from the classroom over the years. Thank you for your continued support.

For my children, Sean, Oisin and Susanna. Thank you for putting the biggest smile on my face every single day; you make everything I do feel truly worthwhile.

For all those working in the field of education during the Covid_19 pandemic. Thank you for going above and beyond the call of duty every single day to educate the nation's children and young people. Your legacy will be etched into the hearts and minds of those whose lives you have made a difference to. One day your name will be shared when people recall their own chronicles from the classroom.

Contents

Chpt. 3 So Much More Than Just a Teacher – 61

Chpt. 4 Expect the Unexpected – 109

Chpt. 5 Collaboration NOT Competition – 141

Chpt. 6 When Things Go Wrong – 167

Chpt. 7 The Challenging Times – 199

Chpt. 8 Things Can Only Get Better – 219

Chpt. 9 Being Employed as a Teacher – 247

Chpt. 10 Top Teacher Tips – 275

Foreword

Why Stories?

Professor Rachel Lofthouse

The life we lead in education organically creates amazing stories. As professionals, we enter the classroom and re-tread school territory that is both strangely familiar and disarmingly new; the story that unfolds there is already the sequel. Doors open to rooms and cupboards we would not have been allowed entry to as children, but the noise, the smells, and the purpose of the places welcome us back. We rub shoulders with our childhood selves. The stories we tell, culled from our teaching experiences, depict both episodes and scenes in which we played central roles or were curious bystanders. These stories represent moments in our past narratives that thread forwards into the future. Our lives as professionals continue to evolve and to evoke emotions, reactions and actions. They entwine with our personal lives as children from our families enter and leave education, and we put on our non-teaching hats and join in the community of parents. They spin into public spaces as we meet the excitable children in the local swimming pool, or the young people we taught when they pull us a pint at the pub.

The wonderful thing about teachers' stories are how they can make us laugh, make us cry, raise our spirits and make us feel less alone. They invite us to imagine the other times and places that our teacher peers have inhabited. They bring to life the characters we taught or colleagues we worked with, and allow us to notice and celebrate their quirks, flaws and flourishes. Our stories, as teachers, connect our daily practices with the grand narratives of our communities and society and with the life-long hopes and dreams of every person we come close to.

Rachel Lofthouse, Professor of Teacher Education
Director of CollectivED, Leeds Beckett University

Introduction

The Art of Storytelling

'Share your knowledge.
It is a way of achieving immortality'
– *Dali Lama*

Everyone working in education has a story to tell. From that dreaded time a child escaped from the classroom by jumping out of the ground floor window to the mystical powers of a wet paper towel used by teachers to 'cure' a myriad of ailments, there are so many memorable moments that happen in classrooms across the country every single day.

There are the inspirational stories which fill our hearts with pride as we recall the student who achieved success in the face of adversity, or the challenging moments in the courses of our careers which we navigated to victory. There are the stories where we find ourselves fighting back tears as we remember the students who turned up to school each day despite navigating dire personal circumstances. And then there are the side-splittingly hilarious stories; the stories that cause us to shake our heads in disbelief at the cringeworthy moments that we simply wish we could forget!

Stories have the power to connect us. It is through storytelling that we share our lived experiences, allowing us to reflect on our own values and viewpoints. A powerful story can capture hearts and minds, and there is no greater story than the educational narrative.

"None of us are to be found in sets of tasks or lists of attributes; we can only be known in the unfolding of our unique stories within the context of everyday events". – Vivian Gussin Paley

This book contains an eclectic collection of narratives from education professionals at all stages of their careers who explore the treats, truths, trials and tribulations of working in education. The stories you will read have been written to inspire, support and entertain you. Some of the narratives may have you laughing out loud, some may offer you an opportunity for reflection—and some may even cause you to shake your head in disagreement! The views expressed in this book are each individual contributor's own, and they may differ from the viewpoints, experiences or research of myself and others. We simply wish to share with you our experiences and perceptions of working in the wonderful world of education.

You are invited to 'dip in and out' of each of the ten chapters in this book, which have been collated into broad themes. You will find recurring themes and patterns, paradoxes and contradictions throughout each chapter, which is illustrative of the very nature of our profession. No two days in the world of education are ever the same, and each author acknowledges that the best professionals are continually growing, developing, and honing our craft so that we can have an evidence-informed understanding of what works best for our learners in our own contexts and settings. This book provides a space for educators to share their reflections, ideas, suggestions and practical tips. We hope you find this book to be engaging, uplifting, inspiring, informative and entertaining!

Teaching is such a wonderful profession. Sure, it has its ups and downs, but the truth is that most of us would agree that there's no other job in the world we would rather do. Whether you are an aspiring teacher, an early career teacher, an experienced teacher, a former teacher, or whether you are interested in learning more about the weird and wonderful things that happen in the classrooms across the country every single day, we hope you enjoy reading our chronicles from the classroom.

Chapter 1

Inspirational Moments

It is the greatest privilege in the world to be a teacher. We have the opportunity to make a difference every single day. Teaching is one of the most important jobs there is: it is the profession that creates all of the other professions. It is teachers who shape the hearts and minds of children for the rest of their lives. It is teachers who are able to help students to maximise their learning potential. Teachers play a fundamental role in giving children and young people the very best start in life.

No two days in the world of education are ever the same, and that's what keeps things interesting. Our hearts could be bursting with pride one moment, whilst we desperately try to stifle laughter following an unexpected humorous moment the next. In classrooms, corridors and playgrounds all over the world, education staff are blessed to be able to watch children learn and grow every single day. Although the job can be challenging at times, there really is no greater reward than to play a small part in a child's life.

In this chapter, authors share the inspirational moments in their careers which made them feel proud to be a member of the teaching profession.

Why We Just Love to Teach

It's because of you that…

What follows on from that phrase has often given me the biggest lift as a teacher—and also a teacher/trainer! It's because of you … that I've decided to study languages at college… It's because of you … that I got my 'B' ... when I didn't even think I'd pass! It's because of you … that I've decided to apply for promotion. And so on. Of course, it's never been 'just because of' me. I've simply been part of that learner's community of educators, and have been following on from the examples and inspiration provided by the so many teachers and mentors who previously supported me along my way. As teachers we get the opportunity to experience those moments when we see the impact of what we do in the classroom and watch learners 'take off'—and as they do, look back and acknowledge the small part we may have had to play. It really is quite wonderful when that happens!

Jackie Hill FCCT, Teacher educator, Co-Founder of WomenEd Northern Ireland, Network Leader for WomenEd North West

It's that magic moment when the student, be they child or adult, suddenly grasps something you are teaching them and makes a step change in their work.

Professor Megan Crawford. Professor at the Research Centre for Global Learning at Coventry University, Fellow of the Academy of Social Sciences (FAcSS), Chair of a Multi-Academy Trust (MAT)

I love working in education, as I think that training the next generation of teachers for our profession is so valuable. We need to develop teachers to think about the system that we are collectively moving forward, to understand what things can change, and to be able to ensure that we have a more inclusive future, that's more diverse and gender equitable. I play a part in that, by helping train early career teachers, working with established teachers in their professional development, and working with teachers who are researching their Doctorates in Education.

Dr Deb Outhwaite, Director of the DTSA, Vice Chair of Belmas, EdD Supervisor at the University of Liverpool.

It is such a privilege to work in education and develop young people. No day is the same and although the job can be a rollercoaster with incredible highs and crashing lows, it has all the thrills of a rollercoaster ride too. I am the kind of teacher, where once you have been in Mrs Hughes' class, you are one of my kids forever. I am still in touch with students I taught fifteen years ago and have loved seeing pictures of their children, keeping up with their careers and even attending their weddings! Until you have been a teacher, it is difficult to grasp the all-consuming career it can be ... but it is also difficult to realise the impact a great teacher can have. I may be exhausted and stressed but I know I make a real difference. How many other careers can really claim this?

Haili Hughes, English teacher, author, TES journalist, founder of @BoostGCSE

I love teaching. Although, I never actually wanted to be a teacher! I hated teachers and I hated schools—things were very different in education in the 1950s. I wanted to be an actress or an artist—don't ask how I became a teacher! But I do remember where I was and what I was doing the first time I thought about it. My launch into teaching was fraught, it was ill-prepared and it was unsupported. However, in 1970 I was sitting on a rocky outcrop under a massive sea-grape tree, reading articles from the Wakefield Express to five children, there were no books in school—or pens or pencils or paper or equipment. I was explaining what the obituaries were as I gazed out across the turquoise Bahamian ocean and I suddenly thought, aren't I lucky? I just love teaching! Since then, I have taught whole classes of children unable to speak a word of standard English in corners of Yorkshire, and whole classes where no one can speak a word of any sort of English in Qatar. I have talked to 600 educationalists in a cinema in Piccadilly Circus and 6,000 parents in an auditorium in Doha. I have queued for planes in Bahrain and Tokyo and Berlin, in Christchurch and Mexico City and Oman, in Seoul and Gibraltar and Cairo—and wherever I have been I have wanted to shout from the rooftops, I just LOVE teaching! Welcome to the wonders of the worldwide classroom!

Ros Wilson has been a teacher for 56 years—and counting! Education consultant, creator of Big Writing/Power Writing, author

Education (not schooling) is one of the most empowering tools of anyone's life. We are all continued learners, day in, day out—relish it!

Dr Shrehan Lynch, Senior Lecturer at the University of East London, Co-founder of @BAME_PE

Education can be transformational at any age. The pinnacle of my career was teaching young soldiers GCSE maths and English in the Army Education Centre in Germany. One boy, because of where he came from and the peer pressure exerted, had no qualifications. Some months later he had two GCSEs, lots of self-esteem, and the ability to communicate with educators. Education can happen anytime and anywhere and we should all be actively looking for ways of supporting others every day.

Dr Victoria Carr, Headteacher, TEDx Speaker, British Army Reservist

I love working in education for the simple fact that it unlocks possibilities for anyone who commits to it. Primary education is the foundation of those habits of work and learning—the platform on which everything else is built. It's key then that personal development is seen to be as important as basic academic skills. Education gives pupils choices and chances—wider opportunities. I'm dedicated to ensuring every child has the same opportunities, regardless of background and circumstances. I want all pupils to benefit from the quality education I was lucky enough to receive.

David Shakeshaft. Headteacher

Working in education is a gateway to supporting students on the right path in life, and this is something that resonates with me closely. My socio-economic background growing up was not the best, my parents did their best to support me academically and financially in school, but this was limited due to their mediocre jobs and lack of further education. I was lucky enough to have teachers that believed in me and ignited my passion for learning as a clear way to break free of the turmoil of my upbringing, something that my sister unfortunately did not get the opportunity to do as she dropped out of school in Year 10 with no GCSEs. Working in education allows me to be that support network for students who come from a similar background and emphasise to them that education can provide different pathways for their future.

Stephen Orford, Mathematics teacher,
Founding member of the teacher network

Education is the beating heart of any society. How we treat it, how we respect it and how we enable it to evolve illustrate where we are as a civilised society. Understanding diversity is our first step into an inclusive system, respecting where our privileges lie and determining how we can empower all is how we turn dreams into plans. What happens in the classroom is key to this—key to the relationships on which learning is built. I have learnt that by changing teachers' attitudes, we impact student experiences—sometimes a little revolution and disruption is needed in our traditional sector to make the evolution for our GenZ students. Growing pains are part of this and that needs to be embraced. For the classroom to be an accessible environment for positive change, for strong brains, hearts and bodies, the learning needs to never stop.

– Nic Ponsford, Teacher, author and doctorate student,
Director of @edtechukhq, Co-founder of @GECCollect

I love the buzz of working with young people. I used to work in the music industry before I retrained to teach and, as exciting as that sounds, nothing compares to greeting your new class on the first day of term, seeing them smiling at you and knowing that you're all going to go on an adventure that year—and no one quite knows what that's going to look or feel like. It's a privilege to be part of the growth, development and happiness of young people—one that should never be taken for granted.

– Adrian Bethune MCCT, Teacher, governor, author of 'Wellbeing in the Primary Classroom' and 'Teacher Wellbeing and Self-Care', Education Policy co-lead at @MindfulNationUK, Founder of #teachappy

After 3 years teaching, I took a break to travel around South East Asia for six months. We were only a week into our trip when I found myself teaching our guide, Diem, English words and phrases as we trekked through Sapa in Vietnam. I had always known that teaching was a profession that I wanted to be a part of, but it was in that moment that I knew that it was in my blood because, no matter where I was, I seemed to stumble across opportunities to teach. And that's what's so wonderful about education—it never stops. No matter who you are, where you are, what you're doing ... we are always teaching and learning from one another. A profession like ours is not one to take for granted: a job that is so unbelievably rewarding, provides so many moments of warmth (from the lightbulb moments to the 'thank you for always being there' hugs), and one that means I laugh every single day, is one that I wouldn't trade.

– Cassie Hayward-Tapp, Year 6 Teacher, piano and choir lead, Creator of #journalingteacher

Those magical instants in the classroom where it all comes together for a pupil and culminates in an 'a-ha' moment, seeing pupils grow in confidence and find their voice, engaging with pupils' natural curiosities, observing pupils developing an enduring passion for unearthing new knowledge—just some of the reasons why I love working in education and couldn't imagine doing anything else! Not to mention the ingenuity, determination and collaboration of educators … there is something really special about a community of professionals coming together to make all of the above possible for pupils everywhere. – *Lekha Sharma, Vice-Principal, Evidence Lead in Education, author of 'Curriculum to Classroom', MSc postgraduate student, Oxford University*

There is a magic that takes place in classrooms all over the world, every single day: the beautiful, curious chemistry we call learning. Something truly beautiful about this process is how it's tied up inextricably with the relationships that supercharge the incredible work that we do. For us, it's this dynamic interplay that makes it all worthwhile. The pandemic highlighted the unquestionable value of schools. It made it crystal clear that we are pillars of our communities, guiding, supporting and encouraging young people to realise their potential, while simultaneously being rocks for their families. For us, teaching is the greatest job in the world. It encapsulates all that it is to be human: curious, caring, compassionate and courageous. It is a position of remarkable privilege and influence. The great irony is that we will probably never realise even a fraction of the impact we've had.

– Dynamic Deps, Russell and Steve (@DynamicDeps) are Deputy Headteachers and close friends. Podcast: 'Don't Shoot the Deputies'. Facebook group: Make an Impact Education

Working in the primary setting excites me because of the challenges and opportunities we experience, but mostly because of the impact we can have on moulding young hearts and minds. Schools are a nurturing and creative learning community, one which values each individual. Schools are places that ensure the needs of all our children are met in all areas of school life and that each child is given a wealth of experience and opportunities. This, in turn, will enable pupils to be extremely confident, responsible and competent members of society. Though our focus remains on achievement for all, and ensuring children have a rich experience of academic excellence, self-discipline and resilience is reflected in all we do. I believe that schools should be happy, caring, spiritual, respectful and hardworking environments in which all staff utilise their skills to enable the children in their care to recognise their true potential and talents. As a community, we celebrate the successes of our children in all areas of school life. My philosophy for education is one which is based around the idea of multiple intelligences and that we can always improve and learn more. I hold a strong child-centred approach to teaching, where consistency, praise, encouragement and challenge are keys to development. I believe that all children are amazing and have unique potential waiting to be unlocked—it is a privilege, as a teacher and a leader, to be able to inspire, enthuse, motivate and nurture children to fully achieve this. I am a strong believer in growth-mindset principles and I am passionate and committed to my core values: forgiveness, friendship and wisdom. I love my job and feel extremely honoured and privileged to work with wonderful pupils and fantastic communities.

– Christalla Jamil, Executive Headteacher of St Paul's and All Hallow's schools, National leader of WomenEd

To be in a profession where no two days are the same is beyond a privilege, but to be in one where a decade later you can bump into an adult who can tell you how much of an impact you had on them, is immeasurable. Especially when, at the time, you had no idea what contribution to their foundations and formative years you were having. Education is far more than the curriculum and the lessons you teach. It is a rich environment for moulding the next generation. They say that youth is wasted on the young, but when you enter the education space, you enter their domain. In doing so, you get to ride along with their youth and experiences and, in turn, bring that to your own life and never be in the position where you can fall foul to the mundane again. The differing day-to-day experiences are why I love to teach, and the stories that come from them.

Ask any teacher if they feel the same and I bet they'll have an anecdote waiting for you!

–Nikki Cunningham-Smith, Assistant Headteacher, SENCO, M.Ed student and author of 'Feel Free to Smile: The Behaviour Management Survival Guide for New Teachers'

Things I Want My Students to Know

Sarah Mullin

Many of us believe that teaching is a vocation: a career to which we are called. We are driven by a desire to contribute towards social change, to provide opportunities for children and young people to survive and thrive as global citizens. As teachers, we often talk about our love for education with our families, friends and colleagues, but there are some things our pupils probably don't know about why we feel privileged to be a member of this wonderful profession.

Here are just some of the things I want all of my students to know:

The best part of our job is you: The best part of being a teacher is having the opportunity to work with children and young people. You make us smile when you make progress. You challenge us with your quick wit and natural curiosity. You make us beam with pride when you learn from your mistakes. You inspire us to become better teachers and better people.

We challenge you because we care: We want the best for you. We want to see you reach your potential. So please understand that, when we ask you to try something again or complete an additional task, we are only trying to help you grow and learn. We want to see you succeed, to achieve your goals; we want to motivate you to strive for excellence.

We work hard to give you the best chance in life: At night, we work late preparing your lessons. We get really excited about a new idea that we want to try in our classrooms. We edit resources that we think will help you understand a topic or concept better. We feel privileged to play a small role in your lives.

We don't want to give out sanctions: None of us signed up to become teachers so that we could give out detentions. When you have to miss your break, we do, too. We just want you to learn right from wrong so that you can make better decisions in the future. We are always looking for opportunities to praise and reward you. We love to see you happy.

We worry about your exams just as much as you do: We don't sleep particularly well the night before your exams, and we'll also be worrying about you the night before results day. We are a team, and we are in this together. We know what your future dreams are, and we want to help you make those dreams a reality.

We care about your views: If you've enjoyed a lesson, please do tell us. It makes us happy to know we've done a job well. Never be afraid to tell us if you're finding something tricky either. Come and see us at an appropriate time, and give us some feedback about how we can improve your learning experience.

We make mistakes: Nobody is perfect. Although we do try our best, we make mistakes. We might have left your exercise book at home, or maybe we forgot to print that exam paper we promised you. We want you to have the best possible learning experience every single day.

We are growing as professionals: We are always growing and developing as teachers, to make sure we can do our jobs the best we can. We might be studying for a qualification ourselves, and many of us spend our time going to events to learn tips from other teachers. We truly believe in the transformational power of education.

We love to feel appreciated: Although we love to receive flowers, chocolates, wine and cards, there really is nothing better than hearing two little words from our pupils: thank you. It fills us with pride to know that you recognise how hard we work.

There's no other job we would rather do: There is no greater honour than being able to watch children and young people grow into confident, articulate global citizens. We do this job because we care about you.

Teaching is more than a profession: it is a lifestyle choice, and there's no other profession we would rather be in.

Sarah Mullin BA (HONS), PGCE, PGCertED, PGDipED, MA, CTE, FCCT, CMgr FCMI, FInstLM, FRSA is a deputy headteacher and Doctor of Education student. She is the author of the number one best-selling book 'What They Didn't Teach Me on My PGCE' and she is the founder of #EduTeacherTips, the YouTube channel for teachers, by teachers. Sarah is on the board of the secondary education committee at the English Association and she is renowned for supporting Early Career Teachers (ECTs) and aspiring school leaders locally, nationally and internationally. She was recently named a 'Rising Star in Education and Academia' and has previously received the 'Contribution to Education of the Year' award.

First Time Behind Bars

Mair Bull

I stood outside the prison, leaning heavily into the solid stone wall, waiting for the security checks before starting my first day teaching in the category B men's prison as part of a university placement.

A member of the prison staff had visited the university and outlined what we should wear, avoiding make-up, perfume and even deodorant. As a group in our early 20s, we were incredibly nervous. Following our drama performance, we were to run sessions on 'choices'–a topic chosen by the prison's education department.

Once through security, we were ushered into the classroom to find the offenders sitting around waiting for us. It was a traditional Victorian classroom, unhelpfully long and thin. As we asked the group to move into a circle, someone indicated the large button on the wall: "Press that for a cuppa," he said. I laughed and played along, recognising it as the emergency trigger. We started by trying to lighten the tension in the room, but within seconds I was deliberately tripped up by an offender. The room froze as they waited for my reaction. Smiling, I said, "Oops, you nearly got me there!" I felt a collective sigh as the atmosphere noticeably eased.

After the introductions, we readied the group for the performance, which began with me seated as a crying character at the train station, head in hand. From the audience, one offender stood, asking if I was alright. I reassured him I was just acting. We restarted and when I slipped a necklace to the floor as part of the plot, a different offender rose and picked it up. I thanked him, once again explaining they could watch for now before it would be their turn to take part.

Following the performance, we started the workshops, each working with one group. With each activity, my group enthusiastically suggested that taking drugs should be part of the plot. "Hmm… interesting idea" I replied, before encouraging them down a different route. This was repeated time and time again.

On day two, my group suggested we create a piece about a wedding where the central character was in love with the bride, but not allowed to marry her, and he has the choice of whether to ruin the wedding or not. I waited for the twist, but it didn't come. Instead, they threw themselves wholeheartedly into this short drama. It was the first time in two full days that the men had fully immersed themselves in a story that focused on choices and life outside prison. In this there was the glimmer of a future and a life beyond the bars.

They went on to create a funny, touching piece about a devastated man, with two endings to show his choices. They performed it with pride and received sincere praise from their peers.

In that experience, I felt the real power of teaching. Education can inspire and encourage others to see the world in a different way. It was one of the most nerve-racking but enjoyable experiences of my career.

Mair Bull is a former Head of Drama who also worked for BBC Bitesize. She now works at Manchester Metropolitan University in the Curriculum and Rise teams. Mair is a governor at an SEMH school and has recently completed an MA in Educational Leadership and Management.

Socks on the Radiator and Ever After Trees

Emma Middlemiss

Twenty-five years ago, I was a young, idealistic graduate, with a pocketful of dreams and a head full of knowledge and wisdom to impart to the young children of England and Wales. Now, I'm the 'Miss Chips' of the staffroom, staring out of the window, and seeing the hundreds of grubby, lovely faces of yesterday blinking back, wide eyed.

They were the best of times, and the worst of times. There were the 'socks on the radiator days'—the days when I'd find myself reflecting on how my years of experience and training, hours of meetings, endless discussions and planning had led to me putting a pair of child's socks on the radiator or mopping up something unmentionable from the floor. Don't get me wrong, though, every day in school is part of the job, and what I get in return makes it all worth it.

In what other job could I amaze my mini-colleagues with my knowledge of Thunderbirds ("how do *you* know about Lady Penelope?"), stun them by laughing along at the sound of farts, and witness it snowing all over the 'astronaut' also known as the AstroTurf. One inquisitive little boy, whose grasp of facts was definitely exceeded by the reach of his curiosity, asked me if the currency in Europe was biros. He was soon put right by the girl on his left, who'd also corrected him when he said, "the fairies have been," by explaining that the glitter on the floor was due to Year 2 using the room for making firework pictures. That same boy said one day that, "I know that there are deciduous trees, but what are the other kind called? Ever After trees?" "They are now," I replied.

When I look out over a playground now, I see echoes of their faces in those of the children out there—a twinkle in an eye here, a smile there, a giggle, or a toss of curls. I recall many, many more delicious moments that outweigh all the socks on the radiator. My career has seen many ups and downs, and some of those socks became metaphorical sledgehammers, but I will have my Ever After trees to wander through.

In a deep, dark forest, there are tall, broad trees, and their leaves are carefully and beautifully written pages, a wonderful Ever After. Anyone can go into the forest, find their tree, which will always be the right one, pick a page, and read it, whenever they need to.

Teachers' Ever After trees are special. Start growing your own.

Emma taught Year One and Reception children in Essex, Buckinghamshire and Shropshire for twenty years, before choosing to work across the primary age range as a Supply Teacher. She lives in Shropshire and is one of eight teachers in her family.

The School Trip

Deborah Kemp

My very first school trip was an activity trip in the Ardennes. Looking back, the significant moment from this trip involved me standing on a precipice, looking into a watery and distant abyss, knowing that I would have to jump in first to encourage the two quaking and terrified Year 9s standing behind me. "If I can do it, you can!" I said. They looked at me, appalled, then a moment of 'we are all in this together' passed between us...

This is what school trips do—they give us the opportunity to really push students to achieve things they have never achieved before; in the process, we get to challenge ourselves.

I started teaching in the late 80s, in the time when teachers had to collect the money for school trips and guard it carefully in their desk drawer, in amongst old registers, paper clips, and pencil shavings. These pots of money never seemed to add up to the exact amount, and it was standard practice for staff to add in that missing £1.72 when it was eventually time to submit the trip money. Teachers, I am sure, heaved a sigh of relief when this responsibility was handed over to the admin team.

I have always leapt at the opportunity to go on the annual school trip, and I am lucky to have had many opportunities. As I became more experienced, I began running these trips; we went to The Gambia, Barcelona, Greece and Norway, and even a school exchange to California—one of the all-time best trips, listening to Red Hot Chili Peppers and driving on Route 21.

Memorable trip moments have included Tai Chi in the mornings in Greece, a staff member being stung by an enormous bee, confiscating contraband on the bus before we had even arrived at the campsite, and getting lost in the middle of the night on the way to the hotel in Italy; getting there meant having to roll out my rusty Italian to the bus driver. So many stories and human experiences can be gained from a school trip. All those long, long coach trips squeezed in the back of the bus, supervising the sick bag and monitoring the DVDs and windows, were bonding experiences.

The coach drivers deserve a paragraph of their own—great company, eager entertainers, sharing many tired (and some dubious) jokes that they no doubt regularly regaled their captive audience with. In my experience, they have all been solid, reliable and good company for the staff and students. There was one exception—a driver who seemed to delight in telling the students about all the coach crashes that had occurred, and then glowered throughout the 26-hour drive to Spain and the subsequent day trips.

Once arrived at a destination, the most challenging aspect of a school trip is not the day supervision and the tramping round numerous exciting (to some) areas of interest; it is the night times when students are waiting for the staff to relax and unwind, so that they can creep about, meeting up with friends and getting up to mischief. I remember in the early days realising that the night was not over until EVERY child had gone to sleep—sometimes having to sit on plastic chairs in the corridors to remind students that we were keeping a close eye on them!

I've been lucky to be part of many school trips in my career, and all have been memorable. It's such a great opportunity to really get to see your students in a new light—and for them to see you as a 'real human,' with equally human fears such as the sheer terror of knowing you were going to have to jump off that cliff! We walked down, by the way, the three of us equally relieved. School trips are the great leveller.

Deborah Kemp is an English and Drama specialist and currently works as an Assistant Principal in South East England. Deborah is a regional lead for WomenEd, presents on a weekly podcast on behaviour with Changing Behaviour UK Ltd and was a contributor to 'What they Didn't Tell Me on my PGCE' by Sarah Mullin.

Chapter 2

Growing as a Professional

Being a teacher means embarking on an exciting career with limitless opportunities. When teachers achieve Qualified Teacher Status (QTS), we know that we are just starting out on our journeys as education professionals.

The very best educators are always a work in progress; teachers are always learning, growing and developing so that we can have an evidence-informed understanding of what works best. It is essential that teachers continue to invest in their subject knowledge, taking time to learn from other teachers so that we can share good practice with one another. I firmly believe that the best resource we have in education is the experience and knowledge of our colleagues.

Very often, our professional growth comes from the everyday events that take place in education settings. We learn from the students we teach. We learn from the issues and events that are taking place in the world around us. We learn from our victories and we learn from our mistakes.

In this chapter, authors share their top tips, words of advice and memorable reflections as they highlight examples of these moments in their experiences of growing and developing as practitioners.

The Problem With the Pandemic for Education Professionals

Sarah Mullin

It is hard to believe that this time last year I was travelling across the country supporting aspiring school leaders. I encouraged women to become the change we want to see in the world because even though gender representation, like other forms of diversity, is essential for society to thrive, women are still vastly underrepresented in leadership positions.

Despite the education workforce consisting of 68% women, just 38% of England's secondary school headteachers are women. Whilst women bring a plethora of positive qualities to leadership positions, many organisations have reported difficulties in recruiting and retaining women leaders, and this may be further exacerbated by the global pandemic.

Covid-19 has impacted the lives of millions across the world. While we are all navigating challenging times, society's biases, inequalities and injustices mean that we are each experiencing these times differently, and there is growing evidence that suggests that women have been disproportionately negatively affected by the pandemic.

Increased demands on women

A study by the Women's Higher Education Network (WHEN) found that women had taken on increasing amounts of childcare, household and other caring responsibilities in addition to their paid work. This has significantly affected their ability to do their jobs in the ways they had prior to the pandemic.

As a deputy headteacher and mother of three young children, I can appreciate the demands on the time of women juggling competing roles in their personal and professional lives. We live in a time when society expects women to raise a family as if they do not work and work as if they do not have a family to raise, leaving many women with a perpetual feeling of guilt. This has never been more apparent than during this crisis.

Teachers and school leaders have had to adopt innovative ways to educate the nation's children and young people; streaming live lessons whilst caring for the children of key workers and vulnerable children before going home to support our own children with their remote learning. We have watched the news in anticipation, learning our fate from leaked documents before official guidance came flooding into our email inboxes at unsociable hours when we should have been spending time with our loved ones. As we supported students with growing stress, anxiety and mental-health related issues, we have struggled to prioritise our own wellbeing, working relentlessly in response to the ever-changing guidance and government U-turns.

It is hardly surprising, therefore, that Education Support's research with YouGov, found that 89% of school leaders have reported feeling stressed or very stressed, with 59% of school leaders considering leaving the profession this academic year. These are, of course, unprecedented times, but the impact of Covid-19 may further perpetuate gender inequality in school leadership as the role of the headteacher may be perceived less favourably by the teaching workforce.

Opportunities for change

Just as the government roadmap for easing lockdown restrictions has offered a glimmer of hope that better times are coming, there is also an opportunity for us to try to mitigate the impact of Covid-19 on women and their aspirations for school leadership.

If we are to recruit and retain loyal, dedicated people who might otherwise be lost to the profession, we must make the wellbeing of our workforce central to our strategic decision making. The flexibility and creativity of education staff has been commendable: we have delivered high quality teaching remotely; shown compassion and empathy to individual staff members and enjoyed contributing to the field of education by delivering CPD from the comfort of our homes, without having to worry about childcare or travel.

In many ways, Covid-19 has helped us to critically reflect on our practice and create positive change by adapting swiftly to the times we are living in. We must continue to look forward with hope, considering flexible working opportunities that are conducive to fostering a healthy work/life balance so that we can promote diversity in educational leadership.

When times change, so must we. So, let's embrace the possibilities. After all, staying positive in a negative situation is far from naïve; it's leadership.

Sarah Mullin BA (HONS), PGCE, PGCertED, PGDipED, MA, CTE, FCCT, CMgr FCMI, FInstLM, FRSA is a deputy headteacher and Doctor of Education student. She is the author of the number one best-selling book 'What They Didn't Teach Me on My PGCE' and she is the founder of #EduTeacherTips, the YouTube channel for teachers, by teachers. Sarah is on the board of the secondary education committee at the English Association and she is renowned for supporting Early Career Teachers (ECTs) and aspiring school leaders locally, nationally and internationally. She was recently named a 'Rising Star in Education and Academia' and has previously received the 'Contribution to Education of the Year' award.

A Work in Progress

Anthony R Hammond

When I started teaching ceramics and sculpture at my current school, my predecessor told me *"Just do ten years; that's what I have done. That will be enough"*. Twenty-six years later, I am still there. People ask me why? It is because it is still so much fun—every day gives me a challenge. The students I teach surprise me every term with their effort, creativity, resilience and their love of learning.

I was unqualified when I started to teach in 1994; I was given General Certificate of Secondary Education (GCSE) and Advanced-Level (A-level) classes, my own department—and no guidance over what to teach. I was on my own. It was very scary, but also an opportunity to reflect upon the previous teachers/lecturers I had from 11-23 years old. There was a theme I recognised in all of them: compassion, patience, empathy, strong subject knowledge, a love for teaching and care for their students. For me, these were the values that were embedded in me, and I knew this was the only way I could teach.

After many roles at my school, I decided in 2010 to become qualified as a teacher. What came next changed me forever. I decided to take all the Special Educational Needs and Disability (SEND) tests to fully understand what challenges students with learning needs have to face. I found out from my Special Educational Needs Co-Ordinator (SENCO) that I am dyslexic. I cried as I realised why I did not achieve well at school. Teaching in my days was just 'chalk and talk'. I look back and no learning really took place in the classes I attended. Being dyslexic and creative go hand in hand, and I realise that it has allowed me to develop strong visual skills, a vivid imagination, strong practical/manipulative skills, and, above all, innovation. Being a teacher, I believe, gives me the opportunity to encourage, support and show my students what you can achieve with a learning difficulty.

Since becoming qualified as a teacher, I now train teachers across the curriculum. Being part of a process that allows me to be at the start of a teacher's career is very rewarding. My first aim is to encourage a student teacher to fall in love with teaching. They need to see the possibilities for their future. It is hard work. I relate starting a new term to getting on an oil rig: you don't get off again until the end of term. It is so busy being a teacher, and the demands placed on you are high. But as I tell my trainees, it's worth it; working in a school allows you to have a positive impact on so many students.

After many years of teaching, I am still learning how to teach. This process never ends. I learn from colleagues and from observing lessons with trainees—I am still 'a work in progress'. This is what keeps me in the profession today.

Anthony Hammond has been 'playing with clay' since he was 11 years old. After studying for a degree and then a Masters in Ceramics, he became Head of Ceramics at Bede's senior school in East Sussex. He is also Head of Teacher Development. He is married to Alison, with one dog, Kassie.

Finding Yourself in the Classroom

Helena Terry

In my training year, I observed a wide array of teachers with different levels of experience, different personalities, and different styles in the classroom. Especially at the beginning, I made notes on every single little thing they did. As a student teacher, I was in awe of everything. I found myself jotting down dozens of key phrases every lesson, so I would know what to say for transitions, to grasp attention or even to start the lesson.

Once you start teaching, you have a multitude of lesson observations to determine whether you are meeting expected standards. However, a lot of teaching and observations are subjective. Data has shown that observations are not wholly reliable, and two observers are unlikely to give the same lesson grading (Cantrell and Kane, 2013). Therefore, the pressure can result in trainees wanting to impress their mentor or classroom teacher, and one way of impressing is by trying to be a less-experienced version of your observer.

Each teacher has their own style, and it can be hard to develop your own when you are taking over someone else's class. I found myself trying to conform to the teacher that was observing me at the time. This was exceedingly difficult, as I had over seven teachers observe me in my training year! Each lesson, I felt like I was putting on a different persona to try and please my observer. I could go from lesson to lesson, and completely change the way I teach. I was not adapting myself for the students: I was aiming to please the teachers.

But then came my NQT year, and with my newfound autonomy, I found I could be who I wanted to be. I quickly learnt that students wanted to see me for who I am, rather than some carbon copy of another teacher at the school. I found that it is okay to share parts of my personality too. It is okay to show off my new nails to the Year 9 girls or to discuss that episode of Love Island with the Year 12s. Those brief moments revealing who you are only make your relationships with students stronger. Students will not respect you any less for showing yourself to be a real person, with likes and interests, rather than an authoritarian robot.

Soon, you also realise that students are remarkably perceptive. They notice when you change up your appearance, have a new poster in the classroom, or even when you are having a bad day. They get to know you, and you get to know them, and that is what makes this whole job even better. To see each student and know them, rather than just treating students as a collective that must be managed.

Good relationships are built on solid foundations, and part of that foundation, for me, is by revealing part of myself. Respect can still be gained and kept if you reveal you are only human.

So, trainees, do not worry. It will seem impossible at first to find the real you and develop your own teacher style, but once you are left alone you can shine and be the teacher you want to be.

References

Cantrell, S and Kane, T. J. (2013). Ensuring Fair and Reliable Measures of Effective Teaching: Culminating Findings from the MET Project's Three-Year Study. Policy and Practice Brief. Bill & Melinda Gates Foundation. Seattle, WA: Author.

Helena is an English RQT in Birmingham. She considers herself on a continuous journey of improvement and is always actively looking for new ways to change up her teaching. Helena is passionate about sharing positive experiences of teaching and removing the stigma surrounding surviving the NQT year.

Being a Visible LGBT Role Model (#outandproud)

Jeanne Rogers

Why 'come out' at all?

I love it when I see posts on social media where someone has been brave enough to tell the world that they are gay or will be expressing their identity in a different way. It makes me smile. Then you scroll down and amongst the positive comments, you often read, "why do people make such a fuss about coming out; you don't see straight people telling the world!", or "who cares if you're gay!?" When any of my friends have asked that question, I tell them how important it is from my own experience and why I made the conscious decision to be open about my sexuality, especially in an educational context.

My story

As a child, I saw nothing in my world that would help me understand what being gay was. I'm of an age that meant there was no internet to shape my sense of self and no social media until I was well into my thirties. Growing up as a working-class kid with limited social mobility, I knew nobody that was visibly gay. The representation of homosexuality on TV was often of a camp, male figure that was there for comedy value. There was nothing in school or college and I didn't have the opportunity to go to university as a young person. Things may have been very different if I did. So, like many others living in a bubble with no diverse role models, I followed the heteronormative path and had what I like to refer to as my 'straight phase' for quite a long time.

I started teaching in further education (FE) when I was 28, and that's when my horizons were expanded. I love the diversity of the sector and the life-changing opportunities it presents for many. At 37, I decided to come out. Being in an inclusive and educated environment, I felt safe. I was happy and no longer wanted to hide who I was. I remember friends at the time warning me that 'being out' could be career limiting, but thankfully that hasn't been my experience. My work family was thrilled for me; other than the odd raised eyebrow, it was just another normal day, as it should be. I think it's important to note that I take a more guarded approach in social settings where it isn't always as safe, so I really value the inclusivity of being in education.

Discussing my sexuality with students has been more measured, but then most teachers are selective in what they share about their personal life. Any conversation should be respectful of your own privacy and professional boundaries. I'm in FE and appreciate it can be different in schools. I have a friend who was a Physical Education (PE) teacher and she was out with colleagues but not openly with students. Sharing in the classroom should always be in context, if it is to add value. Students that I taught at the time of coming out were naturally curious. As new cohorts came along, they got to know about my same sex family in the same way they did with other teachers. I have never shied away from questions a student may have, as I know from experience what a difference it can make having that reference point, regardless of your sexual identity. For many in our schools and colleges, it is the first time they have stepped outside of their cultural sphere of influence, to consider how the world might be different from the societal norms they are used to.

One student's story

I taught a student for two years and we're still in touch 15 years later. "*For me, personally coming to college and having someone who was a visible LGBT role model made my life a lot easier, as at the time I was 'coming out' to my friends and family, which was very difficult. Having Jeanne there was inspiring, liberating and gave me the confidence that I needed, at that point in my life, to be my true self. To this day I am forever grateful, so thank you." (Anonymous, personal communication, 2021)*

One colleague's story

Joanna Barrett is a Deputy Head and a good friend. She is gifted in weaving inclusion into the everyday aspects of college life and is a 24/7 diversity champion. "*The coaching, guidance, safety and friendship I received from Jeanne led to the unimaginable...I came out at work. I've never looked back or had any cause to regret my decision. Having a manager who is open about their sexuality in the workplace most definitely shapes an LGBTQ+ teacher. It allowed me to move deeper into my next chapter—developing my teaching career and reputation. I no longer needed to be fearful, reserved and cautious about my conversations with peers in the staffroom, or students in the classroom. As a manager now, I am open with my team regarding my sexuality, and have ensured that my managerial style reflects the safety and support shown to me, so that if and when my colleagues were ready to come out, they would feel secure in taking this momentous step." (J. Barrett, personal communication, 2021)*

The bigger picture

I am now a senior leader and a school governor and, although I no longer teach in the classroom, I am a strong advocate for LGBT visibility for our students, teachers, leaders, and communities. Creating a culture that is built on the principles of valuing equality, diversity and inclusion can liberate those who are touched by it.

Lisa Jordan, Chair of the Leeds City College Staff LGBT Network, reminds us of the importance of visible role models:

"According to Stonewall, more than a third of LGBT staff (35 per cent) have hidden or disguised that they are LGBT at work in the last year because they were afraid of discrimination.

For an LGBT+ colleague who does not feel safe or confident to be out in the workplace, navigating a simple Monday morning conversation of 'What did you do at the weekend?' can be stressful and exhausting. There is a heavy burden of carefully considering a response that does not disclose the name/gender/existence of partners and family, the location of a social activity, the clothes worn or any other LGBT+ cultural clues. Actively omitting or denying fundamental aspects of self-identity is isolating, and negatively impacts on working relationships and self-esteem.

Colleagues who feel free to be open and authentic in the workplace are able to refocus energy, becoming more motivated, creative, confident, productive, innovative and high performing. Our talents are unlocked, we can make a positive contribution to the workforce with integrity.

Jeanne has been openly gay in the workplace for a number of years and during that time has developed and progressed significantly within her career. For LGBT+ colleagues, charting and sharing Jeanne's journey is empowering; we can envisage ourselves succeeding if we see someone else from our community succeeding.

Coming out and being out is not a decision that is made once. It requires resolve, resilience, and a commitment to continually challenge assumptions, define yourself and represent your diverse communities. Alongside encouraging an increasingly diverse range of visible LGBT+ colleagues, role models influence wider communities. LGBT allies develop awareness, understanding and the confidence to challenge assumptions, stereotypes and discrimination. This impact ripples across our students and the families/communities we serve. As a sector, our scope for positive influence is widespread." (L. Jordan, personal communication, 2021)

These are personal stories shared willingly to illustrate the AWESOME things that can happen, in the right environment. I appreciate that this isn't the same for everyone and that each person needs to make their own choices about how they express their individuality and what will keep them safe and comfortable in their context. Being your authentic self can also be a private matter. What's fabulous is that you are still shaping the lives of those around you through your compassion and understanding. Together, our LGBT+ communities and our allies can all make a difference and be a part of the stories that are told in years to come.

References

Bachmann, C.L. and Gooch, B. (2018) Stonewall LGBT in Britain: Work Report [online] Available at: https://www.stonewall.org.uk/system/files/lgbt_in_britain_work_report.pdf.

Jeanne Rogers is vice principal for Quality Teaching and Learning at Luminate Education Group. She leads a directorate of specialists in quality improvement, teaching and learning, edtech and teacher training. She is part of the central team at the White Rose Academies Trust and is Vice Chair of the Local Accountability Board at Leeds East Academy. Jeanne has an MSc in Leadership and Management and is the Stonewall LGBT SLT Lead for the colleges within the group.

Thriving as a Teacher With Additional Needs

Caroline Powell

Embarking upon a teaching career is thrilling; it provides a fresh start filled with exciting opportunities and an eclectic mix of people. Yet it can also be daunting; it can be a time filled with ups, downs and uncertainties. There are lots of new plates to spin. For many prospective teachers, the role seems unfeasible and impossible. This is especially true for those among us with learning difficulties, illnesses or disabilities who may find the academic work, the rigid teaching days, and the relentless workload incompatible with our own needs and abilities.

If that sounds relatable, I would like to reassure you that I have enjoyed teaching for nearly seven years now, despite a range of serious illnesses. I remain passionate and keen to continue and progress. However, it is not straightforward: on average, I spend around a month each year in hospital, plus many absences for appointments and treatments. Teaching can be quite inflexible and sometimes these hindrances are very difficult to manage. Yet mostly the job satisfaction outweighs the demands.

If you also face some overwhelming challenges, my message is that if you find a supportive school and maintain a determined attitude, overcoming them can be possible. You can still thrive. Here are my suggestions for excelling in teaching whilst managing difficulties and preserving your own wellbeing:

Be as open as you feel comfortable with.

I am not suggesting that you sound off in the staffroom or talk to students in intricate detail about the abscess on your toe. But discussing your needs with your line manager in a professional context is likely to be mutually beneficial. Under the Equality Act (2010), you are not obliged to disclose your circumstances, but your school cannot cater for them if you do not. When undergoing risk assessments and negotiating reasonable adjustments, vocalise your own suggestions and questions. Reflect on the help you require in advance so that you can steer the conversation appropriately. Your manager will probably be grateful for your guidance.

Discussions will vary according to your needs, but here are some examples of questions to explore: will the location of your classroom or duties have an impact on you? Is it important that you have a protected break time each day? Do you need to access health equipment or supportive technology whilst at school? Does any of your equipment or furniture need to be altered?

Consider how your school can help to retain you in the long-term. Could flexible working be an option, so that your health needs can be met? Would you be allowed to go home during planning, preparation and assessment (PPA) time, or slightly adjust your working hours during the day?

Clarify your limits. You should not need to disclose anything you feel uncomfortable with. For example, if you need to provide medical letters as evidence for any adjustments that need to be made, create photocopies and block out any information you do not want to share. Seek advice if you suspect that your school is being unnecessarily intrusive or breaching confidentiality. Your privacy is important.

This all sounds quite severe, but it does not have to be. All of these conversations can be conducted in a friendly, supportive and collaborative way. The outcomes aim to benefit everyone, after all.

Be proactive about overcoming obstacles.

Know where you stand with your school's policies regarding absences and check your rights as someone with a protected characteristic. Seek advice if you have any concerns. Aim to be meticulous when requesting absences and setting cover work in advance. This will be of value to your school, your students and yourself. Do ask for support when needed, and check if your department or school has a bank of cover resources already. It may be best to reserve those for emergencies, as well as develop your own thorough cover lessons for planned absences. This can be hard to set up, especially considering your cover may need to be appropriate for non-specialist teachers with limited resources. However, over time, you may be able to create a set of cover lessons that you can draw upon in upcoming years. If you teach a range of ages, save them in well-labelled clear folders for each year group. Take heart that future absences will be easier to organise.

Be kind to yourself.

Health and family always come first. Whilst I am passionate about recruiting and retaining diverse teachers, I am foremost an advocate for wellbeing. If you know in your heart that teaching is going to make you unwell, I advise thinking creatively about how to forge an equally fulfilling career path.

Realism is vital. I have a progressive disease, so my health will gradually deteriorate. When my needs significantly increase, it will not be sensible to maintain a career as a classroom teacher. So, I am honest and proactive about it. Next year, I am cutting down to part-time. I hope this will enhance the longevity of my career. I also continually undertake personal development so that I can move into a more flexible career when necessary. For example, I am a trained and registered foster carer. I am trying to build a small portfolio of writing. I am looking into part-time PhDs. Creating opportunities for myself keeps me inspired. Having alternative plans at the back of my mind also helps me to stay in teaching, as I am putting myself under no pressure to stick around. I am here because I want to be, and for the time being, I can be. It is essential that we all keep our minds and options open to secure healthy, balanced lives.

Finally, it can be easy to feel like a burden when concessions are made for you. Fear of letting students down can also be fierce. Try to put such thoughts aside. It is important that there are positive role models in schools showing children how to overcome adversity. Children need to see the strength and success of our resilience. How else can they replicate it?

References

Equality Act 2010, c. 15. London: The Stationery Office.

Caroline Powell is Head of English in a Secondary School and Sixth Form College in Cambridge. She gained a PGCE in Secondary English and an MEd in Researching Practice from the University of Cambridge.

Positive Representation Matters

Rochelle McFarlane

Representation matters. I'm going to share my experiences of positive representation in schools. I remember two of my favourite teachers. Miss B always demanded the best. She was Jamaican and had a Caribbean fierceness that reminded me of my Bajan Nana. I looked up to her, and she was one of the first teachers I really respected. Next there was Miss C, she was younger and reminded me of myself. Miss B was like a mother figure and Miss C was like an older sister. I had never been close to any of my teachers before, but I felt like they understood me. They were from a similar background to me, and I saw myself in them. I never really thought about being a teacher before, but they both inspired me to think that if they could do it, I could too. It's only now that I'm older I can appreciate the impact they had on me.

Having these two strong, positive Black women as role models was extremely important for me as a young Black girl who was often distracted at school. Fast forward 7 years, and I am now a teacher, on a placement at a school with a majority of white British students. My experience with some of my Black sixth-form students showed me the power of positive representation. As a sociology teacher, I spoke very openly about ethnicity because of the content of my subject. Through our conversations it quickly became apparent I was more than just a teacher for them. They would often come to see me, and they told me they felt comfortable talking to me about certain things as I understood. I was a young, Black woman trying to navigate a complex world just like them.

As teachers I think sharing personal stories can be powerful. A lot of the issues they faced, I had been through myself. We talked about microaggressions faced by their peers in the workplace (for example, about their hair), or the genre of music they listened to. We discussed why they didn't feel comfortable at prom; Beyoncé's new documentary; embracing natural hair; how they would feel uncomfortable at prom because of the lack of diverse music, or a new African dance move. We had some fantastic conversations and a great open relationship; our students need people they can relate to, who they can share stories with without having to explain certain cultural references; they need people who can understand what they go through.

I remember attending my first Young Black Teachers' Network (YBTN) event in London. It was inspiring to be surrounded by so many knowledgeable Black teachers. Groups like this are doing amazing work trying to increase diversity in education. As I write this, there are protests worldwide after the death of George Floyd and people are starting to have discussions about institutional racism and privilege. Teachers need to move beyond a colour-blind approach. Not seeing colour is not helpful for your students. By not seeing colour, you're not recognising your students and you're ignoring the impact race has on their everyday lives. Black lives matter: we can do better, and our Black students deserve better.

Rochelle is a qualified teacher and Lead Personal Health, Social and Citizenship (PHSCE) Co-ordinator in a secondary school. She teaches Sociology, Psychology, Religious Studies, PHSCE and Criminology. Rochelle is passionate about anti-racism and completed her BA in Sociology and Social Policy. She currently works with Black Teachers Connect and with The Prosperity Project delivering anti-racist workshops to schools.

Why Am I Training to Become a Teacher?

Samantha McMurtry

Becoming a teacher is hard work. I don't think anyone who has ever gone through an Initial Teacher Training (ITT) programme, Post Graduate Certificate in Education (PGCE) or any other route into teaching can dispute that. The long days, the tiredness, the endless to-do lists. You can feel drained and disheartened, coming home some days thinking: why am I doing this?

Then you remember your 'why.' I have wanted to become a teacher since Sixth Form. Back then, I had a rose-tinted view of a teacher's day-to-day life due to just having experienced the student side of education; also, I was so lucky to have been taught by some amazing educators. Despite this, I knew how hard my teachers worked day in, day out and I knew they did not have a simple 9-5 job. I knew how many hours they spent marking our work, making resources, creating a lesson which would ensure our interaction on a grey, Friday afternoon mid-November.

I spent some time conducting work experience within schools and gained a deeper insight as to what was really involved in becoming a teacher. I saw tired teachers getting into school at 7am, leaving at 6pm and taking a pile of books home to mark—yet, didn't fail to turn up to every single one of their lessons with a beaming smile and a passion for their subject which radiated across the classroom. I saw the efforts which teachers put into the pastoral sides of their role, and I saw them demonstrate their care for every child. Something really stood out for me and that was that they all seemed to have one thing in common: every teacher wanted the best outcomes for every single one of their students because they cared. None of this put me off the prospect of becoming a teacher.

I am training to be a teacher because I want to help young people make better choices. I want to teach the upcoming Members of Parliament (MPs), nurses, supermarket workers, cleaners and scientists. Every student should be valued within the classroom and within society. I want to radiate my passion for my subject to my students, like my teachers did to me. I want to learn from my students, and never stop learning. I want my students to know they are cared about, appreciated, and valued. I want to make a difference—and I know that this vocation truly does change lives.

Samantha McMurtry, BA (Hons) is a teacher of English in the East of England.

Never Underestimate the First Time Something Happens

Sara Lewis

When you spend time in a Special Educational Needs (SEN) school, you'll see how dedicated and passionate the staff are about teaching and supporting their pupils. Everyone has high expectations for all pupils, no matter their need. We support pupils to be able to communicate their basic wants and needs using many different communication methods, and we support pupils to become independent learners.

Working in an SEN school has its challenges; however, it is so rewarding. The children became 'my own' and I wanted to do anything I could to help them succeed. The progress in an SEN school may be at a slower rate, but trust me, the moment a child does something for the first time, there is no feeling in the world like it.

Over my time as a PGCE student and a Newly Qualified Teacher (NQT), I had many firsts:

- The first time a pupil takes their first steps independently in the hydrotherapy pool.
- The first time a pupil uses their voice to communicate what they want.
- The first time a pupil writes their name independently.
- The first time a pupil gives you eye contact and smiles at you.
- The first time a pupil uses their communication aid independently to ask for a snack.
- The first time a pupil says your name.
- The first time a pupil engages with you during a sensory session.

- The first time a pupil gets up off the floor during a behaviour incident after giving them 'the look.'
- The first time a pupil supports a peer in class without any intervention from staff.

Those things never happened overnight—it took hard work and dedication. Those are moments you cherish throughout your journey as a teacher. Those moments gave me a 'proud mum' moment; I just wanted to jump and run around the school screaming with pride. Of course, the less exuberant route found me next to the pupil, holding back the tears, and then making a big deal telling everyone about it—my team, phoning parents, during assembly and then telling my family and friends. It is those moments that make me realise why I do this job.

You'll also have some first-time moments unrelated to your classroom efforts; sometimes you'll find yourself holding back from laughter or end up thinking about it the next day and laughing about things like this:

- The first time a pupil decides to use the tannoy in the supermarket to say hello to everyone.
- The first time a pupil decides to throw their toys down the toilet and block the school drainage system!
- The first time a pupil shouts "I've got the gas!" when on a trip in the local museum.
- The first time a pupil tries to grab a stranger's cake when in the local café.
- The first time a pupil decides not to get out of the pool and you jump into the pool fully clothed to get them out!

Never underestimate the first time something happens!

Sara Jayne Lewis, BA (Hons), PGCE, MCCP is an NQT SEND Teacher based in Bristol, UK. Sara is passionate about supporting and teaching SEND pupils. She has worked in SEN schools for 8 years and has extensive experience in supporting SEND pupils, specialising in supporting pupils with Down's syndrome.

A Positive Outlook

Emily Weston

I've thought long and hard about what tip I could offer about being in a classroom. Every day is so different and there are so many different skills we need to have; it makes knowing what the most important thing to do is quite tricky. It will also vary from teacher to teacher; our teaching styles are all unique to us.

But for me, I think it's all about the outlook you have each day and the image you project to the children. It's about the attitude with which you tackle both the good days and the not so good, as well as demonstrating the 'growth mindset' we expect children to have. To be clear, I don't expect you to be positive every single day. It's important we are honest with children about how we feel and allow them to understand that they can express their emotions and also see them demonstrated. But I do think it's important that you don't let yourself become overwhelmed and swallowed by the negative.

Learning walk

You've had a learning walk and you know it's not gone as well as you hoped. The children didn't seem to understand what you wanted them to. You didn't know an answer; you modelled something wrong; you saw the observer raise their eyebrows and look at their notepad, thus putting you off and making you question everything else you do; a child decided now was the perfect time to burst into their own rendition of Dua Lipa's new hit song. Afterwards, you want to shut your classroom door and not come out again until Friday.

We've all been there!

But it won't always be as negative as you think—and I say this from experience! Speak to colleagues—I'm sure they'll all relay to you a story where they felt the same way. Look at children's work; there's always a child who has completed the task brilliantly and makes you see you still taught someone something. Remember you are human, and it is normal for things to go wrong!

You've embarrassed yourself

Your colleague has come to visit your classroom when on maternity leave and you're both having a chat with your class about their new baby, what's happened while they've been off and generally catching up. You turn around and trip over the flip chart, hitting your head on the way down and breaking the flip chart as you fall on it. Silence falls across the classroom until a brave child asks, "Miss Weston, are you okay? There's blood on your head!"

(This is a very specific example so, as I'm sure you've guessed, this actually did happen!)

You'll probably feel like you want the ground to swallow you up. That silence felt like it lasted forever… until I started laughing. Luckily in this situation I wasn't really injured (despite a small cut on my forehead and a very bruised ego…). My class was lovely at the time and genuinely concerned—but as soon as we laughed about it together the situation felt so much better. Funnily enough, that was a memory that cropped up in their leavers' books later that year!

A negative environment

It's so easy when you're in a negative school to feel like there's no positive. Some days you walk through the door and not even the children can cheer you up. You might have reached the point where you're dreading Sunday nights, or don't want the holidays to end. But even in these times, it can be made so much better by finding a positive each day.

It's easier said than done—I know some days I used to drag myself out of bed feeling negative before I started. When other people's actions are the reason you're unhappy, it can feel as if there's no way out. But there is always something positive—whether it is at school or outside of it.

- It could be a light-bulb moment a child has.
- It could be that you saw two magpies on the way to school.
- It could be that you have your favourite dinner on the table when you get home.
- It could be your colleague has come to your classroom to check on you.

Keeping yourself positive helps you to know how and when to make a change. When you're stuck in a circle of negativity, it's harder to break. It sounds like such a simple thing, but, to me, it is one of the most important.

As Albus Dumbledore says, "Happiness can be found in the darkest of times, if one only remembers to turn on the light".

Emily Weston is a transition teacher, teacher of English and book reviewer. She tweets @primaryteachew.

The 'F Word' (AKA a 'Brilliant' Observation Lesson)

Margaret George

In my 4th year of teaching, I taught a Year 8 class in an independent school. The children lacked self-belief due to their 'set 3' status, but were keen to learn and, thankfully, still enjoyed participating. They kept complaining, however, that I misunderstood the meaning of the word 'fun.' ("And now for the FUN part of working with powers!") I enjoyed telling them that my weekend private tutees frequently said the same thing!

The school's Charity Events week came around, and each class had to choose their own charity to support in addition to how they would raise funds for it. My Year 8s insisted that I should donate £1 every time I said 'fun'. My first mentor had frequently warned us that it is good to be aware of overusing catchphrases, so I thanked them for their imaginative idea, and agreed to the challenge.

So… there I was towards the end of the week, with my long-suffering Head of Department who was conducting a mandatory observation of my lesson.

Meanwhile, I was happily enjoying teaching fractions, asking children to come to the front of the room to demonstrate their work on the board. I was feeling on top of things until we reached a new (read challenging) part of the topic. Riding high on the success so far, I exclaimed, "So now we get to the really FUN part!"

My students looked up with glee and I immediately quipped, "Oops! I said the F word, didn't I?", and made a courtly production out of presenting a £1 coin and slotting it into their collection tin.

Needless to say, my Head of Department had excellent peripheral noticing skills and immediately looked up from her note-taking for that last bit! I was so lucky that she knew me well enough to ask for an explanation before typing up that observation!

Margaret studied her BSc and PGCE as a single mum, with two of her three children having Special Needs. She has taught children from Year 4 up to Year 13 in independent, state, large mainstream, and small behavioural establishments, in addition to marking A-level and undergraduate exams.

If at First You Don't Succeed...

Rachael Dargie

If you want to work in the highest stakes classroom of them all, teach the re-sit class. You will encounter a variety of students, some of whom you are surprised to see, and others who you noticed had appeared to check out of your regular lessons a while back and so are less of a surprise. You will meet students who, for whatever reason, missed advancing to the next step on their journey, and require a level of empathy along with your determination to get them through. I have taught the re-sit class for many years, right from the days when it was at the bottom of everyone's list of priorities, and I used to comb the rooming timetable to find a space for us to work in.

Those first September lessons are full of raw emotion: the hurt pride of those who don't think they deserve to be there, the apprehension of the Year-11 class clown who has paid the price for providing the entertainment throughout their GCSE course, and the diligent student who could not have worked any harder but just crumbled at the sight of the exam papers. As a teacher, you navigate through those difficult early days, identifying places where improvements can be made, supporting students with literacy difficulties they have struggled with since Reception, and reassuring students, sometimes those fluent in several additional languages, that they will make progress. Sourcing materials to inspire and stimulate students who have seen and done every paper the exam board has produced is challenging, and inventing ways to make the same skills feel accessible and manageable is difficult.

So, you thought you needed all your positive powers in September? January is when you really earn your stripes as you try to instill enthusiasm and positivity into your potentially jaded charges. But it is also when you see the resilience young people are capable of, and the support of their families; families who never give up and demand that you don't either.

The re-sit class: teaching distilled to its purest form.

Rachael Dargie has been an English teacher for over 20 years, mainly in the north of England. She has mentored trainee teachers for several years.

Be the Change

Shigupta Islam

My first role teaching was in a school heading towards 'Special Measures' and in an area with a strong English Defence League following. Neither of those were my concern when I met my unruly form 9I. It was like a baptism of fire for behaviour management, but perseverance and consistency were my friends. By Easter, things were getting better; Molly even stopped wearing her 'Buddha Rocks' belt once she realised I wasn't going to let up on the uniform policy!

There was one boy in my form who was well known around school as 'that kid'. Carl was a cheeky, lovable rogue, but at the same time he struggled to stay within the confines of the boundaries set by his teachers. He would constantly get into trouble and I would constantly have to have 'the chat' with him. You know the one: 'What do you want to do with your life?'

One Personal Social and Health Education (PSHE) lesson, the children were asked to write a piece about living in a diverse society. It was supposed to be a positive activity. They all handed it in and there were some lovely heart-warming words. Not Carl's though. Carl's piece hit me like a bolt of thunder. I couldn't read the whole piece. The only words I could see were "P**i's should go back to their country". I didn't know what to do with it. In my head I played out a scenario where if I reported it, he would not learn a lesson and his hatred for people of colour would grow stronger. Instead, I confronted him. Carl came from a family where he was taught that Asian people didn't belong in this country. When challenged about his views, he responded "Obviously not about you Miss, you're not a P**i".

I decided not to deal with the situation offensively or aggressively. Instead, I envisioned forging a long journey ahead to challenge and change the community perception by being a role model. Over the years I treated Carl with as much care and attention as I did other students. I went above and beyond, putting on extra sessions and motivating him when he became lazy. One day in Year 11 after a long day of intensive extra revision, Carl hung back to speak to me.

"Thanks for giving up your Saturday. Miss, I want to apologise for something; I doubt you'll remember".

I remembered.

"I've never engaged with people of colour. I know how offensive that piece I wrote in Year 9 was and I'm embarrassed and ashamed by it". He went on to say that at home, he now challenged his father and grandfather on their extreme views, but they won't change. He thanked me for being a positive role model, teaching him values and showing him that change starts with oneself.

I said nothing. The tears rolled down my face. I smiled and cried all at the same time.

Shigupta Islam is a science teacher from the Midlands. She has taught in three of the most challenging schools in the city and has had the pleasure of leading those schools to grow in strength by being part of the leadership teams.

Making a Song and Dance of It

Fiona Ruck

The problem with teaching a knowledge-rich curriculum is that it is full of knowledge. Stating the obvious, I know. Our pupils are capable of incredible things; they are vessels to be filled, lamps to be lit. Knowledge, after all, is power. But for many, retaining this knowledge that we pour into them each day is a daunting prospect. As classroom teachers we need to develop remembering techniques, activities that will inspire, engage and enable our pupils to learn for the long term—to retain that knowledge.

Ask any teacher and they will tell you that teaching is an act. Your classroom is your stage. When you build relationships with your pupils you give them a part of you. And if you walk into one of my lessons, chances are you will see the part of me that I often end up giving is being laughed at. But those are the lessons that my pupils remember. The lessons where I use remembering techniques that involve me singing or dancing, neither of which are my strong points! But my pupils see that I am clearly out of my comfort zone and it helps with me encouraging them to do the same, all in the name of learning.

Using song and dance in lessons acts as sensory input. We need these stimuli to be meaningful and unusual in order to make it into their short-term memory. Try getting your class to sing along to a song about the water cycle, or to rap about plate boundaries, or to sing a song questioning the building of the wall in a case study of Mexico to USA migration, or using the desks as drums in a song about the Mt. St Helens volcanic eruption. These strategies allow us to rehearse this new knowledge with our pupils; you want them to leave your room with the song stuck in their head for repetition to take place. This is critical if this knowledge is to make its way into their long-term memory.

My advice? Put yourself out there. Make a fool of yourself. Use humour. Create remembering techniques that will engage and inspire. Make a song and a dance out of it, all in the quest for knowledge retention. Teach, sing, dance, repeat. And next time you see an excited teacher standing on the beach at Durdle Door, attempting to get a bunch of teenagers to retain their knowledge through dance and song, maybe, just maybe, you'll come and join in!

Fiona Ruck is Second in Geography at a Secondary School in Birmingham.

The Secret and Magical Powers of the Wet Power Towel

Annie Pendrey

Back in 1985, I qualified as a Nursery Nurse (NNEB) and began a career working with children aged 3-4 years in a nursery setting.

At college, I successfully studied a wide range of psychological theories, from Piaget to Vygotsky, and completed over 100 observations of children aged 0-8, evaluating the young child's development and planning for next steps in their play and learning. In addition, I spent hours cementing theory to practice within my academic writing, as well as undertaking many hours of work experience in a nursery through to Year 2, a children's ward, a maternity ward (even having the opportunity to watch a birth), a week being a private nanny to spending two weeks in a residential care home for children with SEN (Special Educational Needs).

All these fabulous opportunities, alongside an amazing set of subject specialist tutors, set me on the path to Early Years—but one thing I was never taught was the secret and magical powers of the 'Paper Towel'!

Our special paper towel was green in colour and arrived in an enormous box in packs of twelve, with each pack encased in a white paper sleeve. You would rip off the sleeve and pop the paper towels into the dispensers located in the children's toilets, the kitchen, and the art area.

This magical paper towel was advertised as absorbent, disposable and extra strong! You would be forgiven for thinking that this humble paper towel was for hand drying only. However, once inside the nursery, this paper towel took on a new life form; it was true, it was extra strong and disposable, but suddenly when put into a dispenser it transformed into a paper towel that possessed super magical powers.

One of its magical powers was 'healing'. When a child fell over in the playground—with a surface which was not grass or some smooth spongy texture as you would find today—out would come the wet paper towel to heal a knee full of gravel and blood.

The paper towel was always there to support you in your creative activities, from sitting beneath your PVA glue pots to absorb the overspill, to wiping up paint from the paint pots (not actually ever really wiping it up of course, more sliding and moving the paint further around from its original spill). You would think that was enough magical power for THE paper towel, but it also was an integral part of snack time. Our incredibly versatile paper towel presented itself as a napkin for toast, a biscuit or fruit, and went on to then double up to wipe the child's sticky face—and of course in the nursery, the runny, snotty nose. It is here the absorbent adjective was questionable—say no more!

However, what this magical paper towel did not lack was resilience, even refusing to believe in its own lack of absorbency as it became an international traveller. Every nursery trip, from trips to the farm to trips to the seaside, the paper towel came out in force. It was so useful, that it would even sit in a bundle of paper towels in the bottom of a sick bucket, alongside cotton wool and a plastic bag as part of the emergency rescue division ready for those oft-feared words…"Miss, I feel sick!"

Strange as it might seem, I firmly believe that in our NNEB training, there should be a section on the amazing benefits of keeping on hand a supply of THE paper towel. The chaos of our environment when in the nursery calls for something with almost magical properties; this almost magical, everyday item certainly served me well in my Early Years days.

Annie Pendrey is a freelance consultant and founder of Creating Spaces. She started her career as a Nursery Nurse and specialises in Early Years, SEN and FE/HE. She holds Advanced Teacher Status and Senior Fellowship HEA. She also serves on the Practitioner Advisory Board for the Society of Education and writes regularly for FE news.

Between the Lessons

Alice Codner

My favourite part of class teaching is, without a doubt, the in-between bits. These are the moments snatched from a packed timetable, after the register but before English, or ten minutes before home time; just enough for a quick game or the sharing of news. Over the weeks, in-jokes and practices unique to that particular group emerge to provide a sense of belonging, which enables children to feel safe enough to take the risks necessary for growth. One of my classes, for example, developed a love for pinecones, and to their delight, each morning we hung a new pinecone that they had collected on a string above the number-line to count the days we had been together.

The trust built up in these times gives teachers the unique opportunity to model healthy ways of responding to circumstances that may arise. One particular moment stands out for me in this regard. It was the day of the Grenfell disaster. Many in my Year 2 class had watched the news that morning and seen images of smoke billowing from flats just five miles away, and babies being thrown from windows to be saved. It was lunchtime, and I had a choice: to get on with lessons as usual, risking modelling the suppression of sadness, or to give the afternoon over to it by writing letters to the emergency services, risking trivialising the disaster by turning it into just another project, or worse, exposing the children to trauma. I was close to tears myself, feeling gutted and powerless, but also aware of the importance of my position.

We started off by sharing honestly about our feelings, just as we practised regularly in Circle Time sessions. The children were fully engaged with the gravity of the situation, and many said they were sad and frightened. We then discussed how to respond. Several children suggested that we pray, so, grateful for the structure of our school reflection times, I told them to "reflect or pray according to your belief". They took up their positions: some prostrate, some with hands together, some sitting calmly with legs crossed and closed eyes.

As I expressed a simple, but heartfelt reflection, the whole class was completely silent. The extraordinary nature of the situation suddenly struck me, taking my breath away: there I was, with thirty incredible individuals, with a whole range of religions, cultures, and life experiences, all united in prayer or reflection, each practised in their own way with total sincerity. It was the purest moment I have ever experienced, and I let a few awe-filled tears fall silently before telling them to open their eyes. I wondered if the world could learn something from these children. Then we sat up and got on with our afternoon lessons as usual.

The privilege of experiencing that moment together with my class was one that will never leave me. It wasn't a formal lesson, but often the most wonderful parts of the job are the in-between bits you don't plan for.

Alice Codner is a teacher at Elsley Primary School in London. She passionately believes in the development of the whole child through education. She is currently the school's outdoor learning leader, and as such has started a school farm, including growing vegetables and keeping a range of animals.

The Way We See It

Uma Tadema

Having switched to teaching after working in completely different fields, like hospitality and aviation administration, my motto has been to always try out new things and keep learning.

The last 15-plus years of face-to-face teaching in varied environments have been very enriching and satisfying. Most days when I finish a class, I feel energised and happy with what I have done.

This March, in order to flatten the curve of the COVID-19 pandemic, the area where I live in Germany had lockdown procedures in place. These meant all in-person classes were cancelled.

Suddenly, like many teachers all over the world, my days were spent in researching online teaching methods, attending the numerous helpful webinars organised by publishers, teaching organisations and much more. I had to think about, in fact teach myself, alternative methods of instruction and learning. I was not entirely new to the experience because even before the pandemic I had already decided to explore online teaching, so I thought this enforced social distancing time would be a good opportunity to try it out. Armed with my one-week information flow about teaching English online, and the enthusiasm to try something new, I asked a couple of my classes if they would be interested in online classes. Some of them said yes and some of them weren't interested, so we decided to go ahead with those who were willing to give it a shot.

The sessions were shorter than the usual ones, and initially some of the students had technical issues which got sorted out later. In fact, during one session, one student took part on the phone for the audio aspect and online for the video. Her computer had some glitches with the audio, but the video worked well. As I had offered to run her through the procedure of entering the virtual classroom, she called and found it easier to speak on the phone and see us on the computer screen. So, she was on the speakerphone the whole time. This was absolute improvisation and learning on the go for all of us.

I felt that my teaching skills were not up to par to the standards of online teaching that the webinars had put forth. Moreover, I thought that it was my lack of skills, not the students', which was hindering the whole process of learning. At the end of the sessions, I felt calling those sessions classes was akin to cheating because I felt that my students had not benefited in any way. However, what took me completely by surprise was that every single student who had attended the online sessions posted positive feedback about the sessions in their respective group chats. These are example of comments I received:

"We had fun".

"It made me feel positive about the whole situation. For a short while I left behind all my worries".

"I enjoyed meeting my classmates online".

"I laughed so much".

As far as they were concerned, while learning English was important, being part of a group, trying out something new, seeing that their teacher was trying her best and going to lengths to make the lesson entertaining as well as informative were all just as important.

While I am fully aware that this kind of lesson may not be the norm for instruction, the example serves to illustrate the point I would like to make. It is worth thinking about how we, as teachers, assess situations or what happens in the classroom and how our learners view these very same situations.

So, sometimes you may think that you are not making a difference, but that may be solely a personal impression based on your perception. Your students might see it quite differently.

Uma Tadema, BA (Economics), PG Dip, CELTA, Cert TEB, M.Ed (Applied Linguistics). After having worked in the service industry in

India, Germany and China, Uma qualified as an ELT teacher in 2002 and has since worked in the field of education in Germany, India and Australia. Uma is interested in technology and agency in the classroom. After gaining her M.Ed (Applied Linguistics) and becoming involved with Cambridge Assessment as a speaking examiner, she is currently running a language school in Germany and considering the option of working towards her doctorate in education.

Chapter 3

So Much More Than Just a Teacher

'Educating the mind without educating the heart is no education at all' - Aristotle

There's no doubt about it, teachers are incredible. During the global pandemic, we educated the nation's children and young people in innovative ways, responding swiftly to the unique times we found ourselves living in. We entered the profession knowing that, unlike many other jobs, our responsibilities extend far beyond imparting our knowledge and wisdom to our learners. And that is why it is important to realise that we are so much more than 'just' teachers.

Teachers are role models who show children how they can make sense of the world they live in. Teachers help children and young people to communicate their thoughts and feelings in a peaceful and respectful way. Teachers prepare their learners to be confident, articulate, and well-rounded individuals so that when they leave school, they are ready to live their lives independently.

Great teachers are committed to giving each and every child the very best start in life, especially when times are tough. In this chapter, educators share their hilarious, honest and heartfelt experiences in the classroom and beyond.

Please Give Teachers the Respect They Deserve

Sarah Mullin

Teaching can be challenging and during the global pandemic, teachers went above and beyond to minimise any disruption to learning for children and young people across the country. As the number of Covid-19 cases and tragic deaths continued to rise, our own fears and anxieties heightened.

As teachers returned home, exhausted after a long day at school, it was heartbreaking to witness unjustified teacher-bashing in the media. You might have thought that 2020 would be the year that we learned to appreciate teachers as key workers. You might have thought that the pandemic would have taught us the importance of kindness and compassion. You might have thought that this year, with parents having to support children with their home-learning during the initial national lockdown, people would have appreciated just how challenging it can be to inspire, engage and motivate children and young people every single day.

Despite the negative ways that teachers continue to be misrepresented in the media, teachers rose above it all and continued to do what we do best: educating our pupils in order to increase their future life choices. Here are five things I would love the world to know about our fabulous teachers and education staff:

1. We do the job because we care

While goodwill and kindheartedness won't pay our mortgages or our bills, most teachers will generally agree that we didn't enter this profession for the money. We could have chosen to pursue a plethora of other careers with far less stressful conditions and far more lucrative salaries, but we didn't. We actively chose to become teachers because we truly believe in the transformational power of education. We are driven by giving each and every child the very best start in life.

2. The educational landscape has changed

It is understandable that some people may have had disappointing—or even unpleasant—experiences in school back when they were children themselves, and this may have affected their perception of teachers. However, the educational landscape has changed considerably over the years. Nowadays, a child who's late to school has a conversation about wellbeing rather than a slap on the knuckles with a ruler.

Today's teachers are driven by doing the best they can for their pupils; often because they want to offer children opportunities that were not available when they were at school. We really do care about the children we teach and we want the very best for them.

3. They are so much more than subject specialists

The role of teachers has expanded exponentially over the years. We have studied hard, gaining multiple degrees and professional qualifications to become subject specialists, so that we can share our knowledge and wisdom with our pupils.

Teachers are fully committed to growing and developing as research-informed educators so that we can help pupils to make the most of their skills. We are dedicated to teaching children to be courteous, responsible and resilient global citizens so that they can survive and thrive as young adults when they leave school.

And, with the number of mental-health cases among children soaring, we are also helping our pupils to learn to cope with the stresses of life.

4. They are adaptable

Teachers have remained calm in the face of adversity and have quickly responded to continually changing rules, advice and guidance.

When teachers were faced with the problem of how to continue educating pupils who were self-isolating, we swiftly adapted to using video-conferencing software in order to minimise any disruption. When parents were no longer allowed to enter school premises, we put virtual parents' evenings in place. We even made sure that no parent missed out on seeing their children in a nativity play or class assembly by offering pre-recorded adaptations.

Teachers have worked tirelessly, under exceptionally difficult circumstances, even when many feared for our own health—and the health of our families—during the global pandemic.

5. Schools are a fundamental part of our society

As the country entered the first national lockdown, we soon realised that while we may all be facing the same pandemic, we would all experience the associated challenges in different ways.

For many children, school was the only place where they could be guaranteed a meal each day. So the primary concern for many headteachers was how they would manage to ensure that their children and young people would eat.

The pandemic proved that schools—and teachers—are a vital part of society. Not only do we bring children together to learn and play but we also provide a safe space for children to disclose safeguarding concerns and access support when they need it.

It is such a great honour to be a teacher—to have the opportunity to play a small part in the lives of children and young people—and although it may be tough at times, there really is no job we would rather do.

Sarah Mullin BA (HONS), PGCE, PGCertED, PGDipED, MA, CTE, FCCT, CMgr FCMI, FInstLM, FRSA is a deputy headteacher and Doctor of Education student. She is the author of the number one best-selling book 'What They Didn't Teach Me on My PGCE' and she is the founder of #EduTeacherTips, the YouTube channel for teachers, by teachers. Sarah is on the board of the secondary education committee at the English Association and she is renowned for supporting Early Career Teachers (ECTs) and aspiring school leaders locally, nationally and internationally. She was recently named a 'Rising Star in Education and Academia' and has previously received the 'Contribution to Education of the Year' award.

The Importance of a Form Family

Raj Khera

It was the summer of 2013 when I found out I would be picking up a form group whose tutor was leaving for pastures new. She came to see me with a handover folder full of behaviour reports and a handwritten list of things to watch out for in the group. I'd heard whisperings about some of these students in the staff room, so I already knew I was in for an interesting time.

The morning before our first form time, I tried to put everything I had heard out of my mind—I wanted them to have a 'clean slate'. Well, the absolute commotion that ensued as the students piled in through the classroom door quickly smeared that clean slate. No, this group needed boundaries and they needed them quick. I was not looking forward to this. Neither were they.

We spent the first term pushing against each other. We practised how to enter form respectfully, how to organise deadlines, how to cope with consequences and take responsibility of poor behaviour, and even how to listen. They hated it. We were afflicted with a whole host of mishaps: there was the Nivea cream phase (where the aim of the game was to smear each other's faces with Nivea cream), followed by the water bomb phase, which was then followed by the entrepreneur phase, and—our grand finale—the throwing furniture at each other phase. The area outside my classroom was regularly filled with my students sitting in various states of dishevelment while I sat trying to eat lunch and doing damage control via email.

As the months went on and the consequences, reflections, phone calls home and conversations about behaviour continued, the realisation that I was not going to let them run riot soon crept in. There were fewer and fewer incidents, and somewhere around February 2014, we became a 'Form Family'. I realised that all they had needed was belief in them and a bit of love. They realised I genuinely cared.

They would come to confess even minor infringements before behaviour points were added to the monitoring system. They would support and regulate each other in lessons so the 'Form Family' could be rewarded. One even sat in the isolation room while his acquaintances tried (unsuccessfully) to burn the door down because he did not want to bring shame on the form by absconding. Most importantly, though, they started taking pride in being part of something successful and loving. They became fiercely protective of each other and their reputation as a form. By 2016, I had a group of well-rounded, respectful, and ambitious teenagers. All secured work experience placements, and all had started to think beyond their GCSE examinations. We reached a point where form time was the best part of the day and the safest space some of them had, and we protected it as such.

Form time in all schools should be sacrosanct and the form tutor should be the tutee's biggest advocate in school. If not, then what is the point in the form system?

Raj is an English teacher and KS5 form tutor. She has worked in multi-disciplinary faith and mainstream schools since training in Amsterdam 10 years ago. Now based in Sandwell, Raj is an advocate for visible diversity in education. She also enjoys her work as a team leader for English Language exam marking.

A Surprise for the Form Teacher

Ellie Clark

I will never forget my first tutor group. I once walked in on a wet Monday morning, tired and harried, to see all the desks cleared back except two pushed together with a tablecloth and full plastic dinnerware set. I was served a 'meal' (canteen muffin), 'wine' (Ribena) and then the designated student got down on one knee and produced a plastic ring. "Miss, we want to be your form forever. On behalf of 822: will you marry us?"

Reader, I did.

Ellie Clark is an English teacher and professional tutor at The Brakenhale Academy in Berkshire. A former deputy headteacher, she now focuses on teacher training and boosting subject knowledge in English; she can be found blogging under teachingin10.wordpress.com and tweeting @ EllieClark_83.

Inspiring Potential

Lorna Baldry

How can anyone learn when they have no roof over their head, no food in their stomach or are worried about violence or other abuse? In these situations, learning becomes superfluous as survival instinct kicks in. We need to help with these pressing issues before we can hope to fully engage learners. If there are too many barriers for it to be the right time for learning in any individual case, then education professionals should note that learner's ambitions and let them know that, while education may not be their priority, it is not a threat either. Learning can be a comfort, and eventually will overcome many problems and pave the way to their dreams.

Treat the learner holistically, ensuring they can focus on learning, in whatever form is best for them, to achieve their full potential. To do this, organisations across sectors must work together to provide flexible, bespoke education with multi-agency wraparound support. This is a method of engagement or re-engagement which can be an effective pathway to learning, further learning and/or employment. Transition advice and support is critical at every level along with early identification of those at risk of disengaging.

Part of building resilience and skills includes enabling understanding, absorption and application of self-assessment, peer assessment and teacher assessment.

In individual lessons, set at least one objective, either universal or per learner/level. The learners should also set at least one for themselves to take ownership. They might do this at the end rather than the beginning of a lesson.

To raise aspirations, people should be exposed to a wide variety of experiences and people. This can be done with tasters from impassioned, expert individuals.

Case study

We established a new model of community learning with wraparound multi-agency support, unique delivery and a unique team.

The young people we worked with on this programme ranged in age from 16 – 25. On occasion, this was adapted to a small bespoke provision with those aged from 4 – 84.

The young people on the core programme had been expelled from or left other education provisions. Some had not regularly attended any formal schooling or learning for many years—in one instance since the age of 10. They showed a desire to engage and to try to identify their own barriers and the solutions to overcome them.

Some had learning variances; some also experienced addictions. We needed to work with these challenges because, despite them, these young people continued to show their wish to engage, simply by being there.

With the help of multi-agency wraparound support, we were able to share best practices with organisations that could help us learn how to work with these challenges. We were able to provide substance-misuse counselling via referral to them and co-working, sometimes even co-location. We could meet with their families and explain how they could support their learning and offer them learning experiences of their own.

We were able to arrange support for court appearances and visiting relatives in prisons.

We used only restorative approaches with no sanctions or punishments of any kind; there were very rarely any behavioural problems, and even when there were, none of them were serious. Outcomes and progression were incredible and significantly above national averages for similar groups.

We considered and planned for things like gang rivalry, former offending, caring responsibilities and mental health problems.

Things such as mood and behaviour are contagious, and surroundings and available resources can set a scene, a feeling, and the level and type of response. We modelled the behaviour we wanted to see. We brought a calm but very motivated mood to our interactions. We shared our feelings, their causes and consequences in circles. We trusted, because trust had often not been encountered before by these young people. We also ensured there was surrounding positivity and encouragement, and basic Maslow needs like warmth, relative comfort, food and water were provided.

In the spirit of transparency, and trusting that nurtured and well-informed young people can and should make decisions that affect them, we took every opportunity to communicate and truly co-produce the plan for their pathway.

Learners sometimes asked us questions that, as we noticed patterns of similarity based on their past experiences, we came to know as our project FAQs (Frequently Asked Questions).

These included:

- What's the point?
- Why is education necessary/important?
- Will you always solve my problems?
- Who are you?
- What do I want to do?
- Who do I want to be?
- What's my place in the world?
- When will I finish learning?
- What will I achieve?

Lorna has 20 years' experience in education, beginning as a law teacher in further education (FE) in 1999. Initially managing law provision at an inner-city college, Lorna then progressed to managing all professional courses and became Social Engagement and Community Collaboration Manager for the college and its community. Lorna worked across curriculum areas and levels of learning, with people aged 5 to 85. Lorna now runs Brightlink Learning.

A Teacher With a Supportive Ear

Tom Griffiths

Never underestimate your worth when working with parents and carers. This year, I've been working closely with one of our Newly Qualified Teachers (NQTs) on safeguarding and the support we are providing to a family. She has been amazed that, even as a teacher without children, she is giving parenting advice. It took me back to my NQT year with my wonderful Year 2 class when I worked closely with a single mum struggling with her child and his behaviour. I often think of them fondly and wonder what happened next after he left Year 6.

Like the NQT at my current school, I regularly went home surprised that 23-year-old me—without children—was being asked such questions as, "What time should he go to bed? How do I get him to sleep? What routines would you suggest?" In my head, I could not comprehend that I had potential answers using my knowledge from the classroom and my own life experience: what do I know?

However, I quickly realised that if you are open and visible for parents/carers, they will open up to you and trust you to support their child (and them). Owning your worth gives you the confidence to do this. Ten years later and with two children myself, the dynamic has changed for me slightly; I can relate more to what is being said, and my school setting is different, so our middle-class parents/carers are more prepared to chat. However, not having children doesn't take away your knowledge and the strategies you use in your classroom each day and how that can help a parent/carer support their child at home.

So, no matter the day you're having, go out at the beginning and end of the day, smile and say hi! You aren't always going to get to speak to all parents and carers, but be the teacher who does not simply go out to speak to a parent/carer about their child's poor behaviour that day—be the one who goes out and sings their praises so both child and parent go home feeling euphoric! That level of trust and approachability will stand you in good stead for the future.

In case you were wondering, the family I mentioned at the beginning are doing really well and relationships have improved amongst the family members. The open and honest discussions we have had has meant everyone's opinions are valued, leading to greater progress being made.

Tom Griffiths LLB PGCE is the assistant headteacher at Tidbury Green School in Solihull. Tom studied law at Nottingham Trent University before working as a teaching assistant in a deprived area of Nottingham. He currently leads on assessment, curriculum and safeguarding, as well as being responsible for mentoring and training middle leaders.

Why I Want to Become a Teacher

Michele Cobb

I have been in the childcare industry for a little over 20 years now, during which time I have worked in a variety of settings and had experience with a range of children, their behaviours, their parents and other practitioners. Even though I dabbled in some other careers, trying my hand at having an office job and even becoming a driving instructor, I gravitated back towards childcare—I knew working with children was what I wanted to do. In the last four years I completed my BA (Hons) degree. All my knowledge, experience and background is within the Early Years, which I absolutely love; no two days are the same and watching and being a part of a child's learning experience as they grasp new concepts is simply amazing. The skills they show when they use their phonetic knowledge to finally begin to blend words, writing their name, using skills to problem solve within their play, resolve conflicts with their peers—and even the huge accomplishment of zipping up their coat independently. The job satisfaction felt is immense and makes me smile every time. There are, however, the days that make my heart sink—days where the children's only safe place is school; I have spent many days where there have been tears and sleepless nights worrying about them.

I am passionate about children's wellbeing and have completed ELSA (Emotional Literacy Support Assistant) training, which gives me the skills to actively listen to a child and look behind any behaviours to search for the why. There is always a reason for a child's behaviour, and I always try to be a calming voice and come down to their level to get some understanding of how they are feeling.

To assist me with this I like to use the fizzy drink analogy, where the child is the fizzy bottle and by the time they reach the classroom door at 8.30 in the morning, it could have been shaken so many times already—for many reasons—that when the lid opens, it explodes. So, when a child arrives in tears or looks sad, instead of guiding them in with a 'you'll be fine in a minute,' I take the time to stop, ask questions to the parents, crouch down to their level and investigate how they are feeling. This helps to build a trusting and secure relationship so that the child knows there is someone that will listen and understand.

I started a School Centred Initial Teacher Training (SCITT) course in September and, as a slightly older trainee, I am hoping that some of the strategies, tools and ideas that I have gained in my years will assist me. Although the thought of leaving my comfort area of the Early Years Foundation Stage (EYFS) petrifies me, I am looking forward to the challenge and learning lots of new ways to scaffold young people's learning experiences. I am looking forward to having my own class and for the children to soak up all the knowledge I will provide for them. I anticipate that my teaching career will be one of hard work but will reap many rewards.

Michele Cobb, BA (Hons) is a Nursery Nurse with a wealth of experience within the childcare sector. She began her Teacher Training in September 2020. She is passionate about the emotional wellbeing of children, understanding the reason behind behaviours, and supporting children to manage their feelings and emotions.

'Just' a Teacher

Claire Smith

First let me say, I do not really like the phrase 'just' a teacher.

I had a conversation with my husband whilst walking our dog the other day. We were discussing our day at work, jobs and future careers. One of his comments was, "Well, you have never been just a teacher, have you?"

Of course, he is right. I have never been 'just' a teacher.

I qualified to be a teacher slightly later in life, after both my children started primary school. My youngest son had his first day at school the same day I started my first job as a secondary school teacher. He still reminds me of the fact that I never took him to school on his first day.

This first job was as an NQT and also a subject leader. I completed my training in December thanks to a flexible PGCE to suit studying and having a young family. I was really worried that I wouldn't get a job in January, but I did—in fact I was offered three jobs! I accepted a position close to home and it came with responsibility for two subject areas. Starting in January and being a subject leader seemed to mean that nobody realised I was actually an NQT. A five minute "this is how you log in and do a register" was my induction before starting a full day of teaching.

I remember attending an NQT conference several months later, hosted by the local authority. It was there that I met my professional mentor, or I should probably say she met me! We were discussing our experiences of being an NQT and sharing stories and tips. Seemingly horrified by my experience, she asked if she could help and what school I was from. "Yours," was my reply. Things changed slightly after that.

Your experiences most definitely shape you and influence the teacher that you become. My NQT experience has most definitely made me the professional mentor that I am now. I am passionate about supporting, mentoring and coaching staff, and I am also responsible for induction in my current role. I do my best to make sure that nobody's first few weeks/months are like mine were. I did survive; in fact, I thrived and spent 11 years at that school. Credit most certainly goes to the NQT mentor I eventually had. She has remained a very good friend and we laugh about the fact that she never knew being my mentor would last so long.

I was 'lucky' enough to be selected by my university when completing my PGCE to experience an Ofsted inspection. The inspector spent the day with me interviewing my mentor and the assistant head responsible for trainees, and of course me too. He watched me teach with laryngitis and virtually no voice. He asked me what I wanted to be. My answer was "a teacher". Where did I see myself in 5 years he asked? "Being a really great teacher" was my reply. He laughed and said that he thought I needed to think bigger than being "just a teacher".

15 years later, from NQT and subject leader to head of department, director of learning, faculty director and Assistant Principal, I still love my job—most of the time. On days when I am dealing with difficult issues and everything seems to be going wrong, my favourite place is still in a classroom being 'just' a teacher. But as teachers, we all know that we are so much more than 'just' teachers: we are a role model, leader, detective, parent (I have been called mum by mistake many times!), data analyst, educator, counsellor, confidant – the list is endless.

We certainly aren't 'just' teachers; we do change lives.

Claire Smith is an assistant principal at a school in Warwickshire where she leads on learning and teaching. She is a professional mentor for trainees, NQT's and Early Career Teachers. She has a Masters in Education (Leadership and Management) and is a Fellow of the Chartered College of Teaching (FCCT).

Teachers of SEND

Lizana Oberholzer

The Special Education Needs and Disabilities (SEND) Code of Practice: 0 – 24 (2014) highlights that we are all teachers of SEND. The Carter Review (2015) echoes this notion, but too often in my teaching career have I witnessed that, at times, only some are teachers of SEND, or only some, buy into this notion. I was very fortunate to meet wonderful young people on my journey as a teacher; many of them were extremely brave, kind and keen to learn. It so happens that one day I was introduced to a shy, tall boy who started in my Year 10 class. He was extremely brave, polite and determined to do well.

The colleague who told me that the student would be joining my group informed me that he, as referred to in those days, was a 'U', and that he had no predicted grades or aspirational grades, and that I would just need to see what I could do. That got my blood boiling, as my firm belief is that for each child I work with, I need to believe three times more than they do that they will do well and can succeed. In my view, no one should be labelled a 'U', and everyone has an opportunity to grow, develop, succeed, gaining the life chances they deserve and work so hard for. My role is to work with them, and to make it happen.

This journey became a personal journey for me as a teacher too, where I had to challenge my practice: how can I become more for my learners and how can I learn more about how I can be a teacher of SEND? I engaged in my own MA studies to extend and develop my understanding in order to support him well. I had to learn strategies, techniques and sometimes developed my own ideas to help him. It became a quest to help give a young man wings; to transform a 'U' into two successful 'Bs' at GCSE and help him to achieve his goals and achieve greatly. I was determined to ensure that he succeeded as I believed—and still do--that every child matters, and every child can succeed.

We worked tirelessly on developing 'recipes' for each exam question he had to answer, and each essay he had to write. He had a love for words, but would often use them out of context, and we had to find ways for him to understand that he needed to construct a clear argument, and be precise. He loved the logic of a discursive piece of writing, and we drew on his strengths with this, developing strategies to use this framework to help frame most of his responses. As a reward, we played scrabble at the end of each session, and needless to say, he was a true master of the game; I had to work very hard to keep up. He read the dictionary for pleasure, and my job was to help him contextualise the words he loved so much in a meaningful way for him to be able to communicate clearly. By working with him, it taught me that each learner finds magic by learning in their own unique way and, as a teacher, my role was to help them to find these moments of magic and embrace it.

On his GCSE Results day, I have never seen a happier child; his disbelief that he had achieved two Bs and the expression on his face will never leave me. He started running in circles on the front lawn of the main school building with his arms stretched out. I remember thinking how liberating it must be for him to know that he is so much more than a U, and that his journey can now truly take flight now that he has the wings he needs to get him there.

Lizana Oberholzer is a senior lecturer and programme lead for the MA (Leadership in Education) at the University of East London. She is the British Educational Research Association (BERA) interest group convenor for teacher education, a BAMEeD Trustee, a WomenEd regional lead, a MAT director and she is also a Principal Fellow of the Higher Education Academy. She tweets @LO_EduforAll.

Changing Lives

Mat Tobin

On a wet Wednesday morning, before school, I scanned the pre-requisites for my interview for the position of university lecturer, which revolved around the importance of literature in children's lives. It was only 8am and I noticed that two girls from my Year 6 class were outside in the rain. I called them in and then had an idea: what if I audio-recorded the three of us sharing our thoughts on a picture book? The purpose was twofold: to challenge any concepts of what we mean by high-quality literature, but also to present the importance of book-talk as a shared, social experience. We bring to the text all that we are and take from it much of what lies within.

The girls dried off and agreed to take part in the discussion. I chose *Not Now, Bernard* by David McKee and recorded the discussion. By the time we had finished sharing our thoughts, the school day was ready to begin; the girls had to get to the classroom and I had to drive off to the interview. As I left, one of the girls asked if I had chosen this book because Bernard was a lot like a boy in their classroom. She wondered whether the boy was angry and violent because he might also suffer from neglect at home by his parents. I replied saying that I had chosen the book because it was a picture book that could be read at many levels, and I knew that both girls would have some interesting thoughts to share on it.

When I returned to class mid-afternoon I noticed that both girls, who were incredibly astute and confident, had moved from their usual seating place to the front in order to be on the same table as this same boy. Much to his bemusement, he was seated next to one of the girls whilst the other sat opposite. I made no comment on this until the school day was over and everyone was going home. Both girls enjoyed lagging behind for a chat with me and were often the last to leave. When the rest of the class had departed, I asked them why they had chosen to move seats; their reply was that they wanted to just help him do well in school and show him that he was a part of the class.

In many respects they were right about the boy's home life. He lived with his father and older brother. His mother had left a few years earlier as the relationship was an abusive one. The boy was mistreated and displayed violent tendencies at school (mostly during play and lunchtime), but he also displayed incredible tenderness in PE sessions to those who struggled. PE, he often said, was the one thing he thought he was good at. He sat at the front of the class with two other timid but kind children, and although he would spend a lot of time off-task and without focus, he was no real trouble.

When the girls sat with him, everything changed. They were supportive yet firm from that day onwards. They would chide him if he wasn't focused, support him with understanding the task, cheer him on and 'tell' me to praise him when they thought he had worked hard. They helped him not to distract or be distracted by some of the other boys. Outside during break, they would play nearby and call him off the field to 'calm down' when he needed it. He never questioned or challenged them—he often looked either shocked or bemused at their level of commitment and control. I watched a transformation occur. With the support of the girls, he blossomed and had a life-changing summer term.

I didn't get the job, but I did get to say goodbye to that most excellent cohort. I worried about what would happen to the boy when they all moved to secondary school. All three were going to the same school and we had worked to ensure they were placed in the same tutor group. I got my answer a few years later when I drove to the university one morning (having gotten the job the second time round). My house is on a street that sits aside the secondary school's campus. I stopped at the end to let the students pass and who did I see? The boy walking between both of the girls. That moment of him laughing at something one of them said will always send a shiver down my spine.

Do books have the capacity to change lives? Absolutely. I often share Meeks' observation that 'reading doesn't happen in a vacuum' with students when discussing texts. Texts offer 'a process of discovery' (Meeks, 1987) about ourselves and others and if we present children with the platform for talking about texts, then we not only invite them to rewrite and reinterpret the story by seeing it through their eyes and those of others, but we also have the potential to rewrite the story of their lives and those of others too.

References

Meeks, M., 1987. *How Texts Teach What Children Learn.* 1st ed. Glocestershire: Thimble Press, p.6.

Mat Tobin teaches English and children's literature in primary Initial Teacher Education (ITE) at Oxford Brookes. Prior to this, he was a primary teacher and leader in Oxfordshire for 16 years.

Pupils Never Forget Their Teacher

Clive Hill

In my first term in the classroom, straight out of my Teach First Summer Institute training, I met 'Sean'. He was a Year 8 lad, much like a Jack Russell—smaller than his peers, full of energy, and fiery, as his stature demanded to keep his place in the pecking order of a tough inner-city secondary school in Derby. He loved to have a laugh and would do anything he could to avoid working. Sean struggled with literacy, and science was just a lesson full of words he couldn't read or spell.

One wet and windy (aren't they always?) Wednesday morning, my Year 8s were just getting settled when Sean thought he had snuck behind a filing cabinet unnoticed; armed with a piece of wood, he leapt out at me with a roar, expecting me to jump out of my skin. I didn't react how he thought I would; the lad saw red when I calmly asked him to sit back in his seat! He ran around the classroom smashing this piece of wood on the workbenches and desks—and he even took a swing at a girl that tried to disarm him. When I got to him, he was threatening to smash my computer up, and then he attacked the fire alarm. I managed to get the wood off him, and when support arrived, we moved the class out to another room and left Sean in there with our Student Engagement Team.

I later found out that Sean had been put into our alternative provision (AP) unit. I knew he blamed me at the time for him being in trouble, and I also knew I didn't want this young man to grow up resenting this bear of an ex-soldier that was twice his size.

I did what I thought was right, and took a Planning, Preparation and Assessment period (PPA) to go and visit him in our AP. As I swiped my fob and stepped in the door, Sean was sitting at a desk, drawing and drinking a cuppa. He looked up from his work and beamed a huge grin: "Alright, Mr Hill?!" Thankfully, he wasn't sitting there plotting my demise. Over the following weeks this was my regular stop; straight after break-duty, I would go and see Sean and find out what he had been up to so far that week. He would insist on making me a brew, and we would talk about whatever he wanted to while I supported him with his work.

When it was time for Sean to return to mainstream lessons, the first class he asked to come back to was mine. I was lost for words. He was still hard work, but worth every ounce of effort we put in together to build a positive relationship. When I left for pastures new, he came to find me on Sports Day—with a bucket of water. I was soaked! Sean thought he had the last laugh…

…but he doesn't know the lasting impact this relationship had on who I am as a teacher.

Clive Hill is a career-changer who trained in the East Midlands, through Teach First in 2017. He is now a lead practitioner for science at a Derby Secondary school and a member of the Chartered College of Teaching Council.

Trust Matters

Chris Reddy

Following a successful NQT year as a PE teacher in 2005, I managed to secure a post as Head of Year 9. My dream role. My NQT mentor told me not to go for it: "You can't have pastoral responsibilities like that if you don't have your own children. You're too young".

Whilst I didn't have the confidence then to debate this with an experienced teacher, I was confident enough to ignore him. A question from many of my colleagues was, "Why would you even want that job? It's the worst year in the school. Liam is in that year".

Liam is what the students called 'the cock of the year'. I've no idea if this is a familiar term nationally, so I'll explain. It essentially means he was tough. You wouldn't want to fight him. 'Who would win in a fight: Liam or Superman?'

The Year 9s were challenging. I had a role in changing not only the way the students viewed themselves but also the language staff used when talking about them.

Whilst Liam was a talented sports performer, he often had no kit. On reflection, this was not his fault. His home life was tough and his family didn't have the organisational skills which I would have liked as a PE teacher. Once again, he arrived to lesson without a kit. I checked the file and this was his 4th time this term. Department policy was now an hour of detention and he couldn't borrow a kit.

During this time, I was helping another PE teacher organise a sports tour to Holland. With online payments not being a thing in 2005, I had the job of collecting the money from the students. I had £210 sitting on my desk needing to go to student finance.

"Liam, come here will you?"

"Yeh?"

"Can you take this to student finance for me?"

"What is it?"

"Cash for the Holland trip".

"How much?"

"Probably about 200 quid. Be quick. We need to get to the top field".

"You want me to take it?"

"Yeah, hurry up!"

"You sure?"

"Just do it".

Whilst this was going on, the other PE teacher arrived.

"What was that you gave him?"

"Cash for the trip".

"How much?"

"200 quid".

"You gave 200 quid to Liam! Are you stupid?"

Let's face it, the chances of him leaving the country with that money were pretty remote. What that 'stupid' act of trust did for my relationship with Liam, and subsequently the rest of the year group, proved to be game changing. I feel that one act was responsible for setting the tone for the year and helped me take them through to Year 11. I had Liam, the 'cock of the year', on my side.

This was my first lesson in leadership. Find a way to trust those around you, even the ones you feel you shouldn't.

Chris Reddy is a pastoral leader, coach and non-executive director of National Careers Week. He has set up Bright Leaders, which focuses on developing the leadership potential in young people to help them recognise their strengths and lead courageous lives.

'Performance' Management

Leanne Herring

Prior to teaching, I worked in the performing arts industry. I entertained children and toured the country. I made little money from it, lived out of a suitcase, never knew where my next job was coming from and had a diet of pure sugar. But as time went by, I watched friends start to settle down, buy property, secure "sensible" jobs, and I decided it was time to join them. So, predictably, my next step was to train as a primary school teacher. Not long after qualifying, I changed my mind... This job is far from sensible!

Now, I'm 'that' teacher—the one who refuses to stick to the plan, writes original Christmas shows, uses green-screen effects in assemblies, runs the 'mini-musicals' club and has a costume for every theme day! Of course, I've had my fair share of eye rolls from colleagues. I still use the same raggedy old puppet in phonics, a top hat and wand in "magic maths" and a personalised clapper board to introduce story time.

Never be afraid to jump into a child's world; embrace imagination and fun— it is far more engaging than turning to page 26 in a textbook you'll never remember the title of. After all, do we look back and think about our favourite worksheet, or the teacher that threw caution to the wind and got us excited about learning? I've seen many changes throughout my career and faced the pressures of curriculum, data and conforming. I recently became disheartened and found myself wanting to leave the profession for a short while. I felt creative teaching was becoming a thing of the past, making way for corporate conformists and generic approaches. I even planned to change jobs before I resented the classroom completely.

Not long after feeling this way, the national lockdown happened; I kept in touch with my class by posting bedtime stories and performing my own via school and social media platforms. The response humbled and overwhelmed me. I received videos of storytelling events, book reviews and puppet shows from both my past and present pupils, using gimmicks and styles I had presented to them in the classroom. They even organised a Happy Birthday montage for me, all waving and singing into the camera. This is the power of teaching, the feel-good moments of confidence and creativity not found in any PowerPoint slide.

The united bond you create with a class is better than any tick sheet or graph. Those moments are forever, and will be throughout each and every generation to come.

Leanne Herring is a primary school teacher based in Essex. She has specialised in Key Stage 1 and Foundation Stage for nearly ten years. She is about to pursue a master's degree in psycholinguistics—and still lives on a diet of sugar.

The First Lesson

Mark Jesnick

You are standing in front of 28 fifteen-year-olds with a picture of a burning car behind you and you have no idea what you're doing.

The picture is the first hit you found searching for the London riots on Google the night before. You are aware these riots originated two miles down the road in Tottenham, and that Mark Duggan was killed less than a month before this lesson.

You imagine that it's the Turkish and Kurdish families of many of the young people sitting in front of you that chased looters away from their shops and businesses on Green Lane and in Dalston and Stoke Newington. You are later told there are students who haven't returned to school after the summer holidays because of their involvement in these riots and the repercussions. Some of these could have friends in this class. One of them is maybe even meant to be in this class.

And yet here you are 'teaching' them how to use adjectives and alliteration to bring the burning car to life and describe the boy in the foreground throwing something, anonymous in his tracksuit and hoodie, but unable to disguise the fact that he's not much older than the young people in front of you. And you have no idea what you're doing.

You've been dreading this lesson, which you've been directed to teach because the school still doesn't know what exam board it's choosing for GCSE and so you need to fill time. You're dreading the fact that these fourteen and fifteen-year-olds will know more than you, that you won't have all the answers, and that they will find you out for what you are—a twenty-two-year-old university graduate with no teaching experience or, at this stage, ability.

But they just don't care. Three are asleep, or at least ostentatiously laying their heads on desks, eyes shut, dead to the world. You don't know which is worse, the idea that your lesson is so dull that they have actually nodded off or that they have no qualms about showing you what they think of your attempts to explain linguistic devices in this most silent manner of protest. Others talk, some in whispering tones that could imply respect but instead create an insistent hum of disregard, like the purring of an inefficient washing machine. One girl has turned her back on you and is talking at full volume to another girl behind. When you pick her up on it, she tells you she is talking "about the work" and, despite the aggression in her voice and the way she kisses her teeth, you leave it there; after all, you really don't want to know what she's saying about this subject matter and are just desperate to avoid conflict.

What makes you feel worse are the three or four in the class who seem genuinely interested, who ask questions about the picture and want to see more like it, and even ask how they can improve their description of the flames rising up towards the sky: "What's a better word for dark sir?" "What about a simile here?"

You feel worse for them because this is what you really have no idea about. Sleeping and whispering and kissing teeth you can sort of deal with: tutting disapprovingly, sighing frustratedly, emptily threatening sanctions and then complaining later when they don't work. But what you know you can't do is teach those who truly want to learn, and you know that they'll soon know this too.

So you tell the class they have twenty minutes to write a description of the car and sit staring at the clock as the talking increases in volume, paper aeroplanes get thrown across the room—and even the three or four who are interested give up and start taunting each other over Manchester United beating Arsenal 8-2 over the weekend.

And you just wait for the bell and the next lesson, when you will do it all again.

Mark became a teacher straight after leaving university, and despite a rocky start (as exemplified in the short story!), stayed at his first school in Enfield for five years, becoming head of English and a lead practitioner.

He is now back in Enfield as an assistant principal five minutes down the road from that original school. He tweets @JesnickMark and blogs about Continuing Professional Development (CPD) and coaching on markmy-words1989@wordpress.com.

A Fresh Start

Devan Creswell

While you should always ask advice on any students in your class you do not know, do not just rely on that judgement; always make your own mind up. One thing that always sticks out for me is a student during one of my first NQT jobs. She never got on with any other teacher and always had issues with staff. I treated her with respect and offered her a clean slate. I ended up being the only teacher she got on with and became someone she could turn to if needed.

I have continued to do that and I always ensure students come into my class knowing that it is a fresh start for them, and any issues from previous lessons do not affect the current lesson.

Devan Cresswell is a teacher of history and an examination marker. She tweets @CresswellMiss.

Learning During an Overseas Project

Lucy Thomas

Last summer I found myself in the middle of nowhere in a secondary school in Uganda as part of a larger education project. I was terrified when thrown into a classroom with upwards of fifty students. I was surprised that the more relaxed setting of sports activities and craft sessions allowed me to gain insight into my passion for teaching. Naively, I thought that—having completed my own education in a socio-economically deprived area—I was ready for anything that this school would throw at me. I was clearly not expecting the emotional challenges that I faced, or the lessons I would learn.

"What do you want to be when you grow up?" "What is your favourite subject to learn?" These basic conversation starters were the only questions I knew to ask in free time, outside of the classroom. I had never found myself in such a new, demanding situation. I was surrounded by hundreds of school children of all ages, all wanting my undivided attention. And I desperately wanted to give it to them. My confidence in this dynamic quickly increased and I was able to develop conversations with pupils, reminiscing and sharing my own schooling experience. It soon became apparent that I had so much more in common with the pupils I met than I ever could have thought.

I immersed myself in the school environment and gauged insight into the way in which the pupils learned. The limited resources were adapted to engage and stimulate the minds of the children in and out of the classroom. I was also part of a team building play materials on the grounds of the school to enhance this aspect of learning. I was fortunate enough to experience first-hand the benefit of creative play and felt lucky to be able to contribute to the school resources. The innovative approach to learning was something that excited me.

I was in awe at the school environment that was created in such a demanding context. For many students, like in the United Kingdom, the classroom provided security and escapism. For many students, the support of a teacher was their motivation to better themselves. I knew that this global system of education was one that I desperately wanted to be part of. These key values are ones that do not differ with the structure or design of a building. They are inherently personal and special, and ones in which I cannot wait to share through my teaching journey.

Lucy Thomas is going into the final year of her undergraduate degree with a desire to start a Secondary English PGCE in 2021. An eye-opening overseas education project in 2019 cemented her desire to begin a journey in the field of education.

Use Your Team

Uma Tadema

I would like to share two completely different situations in diverse parts of the globe that had one aspect in common.

The first situation regards a young girl of 5 who had arrived by boat (as a refugee from Iran), and was placed in the foundation year (the year before Grade 1) in an Australian school. This young girl, (let's call her P) was an only child, severely traumatised from her experience in her home country and journey to Australia. When we initially got to know her, P spoke no English at all, and she refused to let her parents out of her sight. Slowly but surely her parents were able to take a back seat, and P felt confident at school without them.

One incident, that to me defines her transformation, was her first swimming lesson. P refused to go anywhere near the water—perhaps reminiscent of her recent trauma that led to her boat journey to this new country. Her screams and tears were heart wrenching. A judicious mix of patience, encouragement and determination, especially by her PE teacher and parents, helped P to swim just as well as any other child by the end of the academic year. And, by the end of the school year, P was able to transition to Grade 1—albeit as one of the weaker students. By the end of Grade 1 there was nothing distinguishing P from any other child in her class.

The second example is from Germany. R, Grade 2, was asked to leave his elementary school in the middle of the academic year because of discipline issues. As a result, he was enrolled in another elementary school. As the youngest child in a family with many older siblings and a violent father, R was only able to stay in school for a couple of hours before being taken, for the better part of the day, to a centre specialising in troubled youths. In the early weeks, R would literally jump onto tables and be extremely disruptive, abusive and violent at school. By the end of the academic year, his behaviour improved leaps and bounds and R was able to stay in school for the whole time. Although academically he wasn't able to keep up with the rest of the class, he didn't disrupt the class the way he did six months earlier.

In both situations, the class teachers had an ace up their sleeves. Parents, social workers, classmates, the school support network and every possible avenue were explored. In Australia there was a well organised system in place where educators and social workers who had worked with traumatised children could help P. The class teacher was able to get interpreters to communicate frequently with the parents so that they could help reinforce the messages P was getting at school. In Germany, the class teacher was able to take advantage of the interpersonal relationships of a small town to help minimise red tape and organise help for R in terms of supervision or additional help with homework and identifying after school activities which he could be part of. In R's case, he was very good at sports so a football team with a trainer adept at handling troubled youths was found.

No class teacher can devote the resources needed to support any one child intensively over a long period of time. In both examples mentioned, the class teachers made clear communication, practical allocation of duties and excellent coordination among the team a top priority. This helped not only P and R, but the other children were also able to see how everyone plays a part in achieving a goal.

It is a sign of maturity to ask for and accept help; not one of weakness. My takeaway from these experiences is: when there is a team which can help, use it.

Uma Tadema, BA (Economics), PG Dip, CELTA, Cert TEB, M.Ed (Applied Linguistics). After having worked in the service industry in India, Germany and China, Uma qualified as an ELT teacher in 2002 and has since worked in the field of education in Germany, India and Australia. Uma is interested in technology and agency in the classroom.

After gaining her M.Ed (Applied Linguistics) and becoming involved with Cambridge Assessment as a speaking examiner, she is currently running a language school in Germany and considering the option of working towards her doctorate in education.

Be the One

Rani Tiwana

In many ways it only feels like a few years ago since I graduated and passed my Newly Qualified Teacher (NQT) year, but the reality is it's actually 20! I often reminisce about those early days, the people I met and how they shaped me into becoming who I am today. But it goes far deeper than that—by growing up and learning English as a second language I knew I'd be in constant awe and deep admiration for those that went above and beyond.

I was fortunate enough to land my first post, where I completed my final year teaching practice. Getting through that final year came with ups and downs. One great example is that I accidentally swore in class during the penultimate week! I remember it so vividly—a Friday afternoon that very nearly ruined my weekend. I often wonder why I wasn't acquainted with the super-skill of reading a story and scanning for behaviour simultaneously. I lost track of the page and swore in my head … or so I thought. It just so happened that a wonderful teaching assistant (TA) who was by my side, informed the children, 'Miss said, oh sugar' in joint synchronisation as I claimed, 'oh shoot!' At least we both agreed on the same ***'sh'*** digraph! Needless to say, the clued-up class laughed hysterically, and I didn't get sacked.

A few months later, whilst practising lining up, I requested a child to sit back down and re-join the end of the line when he was ready. Upon returning to the classroom an hour or so later, not even noticing one less child in my Information and Communications Technology (ICT) lesson—yes, that's what it was called back then—the said child was still reflecting on whether he was ready or not! Another lucky escape for me!

All humour aside, there are many things I most certainly wasn't prepared for in my first year: informing the class about a member of staff passing away, consoling a child whose dad was in the 9/11 attack, assisting the police in search of a runaway, comforting a colleague dealing with an illness, numerous parents pouring their hearts out and sharing their burdens. I didn't get any training for this side of the job.

If there was anything I soon quickly realised, it was that I was in the right place, the right profession and exactly where I needed to be. Above all, it made me braver. It made me softer. It made me maternal. It made me realise they are *my* children and I am *their* hope.

My advice: If anything, be their rock, their constant. Be the one that listens to them, sticks up for them, is interested in them and finds out more about them. Above all, be the one that makes them laugh, smile and joke. Laugh with them and I guarantee they will remember you more than the best lesson you ever taught.

Rani Tiwana, is an assistant headteacher at Parkgate Primary School, Coventry. She studied English at the University of Cambridge and would love to write and publish a children's picture book one day. Twitter handle @fidsta77.

The Power of Relationships

Thomas Farnell

At my previous school I spent a lot of time as a cover teacher, then I started teaching A-level psychology as an unqualified teacher. Doing so much cover work meant I got to know the majority of the students really well. I was firm in terms of the standards that were expected, but I also put a huge emphasis on building relationships with the students. As I approached a classroom for a cover lesson, the students queuing up for the lesson would be split between cheering and groaning. Groaning because they knew that they would actually have to do work (in a cover lesson!), and cheers because, although they would have to do work, they genuinely liked me.

So, here we had a class that teachers would pull faces at or be trading war stories of poor lessons. They would be worried before even turning up to the class, expecting trouble. Yet I had them asking me to be their teacher because they actually worked MORE. Students actually want to learn, no matter what their actions might say. I didn't do anything spectacularly ground-breaking in that lesson. In fact, I am actually awful at Maths; they really wouldn't want me to be their teacher. But because of the time and effort I had put in previously getting to know them, listening to them and supporting them, behaviour was never an issue because they knew exactly what to expect from me, and they knew what I expected from them.

Thomas is currently a safeguarding and welfare officer at a grammar school in the West Midlands. Thomas was previously a cover teacher and taught A-level psychology as an unqualified teacher. Knowing the importance that relationships can play, Thomas decided to pursue a pastoral role, where he felt he could have the biggest impact.

"But Miss, What's the Point?"

Natalie Fowell

It was a couple of weeks before the GCSE English Literature exam last summer and I was revising *Macbeth* with my Year 11 students. At the time, I was working as an unqualified teacher, at a private education centre, to gain experience ahead of my PGCE. A student who was notorious for his cheeky-but-very-likeable personality interrupted our discussion.

"Miss, English Literature is pointless. It teaches us how to read a text, but what can you do with that information in real life? Nothing!"

"Well … It's not pointless …" I stuttered. I didn't know what to say; I'd never been put on the spot by a student before. He sensed my unease and, to him, my apprehensive reaction seemed to validate his bold claim. With a smug grin emerging across his face, he took a second jab.

"Come on, Miss, how is *Macbeth* going to benefit my life in any way? You know that I'm right—just admit it", he challenged.

I panicked. "Of course it has value! Stop trying to digress; you have an exam to pass!", I quickly muttered. I then continued to teach the theme of sleep to a disengaged student who was, ironically, probably going to nod off now having received confirmation from me, a subject specialist, that English Literature did not have value. It wasn't that I didn't have an answer. I did.

I felt humiliated. Why was I unable to give a calm and collected response in the way that so many of the qualified teachers who surrounded me would have done? Instead, I froze and brushed it off. At the time I was annoyed at myself, but in the days that followed, it made me think hard. The short exchange kept playing on loop in my head.

After lots of self-reflection, I soon realised I was a robot. I wasn't myself. Where had my passion gone? I'd hurl information at them and expect them to absorb it. I was teaching how to pass an exam and that was it. I was frustrated at myself because it went against all of my beliefs. As an individual, I am *so* passionate about English literature. In my view, the study of English is not limited to passing an exam. English is an all-encompassing subject that is enriching to our general knowledge. Every text that we read exposes us to an education that extends beyond the classroom. It gives individuals a voice and we, as teachers, allow those voices to be heard by our students. We learn about social, historical and political issues. We become well-rounded individuals who gain an invaluable awareness of the world.

I had become so consumed with learning *how* to teach and *how* to deliver a lesson that I'd ended up *just* regurgitating information to the class. I wasn't teaching the value of the subject and I was suppressing my passion. It was a wakeup call. I took more away from the lesson than my students did that day.

Natalie Fowell is a trainee teacher, in secondary English, in the Midlands. She has a First Class Honours degree in English and a master's degree in English Literature completed at Keele University between 2014 and 2018. Natalie spent two years working as an unqualified teacher at a private education centre to gain experience before starting her PGCE.

An Ode to My First GCSE Class

Charlotte Broomfield

I had always found boys fairly straightforward. On my PGCE, male students didn't seem all that complicated. The silly ones were silly, not because they hated you but because they were silly. The quiet ones were quiet because they were shy, not because they thought I was a terrible teacher. The disengaged ones were simply disengaged, and it never felt personal to me—if anything, I enjoyed the challenge of trying to enthuse them. Feedback from mentors had always complimented my relationships and rapport with classes. But then I took my first teaching job at an all-girls school.

Don't get me wrong, I had taught loads of lovely girls in my ITT year. I left both placements armed with beautiful goodbye cards, more bunches of flowers and boxes of chocolates than I could carry and the confidence that I was entering the perfect career for me. I did wonder whether an all-girls classroom would have the humour and energy of the mixed-sex classrooms I had experienced. As that September drew nearer, I wondered whether I had made the right decision applying there in the first place.

My form class was sweet, and my first lesson had gone okay, but then I met my Year 10 class. They walked in and looked at me like I was dirt on their brand-new school shoes. They eyed each other as harshly as they eyed me and they were less than impressed when I seated them in alphabetical order, briefly introduced myself, and got to it. I'd ask questions; they'd stare at me blankly. I'd ask them to discuss work with their partner; they'd stare at me blankly. I'd plead with them to show me some signs of life; they'd glare at me blankly. I immediately believed the next two years would be torture for us all.

As you can imagine, everything changed. I don't quite remember exactly when—perhaps a third seating plan change or a sarcastic comment of mine was what broke the ice. By Christmas, I loved this group of girls, and could go from joking about characters we hated and my horrendous handwriting to them working their socks off during an exam response. It hadn't been half as instant as it had been with my Key Stage Three (KS3) groups, but it was so much better. Many of my funniest teaching memories and proudest moments took place with that class. I became the teacher many of them came to when things were tough at home, with friends or with mental health—and that was worth every missed lunch break.

It was a pleasure to watch them grow into witty and wonderful young women and their thank you cards still have me sobbing months later. No group of girls deserved their shot at their GCSE exams more, and I was proud at how they handled it with maturity. In fact, I will never *not* be proud of my amazing first GCSE class—they taught me to be patient, and that good things are definitely worth the wait.

Charlotte is a secondary English and media studies teacher in the north of England.

Winning Over Troublesome Students

Amina Qureshi

Showing students that you genuinely care about them as individuals is paramount to building and sustaining effective professional relationships. Sharing your experiences through stories, your journey in education, and even sharing lunch, builds critical relationships. I once observed a colleague share her lunch. At that moment, I realised she had the most difficult students in the year group eating from the palm of her hand; they were all at once transported to a realm of mathematical equations, spellbound, and consoled by her comfort and care.

Why did they respond, solely, to this member of staff? Perhaps they connected because of their shared experiences. It wasn't a normal revision session; it was definitely more than that. It was a teacher communicating their care, passion and genuine interest in their personal lives.

Since this delightful encounter, I too realised I could make a difference by sharing a bit about myself with my learners. I wanted to be like this teacher. So, I did what any good teacher does; I observed and mirrored the strategy. I shared the good bits about my life, the hardships, the struggles, and gently scaffolded a relationship with my students. I had found that there can be a correlation between disengagement and low ability. I spent time scrutinising their work in rigorous detail, looking at department trackers. How can they make slight improvements to their work for maximum gains? What top tips can I give them?

I often paused and reflected. What has worked with this student in the past? What have they explicitly stated that they found difficult? Was I listening and paying proper attention? I began to think about whether or not they were fully supported in my lesson. How could I adapt activities to support them? At what point could I stop and ask them a question that they had already learned the answer to?

Nelson Mandela stated: “Education is the most powerful weapon which you can use to change the world”. In my case, one-to-one support was all that the student needed to break down the barriers to their learning. They needed a positive role model, someone to listen to their concerns, and someone who sympathised with their story.

Amina Qureshi is an assistant headteacher at a secondary school in England.

Narnia, Oz and Wonderland: Teaching Creative Writing in a Multicultural and Multifaith Context

Matthew Roberts

'Bless me, what do they teach them at these schools?'
C. S. Lewis.

'Modern education includes morality; therefore, the modern child seeks only entertainment in its wonder tales and gladly dispenses with all disagreeable incident.'
L. F. Baum.

"'What is the use of a book,' thought Alice, 'without pictures or conversation?'"
Lewis Carroll.

These were some novels of my childhood. My imaginary worlds. My creative play. Now… a shift in focus is what is needed. Now… an honouring of the identities of the students I serve needs to be celebrated. Now. 'N-O-W' is a liminal space of creative discovery. **'N'**arnia. **'O'**z. '**W**'onderland.

What of the 'NOW' of our students? What are their imaginary worlds? To what extent do the stories they tell reflect the epic events of their history? What imaginative lands will our students invite us in to read? What landscape of their rich cultural and religious heritage will they draw upon? What religious iconography will be depicted?

The lens through which students are able to validate their own experience needs to change. It could be said that characters who are not white, male, middle class and heterosexual are viewed as 'other'. This 'othering' is a form of marginalisation. It is dehumanising. A tangible crippling numbness seeps when a student begins to write 'Mary and Arthur' (absolutely, Ok), when they could write about 'Mohammed and Aleya'. *"I didn't think I was allowed..."* (Did you just feel that metaphysical punch in the gut too?). "You can write about who you are, where you are, how you feel, why you think what you do—in this world and an imaginary other."

NOW is a gateway. NOW is a door. NOW is a space in which students can play on the page and allow themselves to be witnessed, wise, and worldly. I say:

What are the ultimate questions of your existence?

Describe the geometrical shapes in your place of worship?

Tell us about a Mendi Night. *(How do you know about a Mendi night?)*

"Can I use lyrics?" YES!

"Can I 'Shrek' it up?" YES!

"Go all *intertextual* like Malorie did with Stormzy lyrics?" YES!

Write about the local, the national and the international events of our times. "Grenfell?" YES!

Reimagine your world as it is, as it was, as it could be, or as we hope it will never be.

'Being a writer gives you license to be a little bit strange and to break the rules.'

Tanika Gupta.

'What does it mean to be a writer?' 'Learning to make firewood out of self-doubt and turn private wonder into food for others'.

Stephen Kelman.

'In a television interview, I said that diversity in our children's books should include the adventures of disabled children, travellers and gypsies, LGBT teens, different cultures, classes, colours, religions. It shouldn't be a token gesture, nor do such stories need to be "issue-based".'

Malorie Blackman

"Now, begin writing...

...writing...

...your...

...NOW!"

Matthew Roberts has taught English and Drama since 2002; he has worked in a range of contexts, from primary school to university. In April 2020, he was awarded a £5000 scholarship and began his MA in Education: Language and Literacy, accredited by The University of Exeter.

Chapter 4

Expect the Unexpected

It is often the unexpected moments in life which change us the most. That is certainly the case when working in education. Children and young people can be very unpredictable and the truth is, no matter how much experience we have and no matter how much we think we have planned for every possible eventuality in the classroom, sometimes there will be incidents or events that take us completely by surprise!

In this chapter, authors share some hilarious anecdotes about some of those memorable moments that have stayed with them for many years. You will read heartwarming tales that have impacted teachers for the rest of their careers, and you will see that even those of us who have been teaching for many, many years can find ourselves faced with a scenario that could never possibly have been anticipated!

A Child Jumped Out of My Classroom Window

Sarah Mullin

I will never ever forget one particular day during my PGCE year. I was a 23-year-old student teacher on a teaching placement where I had the pleasure of teaching a Year 10 GCSE group. I'd been given a challenging group, as the regular teacher was on maternity leave, and I looked forward to developing my skills by employing all the tips and tricks I had learned about on my course and in my wider reading.

I employed every behaviour-management strategy in the book: specific positive praise, clear and consistent routines, high expectations. I had a row of lovely students at the front of the class who eagerly listened to my every word. However, towards the back of the class, it was sheer chaos. One child sat drawing his tag on a scrap piece of paper. Two girls wrote notes to each other, not at all concerned that I could see exactly what they were doing. Another boy ate a packet of Jaffa Cakes; the crinkling of the plastic wrapper disrupting my train of thought each time he rummaged in his pocket to fetch another one.

Desperately trying to impart some knowledge to at least some of the children, I began annotating a GCSE poem on the overhead projector. And then squeals of laughter erupted.

All heads swiftly turned towards the window. Open-mouthed, I watched a 15-year-old boy climb out the ground-floor window.

I'll never forget the smile on his face as he threw his leg over the window frame before leaping onto the grass verge just below. My heart was beating uncontrollably as I watched him sprinting away, against a backdrop of chuckles and cheers from his classmates.

I froze. I had never encountered an incident like this before—and most certainly had not included anything on the eventuality of a child's escaping from the classroom in my lesson plan.

Anxiously, I tried to focus the class, shushing and waving my arms to signal for quiet. Almost pleading for their support, I moved between the rows of desks, trying to encourage my class of students to gain focus and pick up their highlighter pens.

I had not even completed the referral form to send for on-call support when, cool as a cucumber, my classroom door swung open and the young escapee walked in. He looked sheepishly at me, stifling giggles as he made eye contact with his classmates.

All eyes were on me. What was going to happen next? How would I react? I could feel my cheeks burning as I calmly exhaled a sigh of relief that he had returned unharmed.

The class waited for some kind of a reaction. I gave them none.

Adrenaline got me through the rest of the lesson. At the end of the class, he stayed behind and missed some of his lunchtime in detention. His apology was not sincere; he enjoyed every minute of his out-of-class adventures.

For the rest of the term, he actually ended up behaving much better for me. I'd like to think that perhaps he saw that I was genuinely worried about what had happened to him, although the truth is probably that he anticipated getting into serious trouble.

I can assure you that no child was harmed during the escape of pupil X from the English department. Though the same can't necessarily be said for my ego.

Sarah Mullin BA (HONS), PGCE, PGCertED, PGDipED, MA, CTE, FCCT, CMgr FCMI, FInstLM, FRSA is a deputy headteacher and Doctor of Education student. She is the author of the number one best-selling book 'What They Didn't Teach Me on My PGCE' and she is the founder of #EduTeacherTips, the YouTube channel for teachers, by teachers. Sarah is on the board of the secondary education committee at the English Association and she is renowned for supporting Early Career Teachers (ECTs) and aspiring school leaders locally, nationally and internationally. She was recently named a 'Rising Star in Education and Academia' and has previously received the 'Contribution to Education of the Year' award.

Exploring Their Place in the World

Lucy Williams

My students astounded me with their exploration of self. Let me set the scene. I had two large GCSE art classes. The coursework project title was War. I had taught it before so I amended it to tap into the interests of this cohort to enable them to develop independent working and responses. I changed the title of the project to War/Conflict to support students to explore their place in the world. Teacher-led GCSE art coursework is a big no-no for me; I want my students to become independent, curious, enquiring, and creative young people. We explored images of conflict, we touched on 9/11—I had forgotten they were born in 2002! They all had knowledge of WWII from history lessons and war poetry from English class, and we tapped into that too. We looked at art together—looked at symbolism and meanings—and how it made them feel.

They all created a large body of work, with responses to lots of artwork experimenting with ideas and techniques. It was clear to see many were becoming very self-reflective and self-enquiring. Now for the final piece. They explored the conflicts they felt; we had six responses to Donald Trump, clearly illustrating their concerns, worries and fears for their future. What amazed me the most were those who explored something incredibly personal and how the students created a safe and respectful space to discuss their place in the world, and express their feelings and concerns. Some ideas were very deep-rooted, some explored heritage and conflict. One student who had lived with cancer for three years, and in Year 11 was in remission, created a self-portrait undergoing chemotherapy surrounded by roses, symbolising the love and support of their family and friends. Another student explored representations of their terminally-ill sibling, who they told me was always smiling.

Many students were struggling with their mental health. Bullying was explored by one student who felt they were singled out because they were LGBTQ. Another student suffered with acute anxiety and OCD; their self-portrait showed them wearing a mask of their own face underneath which they were crying. It was powerful stuff. Writing about how their ideas developed was therapeutic. I spoke to the students about how mature their works were and asked if they would be brave enough to make them into posters with a slogan about the conflict. One student asked if they could represent how their friend who had depression felt; their slogan was 'Will the demons ever leave?' A talented student drew the most beautiful portrait of Nelson Mandela and one lesson, out of the corner of my eye, I saw him take an eraser to it. With high-pitched urgency, I asked what he was doing. He said, "I am rubbing him out Ms as his legacy is disappearing." This ability to make such a profound connection made me proud. They talked about their work to friends in the playground and invited them to see their work in the art room. It was joyous.

This is dedicated to those that dare to dream. Dream big.

Lucy Williams FRSA is a senior leader, art teacher and passionate advocate for the arts and wellbeing with a background in museum and gallery education.

Eyes in your Heart

Mandeep Kaur

Children, colleagues, parents—millions of eyes just watching my every move. Below are small anecdotes that I hope make you laugh and help to remove the pressure from all those gawping eyes!

Watching

Freshly prepared resources, straight out of the laminator, sizzling on the crisp, azure backing paper. Rebellious trays show off their 'Comic Sans' typo while the fairy lights dance in the colour-coordinated reading corner. My classroom. My first ever classroom.

But I can't seem to enjoy my masterpiece. I hadn't envisaged thirty curious eyes gazing at me. They are watching me. All of them. Waiting.

Heart pounding, sweaty palms, knees wobbling kind of stuff here!

Am I really r-e-s-p-o-n-s-i-b-l-e for these little people?

For the past sixteen years, Anxiety re-appears every September. The only difference is that she now comes as a friend.

Moral: Your anxiety shows that you genuinely care.

All eyes on me

Hair up. Mask on. Sweat-proof jacket on. Shin pads on. 'Supply Teacher Mode' activated.

A quick room scan and that was when I saw her—'stern face'. Eyes flinching between me and the friends who, I know, are not in their assigned seats. Defiant eyes preparing for battle.

I take a stroll towards her table. Whispers, entwined with fits of devilish giggles become louder.

"Bet you don't know about the Illuminati, do you?"

Slouching further down into her chair, she catches the eye of the smirking boy across the classroom. They are all awaiting my response; only my brain is not acting professionally.

OMG! Girl, please!

Three years of rapping along to Tupac in my green Citroën Saxo (with the bright yellow gear stick!) and 'dis New Born' is questioning me? Y'all need to listen up!...

"Illuminati? Yes, of course! Is there something you'd like to discuss?"

Shocked that someone was willing to listen to her opinions, she began to express her feelings about the world. We listened. We debated. We shared.

Moral: Always remember that once upon a time, you were young.

Watch out!

A beautiful summer's afternoon. Sports Day preparations:

Bean bags: check.

Skipping ropes: check.

Egg and broken spoons: check.

Cones equally measured out with the trundle wheel: check.

Groups 1, 2, 3 and 4 sat wiggling their bottoms on the freshly painted starting line. The race of the year: will Bobby finally be crowned the fastest runner in the class? Or maybe Nicky? Either way, the "cheater" whispers must—one way or another—be eliminated!

Walking backwards, I keep my eye on Group 1, who currently have green hair!

All in position. I lift my whistle as I approach the finish line. One more step back.

THUD!

Silence.

Laughter!

Moral: Always be aware of your surroundings.

Mandeep Kaur BA (Hons), MCCT teaches in the primary education sector. She has a range of experience in leadership, including mentoring and advisory roles. Currently, Mandeep is working part time as she completes her MA in Children's Literature.

Keep Calm and Give It Your All

Mark Noakes

My main teacher training placement was in Year 1 at a small one-form primary school. Within my first half term, sadly, my mentor, who was the main class teacher, had to take time off due to personal reasons. As it is a small school, I had to step in and, alongside the deputy headteacher, I ended up teaching between 60 - 80% of a teaching timetable for a month.

So, my advice to the new students would be to be prepared for anything, but if something unexpected does occur, it's important to just keep calm, go with it and give it your all. In the end, everyone will support you and you will make a great impression and form brilliant relationships.

Mark Noakes was a trainee teacher in a small primary school and he took on extra responsibilities within his training. His advice is to be prepared for anything and to keep calm no matter what. He adds, what you put into the course is what you get out of it.

Ferretgate

Jo McShane

My day in a village secondary school started normally enough. It was bracing cold outside and I'd already done my morning circuit around the local streets, avoiding stepping in dog poo in my Christian Louboutins. I enjoyed the crisp air, exchanging pleasantries with dog owners and patting the occasional passing (generally unaccompanied) lurcher. The tour of the streets every morning gave me the opportunity to reach out into my own past in a similar location, and I'd swear I once caught a fleeting glimpse of myself in non-standard uniform, as I tried to stuff my marble-washed denim jacket into my Gola rucksack. This was the 1980s, when industry on Teesside had declined and a depressive smog seemed to envelop the whole place.

I knew the poverty, the broken-glass-littered streets and the feeling of going to school hungry, and knowing you'd stay hungry all day. These walks around the streets before my own working day also reminded me of the crystalline moment I took a look around me and made the decision that no matter where my life took me, it would be away from 'this'. That is why I teach: to empower other hungry kids to climb out of the damp housing, broken windows and to escape the oppressive sense of fatalism I refused to let claim me. To be reminded by your purpose in education every morning fires you up, readies you for the demands of the day. And believe me, I needed to be ready for the ferret-centered debacle that unfolded when I re-entered the warmth of the school. The names have been changes to protect the innocent, including that of the ferret, whom we will refer to as 'Maurice'.

On entering the dining area, I was greeted by the raised voices of Leo and Archie, two brothers known for their animated displays: "Why did you bring him in anyway? He's dad's best catcher" "I didn't, he climbed in me bag, man!" Having no idea what was going on, and suspecting that a younger sibling had arrived via a non-traditional mode of transport, I gently sought to intervene.

Me: "Morning lads...everything ok?"

Them: Silence, heads down, hands in blazer pockets (shirts hanging out and ties not straight, but I let that slide for now).

Me: "Ok…is there a problem?"

Leo….shuffles feet, mumbles something.

Me (in my mind): Did I catch the word 'Maurice' in there? And 'kidnapped?' But we don't have anyone on roll by that name. Are neighbouring schools missing a pupil? Serious alarm bells rang and my mind thrust straight into safeguarding mode.

Me: "Maurice?"

Archie: "Me dad's … ferret. He's kind of mine as well. He must have jumped in me bag, and now Kevin Spencer has him and wants £20 or he'll let him off over the Dene". Sobs start to flow.

Me: "But you never bring a bag Archie. Did you bring him to school on purpose? For a reason? Where are Kevin and, errrrr, Maurice now?"

Leo: "Back of D Block, Miss".

As the three of us trudged across the yard, a tale of an attempted sale, a resulting ferret kidnapping and attempts to secure funds through illegal means spilled out from the brothers, each adding to the injustice with colourful and rapidly stated embellishments. Kevin was leaning against the corner of D-block, spotted only by his protruding elbow. As we approached, I realised I should have brought another member of staff with me. With rodent-centered feelings of injustice running so high, what if a fight broke out, sending the wiry creature scuttling for cover in the Year 11 social zone? Realising my own vulnerability in this scenario, and the potential chaos of Maurice the ferret affixing himself to another child's new hair extensions, I gestured for a colleague who was probably hoping I wouldn't catch his eye as he scurried across the yard.

When we reached the scene, the bag was situated about a metre away from Kevin's feet as he stood hunched, his face turned away from us. His whole body appeared to be frozen in a permanent shrug as the brothers hurtled towards Maurice's rather tatty mode of carriage. For a second, I felt fear about the contents of the bag; was Kevin a cruel boy? He's quiet, sullen … could he have harmed the ferret? What if Maurice bolts out and attacks my glasses, or worse, runs up my colleague's trouser leg? To everyone's relief, Leo swiftly produced a soft, skinny, creamy-coloured Maurice from the bag with a look that spoke of triumph and relief. As Maurice slinked through his hands like water, Leo forgot himself and planted a kiss on his furry head before returning it gently to the bag with a tenderness I'd never before witnessed in this fierce little lad.

A two-stage process was to ensue, involving the safe repatriation of Maurice and the questioning of his captor. After all, this officially classed as theft since the property of members of the community had been illegally commandeered. The intricacies of the tale saddened me greatly. All three kids were parented by single dads, both families were frequently hungry, waiting for pay day before food and electricity could be re-stocked. All three had woken up cold for at least the past three days. In the midst of this, they had come up with a complex arrangement to lend the hunting animal so that Kevin could learn how to get free rabbit meat, the reliable source of food the brothers appeared to enjoy from their own dad, a skilled poacher when not on night shift 40 miles away. Their circumstances made me feel sadly reminiscent of a time our family was in a similar situation and my uncle provided for us with his ferrets—and Henry, his trusty whippet.

People make do with what they have in the face of hunger and decline of stability, and that is precisely what these three boys had sought to do in the midst of their precarious lives; to trade, up-skill, source and provide. A visit to Leo and Archie's dad established that the police need not be alerted, and that Maurice was quite unshaken by the escapade. He invited us into the council house (the dad, not Maurice) which, though shabby on the outside, smelled of bleach and fabric softener from the lobby inwards. I rebuked myself mentally for expecting something quite different in the middle of this bizarre scenario.

These days, I smile about the story during its various incarnations in my teacher-training lectures about the impact of socioeconomic deprivation on educational achievement. What I never tell students is how I hid in my office and cried for a few minutes that day, because returning a ferret to its chicken-wire outhouse couldn't fix the deeper problem exposed by 'Ferretgate'. That rather than dreaming of their own futures, knuckling down to achieve and aspire, these three lads were wrestling with bigger problems and starting to establish an altogether different set of habits of existence that would go on to shape their lives, for better or worse.

Jo McShane is a Senior Lecturer in Education at the University of Sunderland.

Mischief in Morocco

Daniel Bull

In 2019, I was fortunate enough to be one of the teachers leading a trip to Morocco with a group of students from Years 10 and 11. The trip was a once-in-a-lifetime opportunity for these children: we were spending a week volunteering with a local school in Goulmima and then spending the next week climbing Mount Toubkal, reaching the summit at 4,167m.

Now, as wonderful as it was building school facilities and standing at the summit of the mountain, high above the clouds, my standout memory was of a particular student; let's call him Student A. Student A was a very academic and studious pupil, but could sometimes be a little hesitant to get involved. This was evident on the first evening when we arrived in Marrakech. We asked the group if they wanted to remain in the hotel before leaving to head to Goulmima in the morning or whether they wanted to explore the maze-like winding souks and experience the evening there. The majority of students voted to go and explore. Student A, however, chose to remain at the hotel. When the group returned later that evening with stories, goodies and terrible elephant print trousers, it was clear Student A regretted his decision not to go; he was honest and admitted that he chose not to go because he was too nervous.

The morning came and we left Marrakech for Goulmima. The first week of volunteering flew and it was great to see Student A coming out of his shell; he even offered to be day-leader once and got himself involved in the finance team, making important decisions and budgeting for everyone's food and water. As time progressed you could really see his confidence growing and after conquering the climb up Mount Toubkal, his manner really changed. No more was he withdrawn within the group.

The reason why this memory sticks with me is because of the final night. We returned to Marrakech in preparation to head to the airport in the morning. Again, the group had a choice of staying in and relaxing, which no one would blame them for as they had just climbed a mountain, or going out to explore the souks again. This time the vote was unanimous and the whole group voted to explore, including Student A. It was truly amazing to watch Student A going into the shops, bartering and having fun with the locals. It was so inspiring to see just how much his confidence had developed in a little under two weeks.

When Student A left school, he sent me a lovely email which ended with the poignant line: "finally in Morocco, I wouldn't have felt comfortable or been able to do half the things I did without your constant positive attitude and reinforcement. So sincerely, thank you. You helped me climb 4,167m and gave me your walking poles, not many teachers can say that". It was a beautiful reminder of why I became a teacher.

Teaching is so much more than just a job and it's about so much more than just doing lessons. We can change lives and it's the greatest career on the planet!

Daniel Bull BA PGCE MA MCCT is a teacher of history, both modern and ancient, at Saint Edmund's Catholic School. Graduating with a degree in history from the University of Southampton, he went on to study a PGCE at the University of Chichester, before studying for an MA in Education at the University of Portsmouth.

Bee Prepared

Anoara Mughal

When I decided to train as a teacher almost 14 years ago, many people advised me not to bother—shocking I know! I was told that teaching is hard, but I did not really understand how hard; after all, teachers got approximately 13 weeks off every year, or so I thought.

From the age of 18 my physics teacher tried to persuade me to go into teaching, even asking me to observe one of his lessons from the back of the classroom; at that point the thought about becoming a teacher had never even crossed my mind. Little did I realise that many years later I would indeed become a teacher.

Yes, teaching is hard—but the positives outweigh the challenges of teaching, and I am so proud to be a part of this wonderful profession. There is no other profession where you have the privilege to shape the lives of young people and make a positive contribution to society. Seeing the positives in every situation helps you to get through some of the challenges teachers face on a daily basis—and sometimes you have just got to laugh. You could not make up some of the things that happen in schools, so I thought I would share one of the more unusual experiences with you.

It was early May and the weather was hot. By hot, I mean it was the type of weather where you were sweating from the minute you woke up and where there was no point putting any make-up on as it would start to slide down your already sweaty face as soon as you stepped out of the house.

My classroom was situated in the Victorian part of the building, with really high ceilings, parquet flooring and dark green tiles halfway up the wall. It was sizzling, so I had decided to open two out of the three sash windows, propped open with two Oxford junior dictionaries. As the cool breeze wafted in through the openings, I finished settling some very hot, sweaty and rowdy pubescent Year 6s into doing a quick arithmetic paper (oh how they loved a practice test!).

We had prospective parents coming in to visit the school, and it happened that I was acting head for the morning, so everything had to be perfect as I really wanted to make a good impression on the parents. Although the heat was beginning to get to the Year 6s, they managed to settle and were working diligently. This was going to be great! After five minutes, I began walking around the classroom, peering over each pupil's shoulder to make sure they were on task and that they were attempting all the questions.

After a scorching morning, full of humidity, heat and hair-raising moaning, I had it all covered, and everything was under control. It was going to be the perfect finish to what was a very long morning and I was relieved that I had PPA in the afternoon on such a hot and sizzling day.

Suddenly there was the faint sound of buzzing. I quickly looked around to see if anyone had fallen asleep during the test but everyone was wide awake working really hard on their tests. In fact you could hear how hard they were working. Perhaps it was me? Perhaps I was imagining it? Maybe I was tired and was just hearing things?

Before I knew it, a pupil started screaming and began running around the classroom; I could not understand what they were saying and another pupil followed suit, followed by another and then another, until 30 children were screaming and running around, test papers flung all over the classroom floor and pencils strewn everywhere! It looked like an earthquake had hit the classroom.

To my horror, I finally realised what was causing the commotion—it was the not-so-dulcet tones of an angry, gigantic bumble bee, which I had just spotted out of the corner of my eye, flying quite low around the classroom. The visitors were going to be here any minute: what should I do? Thinking on my feet, I realised I had no choice but to get rid of the bumble bee and settle the children back down before the visitors arrived.

I had an empty box on hand from a book delivery, so I kicked off my shoes and I began running around the classroom with the empty box. By this point the bumble bee was near the side of the classroom closest to the corridor and not near the windows, which were on the opposite side of the room.

I spent what felt like an eternity flapping around like a bird, with a cardboard box in hand, shoeless, on the tables, with my hair out of place and with 30 children screaming hysterically!

Then to my horror, through the classroom window nearest to the corridor—and whilst I was waving a cardboard box around on a desk—I saw the office manager walk around the corner with the prospective family; my class were still screaming but it was too late. Before I could get off the table, the door handle began to turn and my heart skipped a beat. All I heard was, “Mrs Mughal, we have visitors!” I jumped off the table cool and calm as a cucumber, patted my hair back into shape with the box in one hand, held out my other hand and spoke in a calm but high-pitched tone, making sure I was smiling, “Welcome to our school! I am Mrs Mughal. DON’T mind me: I was just chasing a bumble bee around the classroom”.

The parents gave me a knowing nod, peered into the classroom and left. As soon as the parents left, there was no sign of the bumble bee. It had vanished into thin air! We searched everywhere for it, but it was nowhere to be found. After I dismissed the class for lunch, I noticed the bumble bee just casually perched on the windowsill. Thanks for the drama bumble bee! The story was the running joke for the rest of the year, and I haven’t been able to live it down ever since.

About the prospective parents? They had no hesitation about sending their child to our school. Phew!

My Tips:

- Expect things to go wrong and learn from them.
- Remain calm at all times.
- Try to see the positives and/or the humour.
- Balance work, life and wellbeing.
- Laugh—and I mean laugh a lot.

Anoara Mughal has been a primary school teacher for 14 years. She founded @NewToSLTChat in 2017; she is a founding fellow of the Chartered College of Teaching and a fellow of the Royal Society of Arts. Anoara has served as a Network Leader for @WomenEdLondon and served on the steering group @HealthyToolkit for the last three years. As an assistant head teacher, she has led many areas. As well as being an advocate for wellbeing, her passions include reading, language acquisition and translating research into classroom practice. She tweets @anoara_a

Making an Impression

Steve Ladd

Back in 1996, as a young Newly Qualified Teacher (NQT) embarking on an exciting career in a rural Somerset school, I was anxious to impress. The vastly more 'experienced' PE department were a tough nut to crack, but I was determined to prove I was an asset. At the end of the autumn term, we lost use of the sports hall due to mock exams, so the PE department undertook a three-week cross-country curriculum involving team teaching. An advantage this school had was the agreement with a local farmer that we could use his land, so each lesson we would position staff in different points around the course.

As the young, fit newbie, I was given the task of supervising the gate which was halfway around the course. If the gate was open, I simply encouraged the students and completed the rest of the course, making sure all the students were safe. If the gate was shut, I held the gate open for the students, making sure the sheep in the next field did not escape. A senior member of the department, a formidable local woman and someone you did not want to cross, made this instruction abundantly clear. How hard could it be? I know I was a city boy, but I wasn't stupid. She was having none of it. Shut the gate!

On this day, the gate was shut. I opened it and waited for the students to pass. The sheep appeared uninterested in escaping and were busy grazing in their field. Happy days! Once the final student ran through, I swung the gate shut and ran after them. Halfway across the field, I noticed something had caught the attention of the sheep and they were heading for the gate. To my horror, I realised the gate had not clicked shut and the sheep had rapidly escaped. I sprinted into the next field, to try and rectify my monumental mistake, and commenced the near impossible mission of trying to round them up. One man and his dog became one daft city boy and his own legs. In those days I was quite quick so I nearly succeeded in herding them back but every time we bordered the gateway, one sheep would decide that something somewhere else was far more interesting and run off, followed by all their mates. I became convinced they were winding me up because they repeated it on numerous occasions. This spectacle lasted 15 minutes. I was exhausted and panicking, dreading the reaction of the 'formidable woman'. Would we lose use of the farm? Had I ruined years of co-operation between the school and local community? Had my next lesson started yet? Was my career over...?

Suddenly, the sheep were expertly rounded up and through the gate, thanks to the much-appreciated services of a skilled sheep dog. Looking towards the farm, I recognised the farmer, so I apprehensively jogged over to apologise, expecting a deserved outburst. To my eternal relief, he just laughed and said that he'd witnessed the whole escapade—and that that was the funniest thing he'd seen in years! He hadn't wanted to spoil my efforts but, in the end, he felt sorry for me.

I didn't live that day down for the remaining seven years at that school ... but I always shut the gate!

Steve is an experienced PE and English teacher of 24 years. Having taken on many leadership roles, including assistant headteacher, he is enjoying being back on the sports field and in the classroom. Steve leads an active lifestyle with his wife and two sons; he co-presents a sports radio show and is always searching for the next challenge.

The Bodyguard

Dr Brendan O'Sullivan

Many years ago, when I was at the start of my career, I taught in an all-girls school. The proportion of male to female teachers was low, with the former being conferred with almost 'endangered species' status! One event from that time lives in my memory as if it occurred yesterday.

A set of women's toilets were located quite close to the staffroom, something that you would pass several times in one day. One fateful day, I heard a call as I was making my way to the staffroom. There was no one else around and this lone voice made me stop in my tracks.

"Help! Is there anyone there?" called out the lone voice.

Crossing the threshold of this area was not undertaken lightly and I proceeded with caution. I responded with the word "Hello?" repeatedly.

I was greeted with the question, "Who's that?"

I didn't recognise the voice and simply replied with my name: "It's Brendan".

"Oh Brendan, thank goodness, this is Helen".

I wasn't quite sure where this was going and tried to gain more information by asking, "Is everything OK Helen?"

"No, I'm trapped".

At this point I had located the relevant stall door and wondered what trapped meant. I pushed the door and, unsurprisingly, it was locked. I stated the obvious: "The door is locked".

She replied in dismay, "I know. Something fell out of the latch and I'm locked in".

Being resourceful, I asked "Did you try jiggling it?"

"Yes, it's no good, it's stuck solid".

At this point, the logical step would be to seek help elsewhere—or at least find someone with equipment that might ease the situation. I formed a plan that was certain to succeed. "Do you want me to break the door down?" She urged me on with "Yes, do please". Never one to underestimate my non-existent strength, I cautioned her to stand back and brace herself for the destruction that was about to ensue. I charged at the door and my left shoulder received the full impact. The door remained unmoved even though I was expecting it to be hanging from its hinges at that point. Undaunted, I repeated my procedure a second and third time when the wood around the lock gave way. I pushed the door and found Helen waiting to be rescued.

I swept her up in my arms and carried her to safety. The noise of the breaking door had alerted an audience, whose jaws were now dropping at this unexpected scene. News of Helen's entrapment and disproportionate rescue flew around the school. It became one of the school's legends and a comparison was made to the film 'The Bodyguard'. For a long time, far longer than it took the pain in my shoulder to subside, I was greeted by students and not a few teachers with its theme song.

Dr Brendan O'Sullivan is the past chair of the Irish Mathematics Teachers' Association, serving from 2015 to 2020. He previously served as its national secretary from 2011 to 2015. As a post-primary teacher, he is a member of the Teaching Council's Research Engagement Group. He teaches mathematics in Davis College, Mallow, Co. Cork.

Practice What You Preach

Nikki Beech

A class of thirty eight-year-olds using saws as part of their lesson during an Ofsted inspection—what could possibly go wrong? This is a tale of what not to do, and how teachers should always follow their own advice.

Year 3. Wednesday afternoon. Ofsted. What could go wrong? As someone who was relatively new to the teaching profession, I wasn't fazed by 'the big O' and continued working through my medium-term plans. Wednesday afternoon's lesson was Design and Technology (D&T). As staff, we had been assured that because Wednesday was day two of our inspection it was highly unlikely any inspector would be entering our classrooms, but we should be ready … just in case.

The lesson was the 'make' element of our D&T scheme. We'd already evaluated existing products, then designed our own; now it was time to get the saws out in order to make our picture frames. I assigned pupils partners and then meticulously demonstrated the correct method to use a bench hook and saw safely. It was pantomime like—very over the top—just to ensure every child in the room understood the message that if the equipment was used incorrectly, it would result in injury. They were ready. They could relay what to do and how to do it, so, confident I'd done my job, I told them to begin constructing their picture frames.

Everything was perfect. The excitement, the enthusiasm, the care and attention shown was what every teacher dreamed of. I surveyed the room, smiling like the Cheshire Cat, giving a smug thumbs up to my TA just as the inspector walked in. He looked around the room and seemed to nod approvingly before making his way to the back of the room where he took a seat and looked at me. Now, I presumed that this meant I had to do something, so flapping a little inside, I called and gained the class's attention. "I've noticed that X and Y are struggling to saw in a straight line. Can anyone remind me of the steps we need to stop our wood going all wonky?" Like perfectly rehearsed actors, they gave me the answers I'd hoped for. Phew.

I set them off to work again and stayed with child X and Y, who were persevering but still struggling. "Can you show us one more time?" they asked. With the inspector still in the room, I obliged. I took the saw in one hand, held the wood in the bench hook with the other but kept my eyes on the inspector. He was leaving. I watched him walk out whilst sawing the children's wood—only I'd forgotten the safety tip of tucking your thumb in to keep it away from the end of the bench hook and the saw found it.

After the lengthy health and safety talk, and the regular reminders about saw etiquette, the thirty children made thirty picture frames without a single accident that afternoon; however their teacher, the apparent expert, left with a bandaged thumb.

Nikki Beech is a Key Stage 2 teacher from Birmingham who, after a period of time as an assistant headteacher, has taken a step back in to the classroom full time. She is a grammar enthusiast and can currently be found teaching Year 6.

Backwards is the New Forwards

Toria Bono

Lesson plan was done. Resources were ready. My Year 2 class was primed for my lesson observation. All was good to go!

Before I go on, I should say that this was not a formal observation but one of an individual child who was part of the Numbers Count programme. The person observing was a local authority maths advisor who would be leading Numbers Count across the county and had been working on the programme with that child. She probably wasn't interested in me. However, to my mind, there was a maths advisor in my classroom, so *I* was being observed! I think it possibly made it worse that I knew her, so I was desperate to impress her with my brilliance! Hmmm!

Once she'd entered, I told the children that we were going to go outside to practice counting. I thought she'd be very impressed if I did a bit of outdoor learning. As an aside, I hadn't learnt at that point in my career that taking children outside to count did not equate to outdoor learning—I do know that now! The main part of the lesson was subtracting, so I thought the mental starter could be counting back from 100. It was all going well until we got to 90. Then nothing. Complete silence.

I could feel her eyes burning into my back as I silently pleaded with the children to say 89. I discovered at that moment that there is absolutely no way of making a child say 89 just by staring at them! So, I decided to make light of it and shouted the number myself so that they could continue: 89, 88……81, 80—still nothing. Complete silence for the second time.

It was evident at this point that teaching the children to subtract was redundant until we could count backwards. The maths advisor stepped forward and whispered, "It's very common for children to find counting backwards challenging; they only ever count forwards". I had never thought about it before, but she was right. My maths lessons always began with counting forwards. I couldn't recall ever asking the children to count backwards, yet I had planned for them to subtract two-digit numbers on a number line. I knew that there was no way they could do that until they could confidently count backwards.

So, I reframed the lesson and I did it alongside the maths advisor. She suggested we go back inside and use the hundred square, so that the children had a visual representation. We counted back together, and, over the coming weeks, my children became great at counting backwards; this really supported their subtraction work.

I learnt so much that day. Ditch the lesson plan if it isn't working, make sure that early building blocks are in place before moving on—and always teach children to count backwards!

Toria has been teaching for twenty years and is passionate about giving children the very best learning experiences that she can. She loves learning about new ways of teaching and has had many roles in the primary sector. She is currently a class teacher in South East England.

The Curious Minds of Little Learners

Imogen Stark

Whilst you may consider the classroom to be a learning environment, it's also a place of great joy, great laughter, and great love. All these things stem from *those* types of questions, and boy do they test you!

My highlights include:

- "Miss, are you still a virgin?"
- "Why can't you be my learning mentor?"
- "Why are you so enthusiastic all the time? Are you not exhausted?"
- "Are you an Avenger?"
- "How have you made me like writing?!"
- "Are you 42, Miss?" (For the record I'm 24.)
- "Why do you care so much?"

I love the minds of the children we teach, just as they love to question, enquire, and learn—even if they do test us!

Imogen Stark is an English teacher in the South East. She has previously been a Pupil Premium specialist, and holds a Masters in Linguistics from the University of Sussex.

A Symphony in Collaboration

Annie Daniel

Each year end flashes a special moment of introspection in a teacher. Let me share one of my most recent ones.

While people were busy recording the famous Tik Tok switch, we teachers went through a real time switch: The switch to virtual learning in COVID-19 times. Parents attending my Maths Support Group lessons with their children was the most hilarious highlight of many of my days. Virtual class parties, birthday celebrations, and circle times became our 'New Normal'. Amidst working and learning from home, a symphony in collaboration was struck between my students, their parents and myself. Indeed, this was the key to students' success!

Annie Daniel, MA. Annie is an assistant teacher at the British School, India. Annie has been a teacher for the past 8 years. She did her Bachelors in Elementary Education (B.El.Ed.), from Delhi University, India.

The Magic of Teaching: The Sorcerer's Apprentice

Flo Awolaja

Have you ever thought of a hair brained idea and said to yourself, why not? The assumption of what happens when you put students in the driving seat and tell them to drive is a car crash right?! Wrong!

How many of us experience those light bulbs, those eureka moments when the students get it, which can lead to the saying 'When the apprentice is ready, the master will appear'.

The moment students become the teacher is amazing: you see shy individuals bloom into the confident beings you knew they always were. They just needed someone to believe in them before they were able to believe in themselves—they have to be presented with the opportunity.

Time within the class has presented many memorable moments; there are too many to name, of course, but my favourite is when I told both sets of my Year 9 GCSE Art and Photography classes that for the next six weeks they would be the teacher(s) and I the student. The thought of sitting in their place filled me with glee and them with dread. They would deliver the lessons and homework and I would get the opportunity to be the truculent student; then one clever student asked if they could give detentions!

The shock that registered on their faces was priceless! All I encouraged them to do before they started was to ensure all the lessons and homework were planned. To their credit, both groups stepped up to the challenge and their outcomes surprised even me; I thought I knew them, but little did I know.

The lessons flew by and I thoroughly enjoyed the role reversals. Such was my confidence in their ability that when a lesson observation was foisted upon me, I was not fazed. The students would take the lesson—and the observation too! The comments below are testament to their preparation. The lesson was judged 'Good' by my observer and areas of outstanding practice were highlighted. One observer noted that it was "a really enjoyable style of teaching to experience".

After six weeks the students gave feedback as to their experience; the comment by one of them summed up for me the magic of teaching and their experience.

"I believe this topic has made a good difference to my learning. It has made me more confident within my work and made me feel I can achieve more things, I believe this partly because of the feedback I have been receiving from Miss Awolaja and the experience I have had through showing my work and presenting it".

To this day, I have never forgotten those words. I hope in those six weeks the students realised nothing was out of their reach.

My only wish is that when I was their age I had a teacher like me, someone who is always encouraging, goes out on a limb, who is not afraid to take risks and is just as mischievous and impish as they can be; after all, teaching is about building relationships, connecting with them, finding out what makes them tick and what they're interested in.

It is those unexpected light bulb moments that make teaching so worthwhile.

Flo Awolaja is a writer, poet, and photographer, she continues to take delight in all visual pleasures which stimulate the senses. She also has a successful career as a graphic designer and lecturer and combines her passion for art, design, and photography with teaching, working to raise achievement in her learners by encouraging them, raising their self-esteem, and aspiring confidence in them.

Chapter 5

Collaboration NOT Competition

Establishing positive relationships with students, parents and colleagues is essential. Pastoral care and academic outcomes are inextricably linked and so it is important that teachers get to know each and every individual child, working closely with parents/carers so that everyone can share in the child's learning journey. By getting to know the needs, motivations and aspirations of the children we teach, we can maximise the learning potential of every single child.

It is also important for education staff to build up a positive support network so that we are surrounded by teachers, in school and on social media, who will support us every step of the way in our careers. Teaching is a job where we know we should never be afraid to ask for help, advice or clarification. It is important for us to reach out and find those positive, uplifting people who will celebrate our success, support us and even challenge us to achieve our potential. Our children and young people deserve to have teachers who are committed to being the best they can be.

When teachers unite, amazing things happen. In this chapter, contributors share their tips, advice and experiences about the power of collaboration.

We're Not Superheroes: We're All in This Together

Sarah Mullin

All those who work in education are incredible—there is no doubt about it. During the first lockdown in March 2020, teachers were regularly hailed as superheroes—often by parents, struggling to educate their children at home—as we worked in innovative ways to care for the children of key workers, while also supporting the learning of children isolating at home.

Obviously, praise and recognition are very much appreciated. But the narrative of the superhero teacher is not necessarily helpful. Here are five reasons why.

1. We do not have a Kryptonian physique

Unlike Superman, teachers do not have a Kryptonian physique. Teachers work incredibly hard and we need our sleep. With increasing numbers of teachers reporting signs of burnout and work-related stress as a result of the pandemic, it is more important than ever that the wellbeing of all those working in the education sector is given serious consideration.

When teachers feel supported, appreciated and have optimum levels of wellbeing, they are more likely to thrive in their jobs, which, in turn, will have a positive impact on their students.

2. We don't have nerves of steel

Although we love our jobs, it is important to acknowledge that teachers are not superhuman. There are teachers who continue to be genuinely frightened about the very real possibility of contracting

Covid-19 themselves or about spreading it to vulnerable loved ones.

Teachers are proud to be part of our wonderful profession, and have been proud to fulfil our duties diligently during the national lockdowns. But many teachers have genuinely struggled to navigate the worrying times we have found ourselves living in, when it was considered safe to spend the day in a school filled with children, yet it was against the law to go for a coffee with our nearest and dearest.

3. We are qualified professionals

We are not born with superpowers. Teachers spend years studying to become fully qualified. We then continue to grow and develop as professionals by learning from one another, completing additional qualifications and investing in CPD throughout our careers.

As hardworking, dedicated members of staff, it is disheartening for us to see so much teacher-bashing online. Social-distancing measures have been difficult for everyone, including teachers, who have had to adapt to a whole new way of working. So, while the sentiment behind calling teachers superheroes is lovely, what teachers really deserve is respect and recognition for being highly qualified and experienced professionals.

4. We have other responsibilities too

In addition to completing out-of-hours marking, planning and preparation, many teachers have caring responsibilities, a home to maintain and appointments to attend. It is, therefore, important for teachers to establish and maintain personal and professional boundaries, so that we can juggle our roles and responsibilities effectively.

It is also important to consider that, while many teachers feel that teaching is a vocation—that we have been called to the profession in order to make a difference to the lives of others—we also have mortgages and bills that need to be paid. And so we deserve to receive a salary that reflects our worth.

5. We cannot do this on our own

Teachers are able to do the jobs we love because we are part of a team, working together to support one another. From our teaching assistants to the technology team, our caretakers to our cleaners, and our admin staff to our school cooks, we could not do our jobs without the commitment of our loyal colleagues.

We are also aware that children perform best when their teachers, parents and carers all work together with the child to ensure they achieve their potential.

Teachers cannot work in isolation. The best resource we have in education is the skills and experiences of one another. When we all work together, amazing things happen. We are not mysterious masked superheroes, acting alone.

As teachers, we do our best to ensure that when children leave school they will do so as confident, articulate and well-rounded individuals. It is important for children and young people to see that we *really* are not superheroes. We are partners, parents, friends and neighbours, just like everyone else.

Being a teacher comes with a lot of responsibility: we are the profession that creates all other professions. So, while words of praise do make us smile, what teachers really need is the time, funding and support to be able to carry out our roles effectively.

Sarah Mullin BA (HONS), PGCE, PGCertED, PGDipED, MA, CTE, FCCT, CMgr FCMI, FInstLM, FRSA is a deputy headteacher and Doctor of Education student. She is the author of the number one best-selling book 'What They Didn't Teach Me on My PGCE' and she is the founder of #EduTeacherTips, the YouTube channel for teachers, by teachers. Sarah is on the board of the secondary education committee at the English Association and she is renowned for supporting Early Career Teachers (ECTs) and aspiring school leaders locally, nationally and internationally. She was recently named a 'Rising Star in Education and Academia' and has previously received the 'Contribution to Education of the Year' award.

Black Teachers Connect

@blackteachersco

Black Teachers Connect was established in 2018 as a result of my experience when applying to train to teach. When I was writing my application for my PGCE, I wanted to seek advice from other Black educators on their experiences in the classroom and of working in the education system. Unfortunately, I couldn't find a network directly for this.

I created Black Teachers Connect so nobody else would have the same experience as me. The aim of Black Teachers Connect is to bring together Black teachers in the UK, but also worldwide, by providing them with network opportunities, advice and support. It is widely known that some Black educators have experienced racism and discrimination at work, to the point that 53% of BME educators do not see themselves in the profession in the next five years.

Our aim is to have a support system in place to not only help the recruitment of teachers but also the retention of teachers. We have connected with over 1500 individuals via both Twitter and Instagram, and we have recently launched a Facebook page to make it even easier for educators to connect and to create a further safe space for individuals.

We have helped support aspiring teachers and training teachers as they begin their journey into teaching. We are also supporting all educators on how to tackle issues of race and diversity in the classroom, from having uncomfortable conversations to creating inclusive resources.

Educators can connect with us via Instagram (@blackteachersconnect) and Twitter (@blackteachersco). They can join our Facebook group by searching Black Teachers Connect and email us via blackteachersconnect@hotmail.com.

Working With Parents/Carers

Orla Dumond

When I first qualified as a teacher, I felt absolutely unprepared for dealing with building relationships with parents/carers. This was due in part to not understanding their expectations and concerns. I had lots of theoretical knowledge about education but little classroom (or, indeed, life) experience.

I felt out of my depth when parents/carers reached out to me for support and guidance beyond educational matters. I was overwhelmed entirely when confronted by irate parents/carers. Over the years, I have gained much insight, and would like to share a few tips:

Communication is key to any successful relationship. Ensure your first interactions with parents/carers are positive ones. Find ways to reach out to share their child's successes, be they academic or instances where their character shone through. Parents want to know you 'know' their child. Once this is clear, it is easier to discuss concerns and support to address those concerns is likely to be much more forthcoming.

Be honest. Don't try to bluff your way through questions parent/carers may have. If you don't know how best to advise, offer to seek out information for them. Talk to more senior colleagues for guidance if necessary.

Listen carefully and reflect. Our default is to become defensive if we feel attacked. However, pause and take time to reflect. Is what the parent is saying true? Were you insensitive in some way? Did you make a mistake? If so, own this, apologise, and move on.

Understanding is vital. Sometimes we are approached by parents/carers who are struggling and may have their own anxieties around places of authority. Empathy and perspective can go a long way towards providing reassurance and moving forward positively.

Few parents/carers want anything other than the best for their child. This is also true for teachers. Prioritising the development of positive relationships from the outset of your career is critical.

Orla Dumond is a teacher, speaker and learner working in Malaysia. She is passionate about inclusion and research-informed practice.

Finding Your Tribe

Andrea Walker

Music is a haven for some students. This is particularly true for those who arrive at school afraid of their own shadow, the quiet ones, those who find social interaction more complex than others, those lacking in confidence in who they are, or where making friends is concerned. It is one of my favourite things about teaching my subject; seeing these students grow in confidence and slowly, but surely, finding their tribe.

You need to create a safe, welcoming and inclusive environment where students can gather each break and lunch time. It is not something that can be forced. It will start with, "Miss, can I come and practice at lunch?"

They turn up, sometimes on their own, and sit at a keyboard, or with a guitar, quietly strumming in the background. You learn not to ask too many questions about where their friends are, and work quietly to introduce them to other musicians who inhabit the department at every available opportunity. Often, because they come to practice so frequently, they become quite proficient in a short period of time, which in turn draws an audience and positive reactions.

I have seen older students who find their home in music take a younger student under their wing and have them sit with them while they have their lunch. I have also seen younger students include an older student. It creates opportunities to meet someone to say hello to in the corridor around the school, chat to, and in time, rehearse with. This needs to lead to forming friends their own age, or they then face these older students leaving, and find themselves back to square one.

The issue of popularity is a constant source of drama for some students. However, I have found that those who spend their time in the music department tend to have a select group surrounding them, who they trust enough to be themselves. Over time, and as confidence grows, students who were utterly terrified of getting up on stage become confident enough to perform to a full house. Still terrified, but whether as a soloist or part of a large group, they take a deep breath and find the courage—with the support of their tribe. Their sense of achievement after the performance is indescribable yet written all over their face.

I love how the music department becomes a community, a safe port in a storm, a place to share knowledge and skills and express who they are. I love seeing students teaching others, creating their own music, sharing music tastes and arguing about what direction their band is going in because they have their own distinct styles. It is brilliant when a student plays you a song or piece of music that becomes part of your own playlist.

You would think, however, that spending so much time in the department, this little tribe would learn how to tidy away equipment or the cups from a well-deserved tea and biscuit after packing away a concert. Kids will be kids—although the threat of a short banishment from their port usually does the trick (for a while).

Andrea Walker is a teacher of music and drama now based in the North West. She has also taught and been head of department in Kent, Hertfordshire and Buckinghamshire for 20 years.

Unlocking the Secret of Line Management

Judith Hunt

Line management: do we do it well? Do we know why we're doing it? Confession time—it took me 13 years before I figured it out.

For years, I laboured under the assumption that line management was that meeting you had in September where you set yourself vague targets in a rushed discussion with a busy line manager. Those targets went on a bit of paper somewhere and then were never really thought about until the following September—at which point you realised you hadn't really done anything, but your line manager didn't tell you off because they had forgotten to do the mid-year review, so they didn't come out of it well either. There were mutterings of "partially met" and "it'll be different this year", and off we'd go again.

I never minded because I never knew it could be different. I bumbled along, doing my own thing, seeking out my own opportunities and my career progressed nicely. Then I became a faculty leader. I couldn't just bumble anymore; people were relying on me and I needed to rise to the challenge. I tracked down my line manager; he told me it would be fine, he had every faith in me and that we'd catch up in a few weeks. We didn't, so, ever resourceful, I sought wisdom from my fellow middle leaders and calm reigned once more.

But then everything changed. I got a new line manager. One who actually wanted to meet regularly, who wanted to talk about what was going on in the faculty, who asked me challenging questions and who made me analyse data. I must admit, it was a shock, and I wasn't sure I liked it. It was so different. But then I realised that this person was genuinely interested in my faculty, in what I was trying to do and she wanted to help. She was asking the challenging questions to make me reflect and to help me improve. She was giving me the space to try out my ideas and helping me to be confident in them. She taught me how to have difficult conversations and how to be the best Faculty Leader I could be. She didn't give up when I told her I couldn't understand data and she was endlessly patient as she showed me, for the millionth time, how to find what I needed on the computer system—gold star for that! She was happy to celebrate the highs and mop up the lows. We discovered a shared love of educational research and spent hours talking about it and weaving it into our practice.

So now I know the secret of line management. Done well, it is a game changer. It helps you grow as a professional and I will never settle for less again. Insist on time to meet, relish those challenging conversations, talk about the research and embrace the data—you will flourish as a professional—that's the secret.

Jude is faculty leader for Languages and is passionate about all things French. She is currently studying for her Master's in educational leadership and loves the excuse to read all the time. When she isn't reading, she is either eating cake with her best friend or walking her crazy chocolate labrador, Annie.

"What! Another Cover Lesson?!"

Shabnam Khaliq

As a newly qualified teacher (NQT), the one thing that excited me was having my own timetable—my God I was excited. Unfortunately, my timetable had several spots labelled 'Cover'. It was explained that cover means filling in for lessons when staff are absent; cover means you became a maths teacher, a science teacher and a PE teacher—try teaching PE in heels! I despised cover hours and would dread my cover days. I would sit in the staff room and ask, "Why is it always me?", or complain that the "work is never right!" and "Why can't we just have supply teachers?"

Fast forward nine years and my opinions and experiences of cover lessons have completely changed. At the heart of an inner-city school is relationships; in fact, I think this is the heart of any school. I simply believe that children do not learn from teachers when relationships are absent. It does not matter how great a teacher is, how creative or how passionate. Teachers need to have relationships and be known by their students; this, I believe, is the basis of any learning environment. So how does this impact cover lessons and teachers given hours of cover?

Picture the scene. An absent Year 11 teacher. A class of 25. An irritated cover teacher. As a head of department, I see a surge in behaviour issues, I see mediocre attempts at some tasks—and often I see classrooms completely destroyed when cover lessons are taken. Often, covering staff hand out the work and sit at the teacher's desk expecting learners to just 'get on with it'. One particular lesson stands out to me. A learner was given a simple request: "Can you stop throwing that?" Although learners may know you as an 'X teacher', in a cover lesson you are no longer that and become somewhat unknown. And because the human mind fears the unknown, this request was met with a barrage of abuse and a confused teacher saying, "He is not normally like that".

I am not trying to criticise staff taking cover lessons. What I am trying to do is ask you to really consider the emotional and mental wellbeing of learners when you are taking a cover lesson. Just like the teacher in the room feeling emotions of "why am I on cover?", the learners are also managing emotions. Remember as well that they didn't have the time to prepare; they were not given notice that there would be change in their normal day.

I believe there are some simple tricks that can make cover lessons meaningful. I always address the fact that the regular teacher is off. I will always ask for the classroom routine and I show that I trust the learners. You see it is never just 'another cover lesson'. You being in that room will make a difference and it will matter to them.

Shabnam Khaliq BA (Hons), NPQML has been teaching Religious Education (RE) in inner-city schools for nine years. Working as a teaching assistant allowed Shabnam to see the classroom from the perspective of students, and this has shaped the teacher she is today.

Don't Judge a Book by Its Cover

Julia Skinner

She was a woman who stood for no nonsense and looked like she would take no prisoners. She was one of a group of parents who terrified me, which, as the new headteacher, was probably not a good situation to be in. The school was in an area of severe social deprivation where many of the homes had not had a wage coming in for a long time. That did not detract from the passion that most of the parents felt about their children. I found out by my first Christmas there that you never have a class party on a Friday as the amount of food that would be sent in would take a week to eat!

In my third year, I was appointed the head designate of the amalgamation of my junior school with our partner infant school, and I met her again. I had a year to prepare the community for the new school. It was quite a challenge, as I was still head of my school. Anyway, never one to not accept the gauntlet when it is thrown, one of my first meetings was with infant parents. Of course, we met at the infant school so that they would feel comfortable being on home soil.

I dressed to impress—and hopefully to reassure that I knew what I was doing. I explained the vision for the new school and how we would be taking all that was good from both schools. The new school was to be based in the junior building, with the addition of a couple of new classrooms. It wasn't long before she spoke: "I don't know why the littlies have to go over there. They will get bullied and knocked over".

POW! I knew I had my hands full and that this transition was not going to be without its challenges. By working hard and attending lots of joint meetings, I am pleased to say that when the new school opened a year later, everything went smoothly. Both parent communities were comfortable with things and I was feeling positive about moving forward.

One area that needed some work, though, was the governing board. Neither school had strength in governance, so I looked to build capacity and knowledge both from within and without the community. Parent governors play a key role on a school board and I was conscious of the need to encourage parents who were not used to anything 'formal' in school to consider stepping up. I approached the character that this piece is about and was immediately rebuffed with a "Me! Don't be daft!" However, with gentle persuasion—and lots of hand holding—she ended up joining the board and it was a benefit to us that she found her voice in a strategic arena.

I came to rely on her to be the temperature gauge for the playground and beyond; in fact, one of my greatest achievements as head of the primary school was her appointment to chair of the board. If you'd told me at our first meeting that three years later, she would be a pivotal piece in the school's structure, we *both* would have said "don't be daft!"

It just goes to show that you can never judge a book by its cover—especially where parents of your children are concerned!

Julia Skinner is a retired headteacher in Bristol. Since retiring, she has spent a great deal of time supporting schools, leaders and governors to work together and improve the life chances of the pupils. She is a Founding Fellow of the Chartered College of Teaching and sits on their council. Julia is also a designated Leader of Governance and a consultant for the National Governance Association. She is also founder of the award-winning '100 Word Challenge'—an international writing project linked to blogging. @theheadsoffice

What Can Social Media Do for You?

Jessica Moody

In January 2018, I was fresh out of a breakup, struggling with my sense of self; having moved areas to be with my then boyfriend. I felt I had no true identity. I had lost who I was as a result of giving myself entirely to someone else. I was working at a school where everyone knew me as Mr. X's girlfriend and in a town where I didn't know anyone. Determined to complete the school year with my current Year 11s while still working with my ex, I realised I really needed something for myself.

A colleague, and now friend, asked me to come along to a WomenEd event being held in Birmingham. It was my first journey into spending my Saturdays at educational events, a journey I would never have done if I was still with my ex. I turned up stupidly early and was greeted by the powerhouse that is Hannah Wilson. They welcomed me to the event and I offered to help as much as I could, which turned out not to be a lot, so I was left in the staff room drinking coffee on my own until everyone else arrived. I was so nervous it was unbelievable—I didn't even really know the colleagues I was attending the event with and was very aware that they were a 'clique' in the friendliest of senses. There are two sessions that stand out to me from my first event, and the lessons I took from them have stayed with me since. First, Anne-Marie Williams asked us to do our elevator pitch, so—terrified—I shared mine. "I'd love to work in your department"; this was the first reassuring message from another person that I could do the job I'd been so determined to do since qualifying as a science teacher in 2013. The second was from Jill Berry, whose closing keynote had me in tears and had me determined that I would find happiness (side note I have; not romantically, but in who I am).

That day, I launched myself into the world of #EduTwitter, started building a network of people who inspire and educate me every day. I'm not a 'big name' on Twitter with thousands of followers, but even within the 1000 or so I have now, I am encouraged every day by the joy the social network brings. I will add a caveat here: it's an echo chamber; you follow the people you like and mute or block people who disagree with you. I never involve myself with the arguments over teaching and learning ideas, booths or lists. I have created a network that gives me balance, challenges my ideas and gives me space to think about alternatives.

It's through Twitter that I now speak at TeachMeets, I'm a local governor, a regional lead for WomenEd and I am completing a master's degree in education. All things that, two years ago, I would never have imagined myself doing. I have developed friendships with people I never thought I would. I spend my weekends and evenings with virtual friends who have become real friends. I enjoyed a hilarious night out in Sheffield with people I met at an event and had countless conversations that have developed me as a person, teacher and leader. I even threw myself into the foray of Edudate, a dating service for educators—who am I?!

My chronicle is not from the classroom, it's from Twitter—but the impact of Twitter on who I am in the classroom is immense. I have never been more involved in educational research and literature. I would never have had over 200 people respond to questions such as "if you could have anything in your middle leadership training what would you have?" to enable me to listen and improve training. I wouldn't have changed my practice to be more evidence informed and subsequently the practice of the science department. I wouldn't be the person I am today if it wasn't for being 10% braver and attending my first WomenEd event. If there's one thing you do after reading this, get on Twitter. You don't have to comment on everything, like everything, or even get involved, but you never know when you'll read something that changes how you do something, makes you realise you can write a book or speak at an event or give you new opportunities for friendship that go beyond the web.

People really are amazing, and if you gain half as much as I have from getting involved, I can promise you, you'll be happier.

Jessica Moody BSc. MCCT is the head of science at Park Hall Academy, @JEM_Science on Twitter and WomenEd regional lead for the West Midlands.

What Goes Around Comes Around

Heather Moore

A piece of advice for any new teacher: "Everyone knows everyone". What you say, do and how you act are all going to be remembered.

In the past 15 years of teaching, I have met so many teachers over and over again. Interviews, work that I am employed to do in their school, or through moving schools. You never know who you will meet again, and who will be in touch about someone or something. Not a week will go by without someone asking if I know such and such!

My second PGCE placement was a contrast to my first, where I was placed in one of the largest council estates in the country at a "rough and failing" school.

My mentor was great. Head of Physics, enthusiastic, young, passionate and realistic. I recall a fateful day when Year 11 lined up outside his class—if it could be classed as a "line"—and he locked the classroom door, with us on one side and them on the other. He had no intention of his trainee being involved in the fight that he could see ensuing.

Days later, we were having a professional conversation in the corridor, as many productive conversations can happen there. A la 'The West Wing", staff often pass each other while walking and no one stops; they just talk as they move away from each other. Teaching is fast-paced, with decisions often made like this! Due to unforeseen circumstances, my mentor was absent from school for some time and I was left to teach a full physics timetable on my own. I tried my best to treat the situation with professionalism. I was still in training, and always endeavoured to do my best for the students.

During all of this, I continued to—unsuccessfully—apply for jobs. Wondering why, I called one of the schools and asked if there was a reason; I was told, "You don't have a reference from your current teaching placement school". When I asked the Head of Department (HOD), his response was, "I don't have time". I changed my referee, and landed the next job.

Years later, I interviewed for a second in department, and it turned out the HOD from my 2nd placement school was now the HOD there. I wasn't interested in working for a HOD who had little time for his staff, trainees or not.

Three years later, I was requested to go in to support a science department in a local school—and it turned out that I was training and supporting my old second placement mentor! Recalling his inspirational influence, I was determined to help in any way I could.

The moral of this story is that there is no experience that will not lead you to the next opportunity. Remember to remain professional and positive. Take from an experience, but also manage what you leave behind.

Heather Moore BSc (Hons), PGCE, NPQML, MCCT is currently a lead practitioner in a leading North West secondary school. She has held positions as Key Stage 4 Coordinator, second in department and head of department in science. Alongside her day-to-day role, she supports other North West schools to improve attainment.

The Magical Mentor

Tejal Shah

"Years from now, you're going to look back on this moment and wonder how on earth you managed the last few months. But you will".

I was stumped. It wasn't like I hadn't heard similar, but it was the absolute conviction that Maria spoke with—and that it was Maria saying it—that made me believe her.

In November 2010, my best friend Jasmin died at the age of 19. We met in nursery and she was the sister I never had. When she passed from meningitis, I felt like I'd been winded. What 19-year-old dies with no warning?

I was so painfully lonely: the person I spoke to the most was gone.

So, imagine the gut-wrenching, world-flipping, colour-draining sadness when three months later I heard: "Nik died".

It's impossible to convey the full extent that my brother's death affects me, but the few months after were a particularly potent cocktail of emotion. I would flit between flurries of passion and weeks in bed. I rarely attended my Italian seminars and fell severely behind.

My tutor, Maria, kindly took the time to run through the grammar I'd missed. Why would I care about 'il uture'? I nodded politely at something I didn't understand and suddenly she paused, broke into English and said those first two sentences to me.

She then snapped back to conjugations.

It would be a lie to say Maria is the reason I became a teacher, but she definitely deepened my understanding of what a teacher's role is. Teachers give faith AND grammar lessons.

It took a long time for my grief to transform into gratitude. Over the years, I had various jobs and experiences until I somehow wound-up teaching at the very school my brother went to as a teen. It felt like a cosmic wink.

'H' was a handful of a student. He successfully enraged every member of staff at least once. He was also one of those kids that are impossible to stay angry with. H might be defying you, but at least he does it with a cheesy grin.

One day I saw H meandering around the school corridors when he should have been in a lesson. His sister had passed away months before, and his grades had plummeted. He was bunking, and I saw myself in him.

"Do you want to help tidy my classroom?"

It didn't take much tidying before he spilled—the changing dynamics, the lack of attention, the self-destructive behaviour. H also told me he climbed the school gate to sleep in the field after a fight with his parents.

This happened a few years ago, but it still moves me that this student who, despite claiming he hated it, saw school as his safe space. School was his stability. H couldn't see beyond his grief, and I can't imagine how much worse grief feels when all the adults decide how you're going to manage it. He just needed to know it was going to be okay.

There was a lull in our conversation and then I heard Maria's words come out of my mouth. After all, the foundation of all teaching is having faith in a brighter future and imparting that faith.

"Years from now, you're going to look back on this moment and wonder how on earth you managed the last few months. But you will".

Tejal is a 29-year-old secondary teacher in London. She has a love of guinea pigs, Italy and over-analysing the writer's choices.

It's Not Me, It's You

Rebecca Lynch

All schools are the same … except when they're not. Staff are the beating heart and engine room of any school. They can make your journey heaven or hell; this section reflects on the experience of both.

In 2013, I started my newly qualified teacher (NQT) year—and I was SO excited! I took the first job I interviewed for, without any research or even looking at the website. That was my first mistake; I was just excited to qualify and teach.

I started in September and was shown to my classroom, and to my dismay it was a computer room. Great if you're a subject that relies on computers, not so great for an NQT maths teacher. I started to meet my department and that's when I started to think I'd made a mistake. There were seven of us, and only two of them were interested in any communication. I later learned that staff turnover was so high, they expected me to leave by Christmas like the majority of young teachers.

I struggled—and I mean really struggled (crying on the way to work, crying at home). The kids didn't listen to me, I had minimal resources and those computers were in my way. I had my first NQT observation and was asked why I was teaching in computer room. Of course, my answer was "that's the classroom I was given"; fortunately, it was decided that the room wasn't appropriate. I was switched classrooms with one of the few teachers who bothered to talk to me, and this did not go well. From that point, I was ignored by all but one member of the team. I didn't leave by Christmas but two of the team did leave by Easter. The new staff arrived and, again, I found it hard to bond with them. This continued into my second year. I was miserable. Miserable to the point I wanted to quit teaching forever.

I spoke to a friend who was teaching at her old secondary school and she had a completely different outlook. A few weeks later, there was a job vacancy and after another morning of crying in the staffroom, I decided enough was enough. I wrote my application on Friday during a break time, and got it in just in time for the 12PM deadline. That same afternoon, I was offered an interview on Monday morning.

I got to the school and within five minutes I knew I'd found my home. I walked through the school with the head of maths (who later became headteacher) and he spoke to everyone we walked past. Students, teachers and site staff: everyone! There was no hierarchy and definitely a warm culture. During the course of the day, I met teaching assistants and teachers and every single one of them was so positive and encouraging. I was the only person interviewing that day and I got the job.

That was the best decision I ever made; five years later I still can't believe I got so lucky. The team I work with now are like family. We eat lunch together every day and we spend time together outside work. We've celebrated weddings, engagements, babies, new homes, birthdays and promotions together. I found the place where I belong.

Remember that the issue might not be you, but the place you work. Try a new school and do your research.

Rebecca Lynch is a Lead Practitioner in Mathematics for Ninestiles, An Academy and Summit Learning Trust, and is currently studying a Masters in Expert Teaching.

The Power of Making Connections on #EduTwitter

James Grocott

Have you ever been to a gathering or a party or a wedding where you don't really know anyone and it's clear that everyone else there have met before and know each other? Everyone is really friendly and they walk around chatting to one another about things they've got in common. You might try and join a conversation about something you have in common with them, and thankfully there are usually one or two who might chat back to you—but they're soon off on their way back to their group.

This is my analogy of how #EduTwitter is for people that are new to using it. It's like that party (and sometimes it really is like a party as it's such an amazing thing to be involved in with so many amazing people) and even though you've been invited and are welcome to be there, it can feel like you're not quite 'in the room'. You might have pressing questions; you might have great ideas; you might actually have so much that is worth hearing, but it's like you're on the outside looking in. You might pose a question; you might share a resource or you might make an amazing statement about how we can better the education of our children, but it's hard to be heard.

I've been lucky over the past year or so as I have become one of the 'in the room' people. And it really was luck for me. I shared a few resources, made a few comments and, most importantly, got involved in conversations. The one thing that really got me 'in the room' was my idea to try and get everyone connecting with one another at the #EduTwitter 'party', and that's when Follow/Follow Back Wednesday

(#FFBWednesday) began. It was precisely because of my party analogy that I invented it and, once again, I got lucky. I'm sure people have tried for years, and in different ways, to invent something similar to #FFBWednesday; perhaps it has worked to an extent but didn't quite take off, so I'm not claiming to have invented a brand new 'thing'. It's just that I was lucky and it worked!

I knew it was working because it began to grow and grow, week after week. What started with 50 or so people on the thread now has nearly 800 every week—which is amazing! Educators from all over the world take part!

The whole point in #FFBWednesday is about 'making connections'. It's not about following for the sake of following. It's a thread for people involved in education where they can connect and then, hopefully, this can lead to everyone growing their Personal Learning Network (PLN), which in turn gets people the support and help they might be needing from #EduTwitter. Essentially it gets people 'in the room'.

It has worked phenomenally well, and it's great to hear from people each week saying that they've made new connections or have managed to get an answer to a question that they've posed because of it. Join us every Wednesday on Twitter!

James Grocott is a primary school deputy headteacher from Suffolk who currently teaches Year 5 and 6. He has been teaching for 16 years and in that time has been a subject leader, phase leader and SENDCO.

Chapter 6

When Things Go Wrong

Who would have thought that teachers might end up in the local hospital due to a regrettable encounter with a piece of classroom equipment? Have you ever found yourself clutching a paper bag filled with a child's vomit on a coach trip? Who can relate to the shrieks of horror when a bumblebee decides to enter your classroom during a class examination?

This chapter should really come with a disclaimer. The narratives you are about to read will have you laughing out loud, wincing in pain—and you may even feel a little queasy! Working in schools can be very unpredictable: sometimes teachers can find themselves in the most unfortunate scenarios.

A Sing-Song is Always the Answer

Emma Turner

My NQT year was the year of my career which probably I remember most clearly. Some parts are viewed through the rose-tinted glasses of 22 years of teaching—and a little like a dreamy slow-mo flashback sequence from a schmaltzy Hollywood film—while other moments remain etched on my retina forevermore, producing cringes which still curl my toes so tightly, I'm likely to get an immediate cramp.

I should have guessed from my first teaching interview that I was perhaps not destined for crisp and polished professionalism. After being led out onto a large raised patio overlooking the school field, other candidates commented to each other on the potential for outdoor learning, extended sports offers and nature walks. I found myself turning around on the gusty slabs and pronouncing, "Blimey, that wind comes straight off that field and up your trouser leg, doesn't it!" Sadly, I had chosen to say this to the chair of governors, who was as bewildered as I was as to why I'd thought that an appropriate observation during an interview. I spent the rest of the interview berating myself for my inability to think of a pertinent question or observation, and instead busied myself by accidentally offending everyone else in the staff room. I sat in the wrong chair; I used the wrong mug; I called one lady by the wrong name for the entire lunchtime until one other staff member could stand it no longer and corrected me. I spent a disproportionate amount of time silently bemoaning the fact that my surname began with a 'T' and I was last up for every aspect of the day.

By the time my turn for the formal interview had come around, I'd been at the school for almost 8 hours and was fully acquainted with the tea urn—and subsequently the school plumbing facilities. I was borderline high on caffeine and bleach fumes so I went into the interview a mix of the arrogance of youth, a desperation to just get it over with—and an overwhelming urge to visit the ladies again.

As I was asked standard question after standard question, I trotted out the well-rehearsed answers my university had drilled in me, and that my peers had also said they'd given in interviews. I sort of relaxed into the process, although my newly bought suit was not only uncomfortable but also ill-fitting. I spent most of the interview sitting like an amateur contortionist as I tried to ensure my top didn't gape, my waistband didn't fall down and I didn't pee myself thanks to the copious amounts of tea and adrenaline.

It was with huge relief that the final question was answered, and I congratulated myself silently that I had managed to dodge making myself look like a Class A doofus—which usually happens whenever I'm nervous. As I went to stand, the assembled panel shuffled their papers and the chair of governors smiled warmly and asked another question: "Where will you go from here Miss Turner?"

I replied, "Probably home for a gin and tonic but if I'm honest, I need a wee first," and I gestured towards the door—but then noticed the rest of the panel had looks varying between "aghast", "amused" and "horrified".

"Miss Turner, I meant where will you go from here … with your career?" I stood there in my ill-fitting suit, burning cheeks, desperate for a wee, and said the first thing that came into my head, "Well … you tell me; I'm kind of hoping I'll be here." I figured that I had nothing to lose. I'd drunk out of the wrong mugs all day, offended the staff, commented on breezes up trouser legs, sat in the wrong seats, spent most of the day in the toilet—and now alluded to alcohol being part of my career plan.

Imagine my surprise, then, when I got the phone call later to say I'd gotten the job.

I spent the summer celebrating and amassing resources for my new job. I laminated everything that wasn't nailed down and was ready to meet my first class. Except I wasn't prepared at all. I was in a draughty, rotten, old mobile classroom set in the furthest reaches of the playground. There was an actual tree growing up through the floor of the resources cupboard; when you opened the door to put anything in it, you were faced, not with neat shelves, but with the subject of a nature documentary. The ceiling was collapsing in the main teaching area and was held up with a series of columns, all seemingly placed by someone who was either doing some kind of magic art installation or who hadn't realised that children actually needed to see the board when they were working. Wherever you sat, one of those columns would skew your view of the board, so my class looked like the crowd at Wimbledon whenever I taught as they leant left and right with metronomic regularity as I attempted to teach.

I made so many errors in that damp—and frankly condemnable—shambles of a mobile. The number of times we accidentally got locked out of it too meant that I became a master of the impromptu resource-free outdoor lesson; often it was because I'd, yet again, left the keys to the mobile somewhere between the mobile steps and the staff room. However, on one occasion it was not my fault—one of my pupils had jammed a Smartie in the keyhole rendering it completely useless until the premises officer could remove the entire lock and handle and we could all get back in again. I had to ensure I always locked it whenever we left, as I began teaching in the days when school sites were completely open and had very few security measures to prevent anyone getting onto the site. I discovered that it was definitely not secure that same sunny afternoon of "Smartie in the keyhole", during a Geography lesson, when I turned around to find a pupil's father, clearly agitated and obviously wanting an immediate discussion.

I wasn't quite sure what the protocol was for dealing with an angry parent who just appeared in your classroom clutching a large carrier bag, but I duly dispatched two children to hunt down the Senior Leadership Team (SLT) for support and then politely asked the father if I could help him. He looked my board up and down, as if assessing my lesson content, then tipped the contents of his plastic bag onto my desk. Out clattered a huge pile of music cassette tapes and as my class craned their necks to try and see around the pillars and work out what was going on, I noticed one of my pupils had gone puce and was trying to slide down his chair. I figured correctly that this must have been his dad, and he leant over my desk and pointed at the board full of geography before pointing at my badly drawn map of the British Isles and asked, "When are you going to teach Bradley to stop nicking cassettes from Woolworths?" And frankly, there's not really an answer to that when you have 30 inquisitive children delighted at the unfolding drama, a member of SLT looming in your doorway, a pile of stolen cassettes on your desk and an irate parent in your classroom.

Luckily, my SLT broke the silence by gesturing, puzzled at the table nearest the door, and simply asking. "Why is your door handle not on your door and why is it in pieces on the table?" Of course, there is no good answer to that either, so I was relieved when my class broke into the song they'd made up when I'd first shouted "Who put the Smartie in the keyhole?". They'd sung back, to the tune of "Who put the colours in the rainbow?", "Who put the Smartie in the keyhole?" And so, should you ever need to know the appropriate response to a missing door handle, an irate parent, stolen goods in your classroom and a bemused SLT member, the answer is always a good sing song.

But I'll tell you one thing; that night I definitely went home for that gin and tonic!

Emma Turner FCCT is Research and CPD Lead for DSAT. She worked in primary schools as a class teacher, leader and coheadteacher for over 20 years. She is a columnist for the TES, Ambassador for the GEC, author of "Be More Toddler" and passionate advocate for flexible working.

Narrow Escape

Professor Colin Richards

It was early July. The weather was hot and getting hotter; the sun was high in the sky. My class of eleven-year-olds were feeling the heat. Even with the windows fully open they abandoned the pretence of working and flaked out in the heat, heads on desks, eyes closed.

I looked out of the window. The young teacher whose class was in a mobile across the playground had not got any windows open despite the soaring temperature! "It must be like an oven in there", I thought. "I need to do something."

I rushed out of my classroom and headed for the mobile. I could hear a faint but growing buzzing sound but disregarded it in my haste to rescue the hapless class and its young teacher from the Sahara-like temperature.

I reached the mobile door, threw it open and was about get the class out of that "hot-spot" when I heard a loud voice coming from the main building. It cried: "Shut the door and stay inside!" I hesitated for one second … but only for one second … luckily…

There was a rushing sound, the sunlight was suddenly dimmed, and there was a fierce, incredibly loud, splattering noise—as if a hail-storm had broken loose. It couldn't be … not on a cloudless day in high summer?

It wasn't. It was the sound of a swarm of bees whirling in a black cloud around the mobile and smashing themselves, thousands of them, across all the windows. All of us were rooted to the spot, the heat forgotten, as the mass of bees hurled themselves at the glass. Luckily, very luckily, not a single window had been opened—despite the heat. No bee could penetrate into the mobile. Had there been the smallest window open all hell would have been let loose with thousands of bees attacking us.

Stunned by the carnage—but not stung by the swarm—we watched as the swirling mass finally moved on across the playground and into a neighbouring field. We waited anxiously, getting ever hotter, until I was satisfied the swarm had disappeared and I could get the class and its traumatised teacher back to the main school. It was the closest I ever came to experiencing hysteria, mayhem and possibly near-death in a career of over forty years in primary education.

At the time of this incident, Colin Richards was deputy head in a Warwickshire primary school. He later became a primary HMI and a professor of education.

Colin Richards is currently Emeritus Professor of Education at the University of Cumbria and has been a visiting professor at the Universities of Leicester, Warwick and Newcastle. A former primary school teacher and deputy head, he was an HMI from 1983 to 1996, specialising in primary education and in teacher education. He is the chair of governors of a Cumbrian secondary school, has served on a number of primary school governing bodies and has recently stood down as a National Leader of Governance. As a critic of much (though not all) past and present government education policy, he is a frequent contributor to the national press (in particular, to the Guardian, the Observer, the Independent, the Times Educational Supplement, Schools Week and Education Journal). He also tweets at @colinsparkbridg.

Only Fools and Parents

Tom Rowan

Without sounding too defeatist, stepping into a primary classroom for the first time as a class teacher is truly terrifying. When 30 pairs of eyes are staring up at you and you are responsible for their academic progress, it does tend to raise the heart rate a little. To add to this, a 10-month PGCE barely scratches the surface when it comes to preparing you for that first day in September as a Newly Qualified Teacher (NQT). Teacher education programmes are often blamed for the fact that many teachers are unprepared for their roles (Worthy, 2005, p. 2). Talking from experience, there is a chasm between the educational theory that you learn at university and what challenges you face when you enter the classroom.

For example: my first ever parents' evening. Whilst sitting next to an experienced teacher, I foolishly nodded and thought how easily I could replicate the conversations she was having with parents about their child's progress. However, this was far from the truth. Just eight weeks into my NQT year, there I was placing two chairs opposite me whilst wiping the sweat off my forehead. A large intake of breath and a sip of water did my nerves all kinds of good (for all of three seconds) until two adults stared at me across the four-foot table. Holding it together as best I could, I cleverly diverted the conversation straight back on to them by asking the classic teacher question, "So, how do you feel the year's gone so far?"; the added bonus being it gave me the chance to scrabble around for the right paperwork. With it being a nice way to gauge their opinions, I confidently rose in my chair, foolishly believing that nothing could go wrong now. I was highly mistaken. The conversation continued in a professional manner. Discussions around how their child had settled into Year 3 and the early progress they had made went down well.

The events that unfolded subsequently were received with less enthusiasm. After 10 intense minutes, I decided to reach for my glass of water to wrap up the proceedings. Remembering tips provided to me by my mentor 6 months before, I maintained eye contact with the parents. In a moment of my life I will never forget, my fingertips smashed against the glass and it toppled over onto the table. It was like one of those slow-motion events that you see in films where the actor shouts "Nooooooo!" Clawing at the exterior of the glass, my heart rose up into my mouth. "Oh my, I'm so sorry!", I said to the parents glaring angrily at me. Drenched from the resulting splash, they said nothing, rose from their seated positions and left the room, leaving me to contemplate whether teaching was the right profession for me.

As stated earlier, a PGCE can't prepare you for everything! I guess my top tip before starting your teaching career would be to expect the unexpected—and buy a water bottle with a securely fastened lid!

References

Worthy, J., 2005. 'It didn't have to be so hard': the first years of teaching in an urban school. *International Journal of Qualitative Studies in Education, 18*(3), pp.379-398.

Tom Rowan is a Recently Qualified Teacher (RQT) who began his journey into teaching at The University of Nottingham. He gained a PGCE from the establishment and has enjoyed 18 months submerged into the hectic classroom environment. He currently works at Lantern Lane Primary School in East Leake, Nottinghamshire.

The Chronicles of My Foot

Anonymous

It was May 2019 when the 'Chronicles of My Foot' began. The first bell had gone for morning registration and students had started filing into form rooms. I was standing in a doorway speaking with a colleague. We had just about wrapped up our conversation and I turned towards my room. At this point, a truly indescribable pain shot up from my right foot into my leg and through my whole body. At first, I did not know what was happening. All I knew was that my foot felt like it was being crushed and simultaneously set on fire. I looked down and saw one of our wheelchair-user students parked on my foot. He had sped around the corner and had misjudged the gap between the doorway and where I was. The consequence: an electric wheelchair parked on my foot.

Unsurprisingly, I panicked and tried to drag my foot out. My colleague, at this point, had realised from the colour draining from my face (and the words tumbling out of my mouth) what was happening. She tried to help move the wheelchair but it was heavy and practically immovable. The student did not realise what exactly was happening and so hit his emergency brake on my foot. I was now stuck with the wheel firmly parked on my foot. Eventually, we managed to get the student to move the wheelchair; regrettably, for my foot and me, it was in a three-point reverse turn motion back over my foot.

Reader, I don't know how I didn't throw up, pass out or cry. I limped back to my room and watched my foot balloon over the next few minutes.

Several accident statements, ice-gel patches and Ibuprofens later, I ended up in Accident and Emergency (A&E). I had broken the bones in the top of my foot. They couldn't cast or boot it because of where the breakage was. I spent the summer term at work confined to my classroom due to being in flip-flops. My work family was great and brought me refreshments throughout the day. They even 'transported' me to places I needed to go when the swelling was bad (and the corridors were clear). My foot started healing after further medical intervention and, thankfully, by the end of the term my limp had gone.

Summer holidays came and went; it was now September and we were back at work. It was a Friday and I had double Year 10. One of the girls came running in, waving her homework towards me. In the process of getting to me, she knocked the paper trimmer. We watched it, in slow motion, fall diagonally and land on my foot. I don't know if it was a rush of adrenaline or utter disbelief at my luck, but I convinced myself the tingling I felt in my foot was nothing. By lunch, I could not ignore the now swollen and bruised foot attached to me. Another trip to A&E. No re-break thankfully, but extensive soft-tissue damage on top of my other damage.

Rather embarrassingly, the X-Ray technician recognised me from the wheelchair incident and declared that I should "keep away from kids if you want to keep your feet". We are given lots of advice as teachers—I feel this was amongst the most noteworthy of my career.

The Worst and the Best Memory

Fiona McSorley

In 1979, I was an enthusiastic Newly Qualified Teacher (NQT) in geography, hoping to inspire my love of the world to the next generation. I was teaching at a school in Croydon where one of my friends from university taught. Schools were very different then. My classroom had the old wooden desks with lids and generations of graffiti etched into them. I was once asked if I wanted a misbehaving boy caned; I declined on the boy's behalf. I cannot remember any NQT meetings or support. I knew I had passed my probationary year when a gentleman from the borough popped into the classroom to tell me I had passed—without him ever seeing me teach. Perhaps that's why I lasted 38 years, accumulating all sorts of memories along the journey.

My worst and best memory came from an incident that occurred one sunny Monday afternoon.

There was going to be a fight. Boys from a school down the road had threatened our students and male staff were called to help. My friend, always one of the good guys, rushed to go help and asked me to look after his Year 10 class. This was not a class that one would immediately call likable. There were characters in it, and some I knew well already. I was not deterred, but marched in boldly and inquired what they had been doing last lesson and attempted to sort out some work. The stock cupboard was at the back of the classroom and, after settling the class down, I went in search of some textbooks to keep them occupied until their 'real' teacher returned.

Disaster struck as I stepped out from the cupboard with a pile of books in my arms. As I placed my foot on the step down (about 18 inches above the floor), the step moved away from the wall and I flew up in the air, scattering books everywhere, and hitting my head on the stone lip of the cupboard floor. I thought I heard a pupil laugh but it stopped quickly when I didn't get up. Then, two of the most troublesome students came to see if I was alright; the last thing I remember is them leaning over me asking if I was ok before I lost consciousness.

I later learned that said two characters went to get help whilst the others kept an eye on me. This brought out the best in them. They were young, and a bit scared, but knew I was hurt and needed help. I was not out for long and had a huge bump and headache afterwards, but will always remember their care. Young people are often dismissed as trouble or indifferent, but I disagree.

In today's world, this would have been a health and safety nightmare. Back then, a note in the accident book and a cup of tea sufficed. The caretaker had the last word when he accused me of breaking the step he had built!

Fiona McSorley FCCT recently retired from a long teaching career as a Senior Leader and from running a Teaching School. Now she is able to 'pay it back' through helping the schools as an Associate for PiXL6. Fiona is a Trustee at her local MAT, a Fellow of the Chartered College of Teaching and a Regional Leader for WomenEd.

The Day It All Went Wrong

Vicky Ball

The day in question was a Thursday; the day I have the same Year 8 class three times in one day. This particular day, I had missed the memo telling us it is Year 8 injections.

First lesson: only a few turn up. "Injections", says a girl with fear in her eyes. It's ok, I think. We got this. Starters are on the board, so they can just do that until everyone else arrives. I didn't factor in the panic attacks that the ones still waiting are having.

"I'm scared it's going to hurt".

"It's just an injection. You'll be fine".

Kids start arriving in dribs and drabs, and every one of them is asked "How was it?" Stories of the size of the needle echo around the room. Some don't make it back because they fainted.

Some of the original ones go off for their injections. Some have finished the starter while some have barely started. Already it's starting to go wrong. The returning ones are clutching their arms in pain and others start getting out their lunch boxes.

"What are you doing?" I ask.

"The nurse said we had to eat something after".

"I think she meant a biscuit, not a whole picnic".

"Oh, we're allowed to eat".

After more get out their lunch boxes, "NO".

The lesson continues in a similar thread, and not much work is done.

Second lesson: most have had their injections, some have gone home, the trauma being too much for them, but a few are still waiting—and their panic has increased.

Then, as if injections are not enough, a giant hornet flies in the room. At this point I think I may as well go home; this day is not going to get any better. Most of the class run outside of the room, screaming, leaving me to flap at it hopelessly, trying to get it out of the window without killing it. After a few minutes of doing this, while trying to stop the class from disturbing other classes, I decide enough is enough; it is either the hornet or my lesson. I grab the nearest exercise book. One whack and it falls dead behind the radiator.

I try desperately to get back some semblance of a normal lesson until Billy walks in and stands in the middle of the room rotating his arm like a propeller.

"What are you doing Billy?"

"The nurse told me to keep moving my arm".

Third lesson: everyone has had their injections, so it's time to do some actual work. Halfway through the lesson, the deputy head comes in and I tell him about hornet incident.

"Oh", he says. "You know, dead hornets attract more hornets".

Cue student crawling under the radiator trying to rescue the dead hornet. I give up!

Vicky Ball is a teacher of English and religious studies in Suffolk. She is also mother to two teenage girls.

Pigeons: An Unexpected Irritation

Nick Tingley

There are certain situations that no amount of training will ever truly prepare you for, and there are those that no one ever thinks to train you in. The bizarre moments—the sort of things that come totally out of left-field—certainly add a bit of spice to your day… Had I left to go home one minute earlier, I would never have been involved.

"Sir, sir!" There is something amazing about how high-pitched excited voices can get as they bellow at you down an empty corridor. "Der da birf ala contee".

It took me three attempts before I finally realised what they meant. A bird had wandered into the canteen; given that my room was nearest, they had come to me for help (it's amazing how they can always think sensibly when there actually is a problem).

What on earth was I going to do? The last time I even came close to handling a bird was when my-six-year-old-self had a rather regrettable encounter with a grumpy owl (side note: owls do not like to be prodded, no matter how amusing it might look), and I wasn't really relishing the idea of chasing a bird around a massive, glass-walled dining room. But my students had come to me, and I was naïve enough to answer the call.

I had hoped that the girls would simply wander off, having fulfilled their duty to inform someone of the avian invasion, allowing me to try—and fail—to ward off the bird in peace. I had hoped wrong.

Thus, I found myself standing in the canteen observing a fat, slightly over-energetic pigeon, who had decided to nestle in amongst a collection of folded-up tables, whilst a group of three teenage girls took up seats at the far side of the room to observe the inevitable chaos. They watched with bated breath as I slowly approached the bird; one of them opened her bag, took out a family-size pack of popcorn and proceeded to munch with such glee that you'd think it was a Saturday at the cinema.

I was all alone—a hunter stalking his prey...

I looked at the pigeon. And he looked at me.

"I'm not going to make this easy for you", he seemed to say, as he spread out his wings and launched himself directly at me. He fluttered and dived and waddled and swooped. With each pass, I attempted to coax him towards the open door, finally managing to direct him towards the outside world and freedom.

One of the girls gasped; the pigeon altered its course, swerving this way and that, and collided with the window with a sickening crunch.

I took away two positives from that day: I learned how to talk to students about death, and I got a free family-size bag of popcorn. I call that a pretty successful day.

Nick has been teaching English for two years, having passed his initial teacher training last June. He currently teaches at a large, comprehensive school in Surrey and delivers occasional seminars for trainee teachers at the University of Brighton.

Sick

Rosie Birks

Once upon a time, the word 'sick' was used to mean 'cool'. This is not what this is about. This is about vomit. As a secondary school teacher, I did not think I would have to deal with vomit.

I was wrong.

It was nearly the end of my Year 9 lesson. The children had just started to pack away and stand behind their chairs. A boy put his hand up.

"Miss, I'm going to be sick".

I am not built for speed or elegance. I clutched the bin, which I always keep at the front of the classroom for easy access, before dodging gangly arms clutching on rucksacks, unaware of the impending danger.

The boy sat two rows back and, fortunately, close to the middle aisle. As I stretched towards his table, I saw his cheeks bulge. It was coming. He put his head forward. His mouth opened.

I looked away (I might have even closed my eyes a bit) as I thrust the bin towards the boy. A splatter made the bin tremble, then it was still. I put it down on the table just as shrieks of horror escaped from the nearby students.

Quickly, the class was dismissed, whilst the boy dabbed his mouth WITH HIS SLEEVE. Bravely, I inspected the damage; I checked the table. There was nothing there. I checked the boy's shirt; there was nothing there either. I take a quick peek at the chair and the carpet and even the side of the bin. There was nothing there.

I caught every drop in the bin. As I filled with pride and made a terrible joke about being in the cricket team, I scribbled a medical note and let the boy take my bin with him.

But that wasn't the last time. We were on the way home from a theatre trip in Manchester. It was late and the sixth form students were tired. We still had a couple of hours to go when a shadow fell across my seat. A big lad, 18 years old, felt sick.

Two minutes later, after I passed him a sick bag and sat him at the front, he did indeed start to puke. My colleague said she could not cope with sick and moved to the back. She abandoned me. Traitor.

I watched, helpless, as the sick continued. It was going to fill the little sick bag. We needed to swap bags. But how? When? And why are sick bags so often made from paper?

I was hypnotised by the dark stains spreading relentlessly through the bottom of the bag.

I had two plastic bags ready, although I did not know if they had holes in them. I had told the boy the plan…

3. 2. 1. GO!

There was some fumbling. Some sick slopped out of the bag but I caught it with the second plastic bag. I asked the bus driver where the bin was. It was bursting with plastic bottles and sweet packets. There was no room. I could not put it on the floor because the first aid kit, the trip pack and my handbag were all stuffed down there.

I could not put a bag of sick next to the boy still retching, so I held the bag of puke, dangling over the front passenger seat, for the rest of the journey. My arm ached from the sheer weight of it.

When we got off the bus, he didn't even say thank you; I could barely raise my arm to wave goodbye.

And because things often come in threes, here's another example: We were nearly at Manchester Airport. It was the Danish Exchange Trip and I had just done the final rubbish run with my bin bag, making sure everyone was ok and reminding them to take everything with them. Google maps said we had 8 minutes left of our journey.

That is when it happened. A 14-year-old boy had been very sick. Everywhere. Luckily, he was sitting on his own. Unluckily, his sick was yellow and like cottage cheese in texture.

The smell was overwhelming. We moved as many kids as we could away from it. We were nearly at the airport and we could not waste time scrubbing the bus—or him. We did not have the equipment for it either. I grabbed some toilet tissue and began scooping the worst of it up. The wave of stench made me gag.

I am glad we moved the kids away so they did not witness this.

It was a terrible clean-up effort and the kids raced off the bus, desperate for fresh air. The boy had left his iPad face down in the puke; it had clogged the earphone socket. I tried to flick it free. As I used my longest nail in the socket, the toilet paper ripped, leaving a little nugget of sick on my finger.

Inside the airport, I asked if he could change his clothes and shoes before we went any further. It really did stink. His reply horrified me. He had only brought one pair of brand new, once white, Nike trainers. They were blotched with yellow and they reeked. So, we had to get a flight, and then a train, with this boy wearing sick shoes.

I have no idea what his host family thought as they collected this student wearing his own vomit, but I do know that his host family rolled with it and helped clean his shoes. When I saw him the next day, they were brilliantly white and spotless.

Being a teacher, or hosting exchange students, is a pledge of commitment for better, for worse, in sickness and in health.

Rosie Birks MA FCCT teaches English and mathematics at a secondary school in Derbyshire. Alongside her work as head of house, she is in the third year of her education doctorate focussing on creativity and student voice.

Beware the USB

Michael Roberts

I was working as an IT technician at the time, and I was responsible for setting up laptops and tech stuff for visitors. We had an interview that day for head of computer science. The teacher had to deliver a lesson that was in front of Year 10/11 students, whilst being assessed by the head and interview panel.

I received a call to go down because the man's USB stick wasn't working (we've all been there). Anyway, I went down, pushed a few buttons, kicked a few components (utilising my highly developed IT skills, of course) and, unfortunately, there was a problem with the USB stick. "Not to fear" the candidate said as he whipped out a second stick and popped it in the back; unfortunately, for him, on the screen, in front of all the students and all the staff, popped up some rather inappropriate photos.

As you would suspect the staffroom afterwards was full of commentary! He didn't get the job, but he is somewhat of a legend—for all the wrong reasons.

Eyes in the Back of Your Head!

Rachael Rivers

Here is a top tip for new teachers: if you have your photograph taken at school, make sure it is a good one and that you are completely happy with it, because—mirroring Frankenstein's unhappy realisation—once created, it will follow you.

Despite arguments to the contrary, I do not believe I am photogenic. It is a truth universally endured by the teaching profession that we are surrounded with images of ourselves. Every day I am confronted by pictures of myself: on the school staff notice board, in the school entrance, on the school website and—worst of all—around my neck on a lanyard. To further my pain, my image also appears on a screen every morning when I sign into work and every evening when I sign out, as if to seek confirmation of my discomfort. There is simply no way of getting away from your image.

Some years ago, I was involved in a hugely successful teaching and learning project which required me to have a camera installed in the roof of my classroom so that my teaching was recorded and used in mentoring sessions with a remote mentor. Shortly after the project ended, my headteacher asked me to provide him with a photograph; my image was required so that it could be used on display boards at an educational exhibition, on a stand promoting the use of cameras in the classroom. Feeling slightly apprehensive, I asked a friend if she could pop into a lesson and take some snaps of me in action, teaching my Year 1 class; I figured that casual shots of me in the classroom would look better than posed images. This she did, very kindly taking lots of pictures of me teaching a twenty-minute phonics lesson before playtime. The new trigraph I was teaching that day was 'ure' and with my beloved pupils' help, I wrote a number of words containing this sound on the whiteboard, over the course of the session. Phonics went well; the children had once again learned well, they had had fun and I felt happy about my teaching. Surely one picture, at least, would convey all this.

And so, having sent the children out to playtime, I felt optimistic as I opened the iPad and started to view the images; I was confident that my lovely colleague and friend would definitely have captured some pictures suitable for the exhibition. To be precise, there were actually twenty-three images, every one conveying with crystal clarity the word "manure" behind my head.

Needless to say, none of these images were used for the exhibition. Once he managed to stop laughing, my headteacher simply took a quick snap of me on his phone and commented how the Phonics images had brightened an otherwise ordinary day.

The moral of the story? Teachers really do need eyes in the back of their heads!

Rachael Rivers is the CPD leader for the Learning for Life Partnership in Cheshire East where she has the opportunity to mentor, support and source training for teachers of all ages and levels of experience. Prior to this, she spent over 30 years educating children in different settings, from playgroups to primary schools, high schools to higher education establishments.

Watch Out for the Zipper!

Callum Waters-Court

In 2019, I was teaching an excitable Reception cohort in a two-form entry school; it was my second year of teaching reception and third year of teaching in total.

Picture a sweltering day in the middle of July as we rapidly hurtled towards the end of the year. We had 60 children, between the ages of four and five, crammed into one classroom playing party games; pass the parcel, musical statues and musical chairs—the classics.

Now, I am sure you are beginning to get a picture of what the classroom looked and smelled like! After a rather raucous time, we decided to sit and eat some food. In the middle of eating, one of the boys walked into the classroom from the cloakroom with a face full of terror. I had never seen a face like it before, and I have never seen a face like it since. Tears were streaming down his face and he was sobbing uncontrollably, unable to get a word out. All of the adults turned to look and see what was happening, as is the natural instinct. What we saw was something out of a horror film. A young boy distraught, clearly in agony, with his trousers pulled down to halfway on his thighs and his groin covered in blood.

Everybody froze. What do you do? No one prepares you for this scenario! Had *it* fallen off? Gotten caught in his zipper? No one particularly wanted to get too close to assess the damage!

The teaching assistant closest to him, let's call her Joan, rushed him into the cloakroom to begin dealing with it, followed quickly by another teaching assistant—we'll call her Barbara. From the other side of the room, I tried to keep the children calm and focused on their snacks while I wondered what was going on in the adjoining room. Did we need to call an ambulance? His parents? I could still hear his wailing in my mind and the thoughts of what might be happening were swirling around in my head, leaving me lightheaded. I trained to be a teacher, not an A&E doctor!

The next thing I knew, Joan walks back into the classroom, doubled over holding her stomach, making a wheezing sound. Oh dear. It must be horrific as she looks like she's going to be sick! But wait … is that … laughter? Barbara quickly follows behind, also unable to speak because she was laughing too much. Through their squealing and stumbling for the words before cracking up again I hear, "it … was … fluff from his underwear!"

As it turned out, he had been wearing a brand-new pair of red pants and all of the frivolities had meant his sweat had mixed with the fluff and, from across a classroom, it only looked like blood.

As soon as he realised it was fluff and that he wasn't actually in pain—it was just the sight of the 'blood'—he stopped crying and went back to enjoying the party!

Callum Waters-Court BA QTS studied education at the University of Greenwich before completing a PGCE in Peterborough. He is a primary school teacher with experience across the Years who absolutely loves his job … and all of the wacky things you see and hear in school!

Żart

Pippa McKeown

Picture the scene: it's my second day as a cover supervisor in a tough school in a small Yorkshire town. On my timetable is an English lesson (great—that's my subject) with Year 9. The bell sounds and off I go…

It was a school (since-closed) in difficult circumstances in a town with high unemployment; they faced falling numbers and results, rapid staff changes, and a devastating fire. There was a high proportion of students with SEN (with retrospect, an even higher proportion went undiagnosed) including English as an Additional Language students (EAL); as is so often the case, neither was well-funded. However, the hardships the school had faced gave rise to a strong sense of community, rooted in the identity of their town. I should clarify: I am not from round these parts. Boy, did they know it.

The lesson began with the usual shuffling, lateness and wandering often associated with testing out cover teachers, especially when cover had been inconsistent and impersonal previously. The class was a little suspicious, but not unpleasant. One boy stared blankly as I handed out the work; those sitting near him explained that he was new and didn't speak English, but he did *attempt* to understand the task.

It would be dishonest to say I settled the class: I was inexperienced, nervous and in their territory. But they sat in their seats, they chatted and they did some work. I focused on helping a student with severe dyslexia and the new boy who knew little English. I drew symbols to try to explain the core elements of the task, made a list of key words, used my phone to Google the Polish versions, and even attempted to self-consciously pronounce one or two, which amused him (and the class) a *lot*. And so, as the lesson continued, I focused on these two students and felt I was doing something worthwhile. At least they felt truly supported.

Of course, he wasn't new and he wasn't Polish. He was as Yorkshire as proper tea and as the lesson reached its closing minutes, he could maintain his role no more. He leaned back in his chair, looked to his friends and said, "Mate, how much longer?", before they all burst out laughing. In fairness, although they were laughing at me, they were not particularly unkind: "Miss, your Polish accent needs work" is entirely accurate.

So, what did I learn?

That kids are kids. They will avoid that grammar exercise, the experiment write-up or the next page of the textbook if they possibly can. I was a compliant, respectful student, but, like every other teenager, I relished the times we got a teacher off-topic: "When is your wedding Miss?" "What's your cat called again?" If we had convinced a new teacher to unnecessarily attempt to become bilingual, I would have found it hilarious! The challenge for us as teachers is that they don't (perhaps can't) appreciate the importance of the missed moment until it appears in an exam. It is *our* job to make them learn.

After a year as a cover supervisor, Pippa McKeown MA PGCE qualified as an English teacher and has since spent over a decade in secondary school classrooms. She believes in high standards, support and challenge, and the occasional opportunity for laughter.

Keep Calm and Carry On

Stuart Pryke

Picture the scene. I'm a PGCE trainee on my second placement, standing in front of a class of cheeky Year 7 students who are listening to me wax lyrical about Shakespeare. Some are alert and ready, others bored and thinking about what they've got for tea that evening. Me? I'm in my own little world, talking about the Globe Theatre with such enthusiasm that I'm completely unaware of … well … everything really. I'm near my desk and so convinced my chair is behind me that I go to sit down without looking, still jabbering away about the groundlings and lords and ladies of Shakespeare's London. Imagine, then, my surprise, when instead of sitting down gracefully on my chair, I completely collapse onto the floor; registering perhaps only two seconds before I hit the ground, that there's no chair behind me and this isn't going to end well.

There's a long silence. Too long.

Then, slowly, an eruption of raucous laughter builds until I can't hear myself think. I'm still laying on the floor at this point, a little stunned, my face a bright shade of crimson as I desperately think of some scenario where I emerge out of this relatively unscathed. There's no way out. None at all. I pop my head above the desk and quickly clamber up to greet the uncontrolled hilarity filling the room.

In that moment, a slight spark of anger flickers within me, caused by embarrassment and close to making me shout in an effort to get them all to be quiet. I open my mouth, take a deep breath … and burst out laughing too—that spark extinguishing as quickly as it threatened to ignite. Why? Because it was *funny*. It must have looked completely ridiculous—and at that age, I probably would have done the same. Thankfully, I was asked if I was OK by one particularly shocked student at the front and, after a couple of boys decided they'd like to re-enact the moment (without permission I might add!), I finally managed to regain control.

Why am I telling you this? Because whenever I'm asked for my top tips by those who aspire to join our amazing profession, *"don't take yourself too seriously"* is most certainly up there. There are always going to be times when we have to laugh at ourselves, times when we look like complete fools (either intentionally or not!) and times when we wish there weren't thirty-odd witnesses to see us spectacularly mess up. But we keep calm and carry on! We, as teachers, are human and we should not pretend otherwise. Advice like 'Don't smile before Christmas', in my opinion, is wrong. One can still set consistent, high standards whilst maintaining a sense of humour. Such a mantra is too dismissive of the emotions rampant within our classrooms and stops our students from seeing their teachers as individuals. I'm not saying we should all suddenly become jokers or be unprofessional, but fostering an appreciation for the power of emotion in our classrooms is essential.

Classrooms should be happy, joyful and energetic. They are where our relationships thrive. They are where students thrive.

They are where *we* thrive.

Stuart Pryke is a teacher in charge of teaching and learning at a rural secondary school in Suffolk. He is co-author of 'Ready to Teach: Macbeth' and tweets @SPryke2.

Freeze! Caught Red-Faced

Maisie Tickner

In my first year of teaching, I was given a rather challenging Year 10 maths class. In an effort to engage them with their learning, I decided to start taking them to a computer suite for their Friday lesson every fortnight. During these lessons, the students were able to use interactive maths software that complimented their classroom learning. Every student started each two-week period with three lives. If a student lost all three lives throughout that period, they had to remain in the classroom with the head of department during the lesson in the computer suite.

At the end of the first half term, I was elated that behaviour had significantly improved, along with the relationship between myself and the students. However, several colleagues of mine were regularly reciting stories of awful behaviour from some of the students when in a computer suite during their lessons. Sadly, I was not naïve to the fact that some would likely try to misuse the computers—for example, for online shopping or gaming—when I was not watching. Consequently, I arranged some training with the IT Department to learn how to use the screen monitoring software, which allows teachers to see, freeze and control all the screens around the room on their screen. During lessons, I made sure that the monitoring software was projected onto the whiteboard so students knew I could see their screens from every position in the classroom.

The week we broke up for the Christmas holiday, I had taken the class up to the computer suite. Ten minutes before the end of the lesson I noticed that the screen belonging to a relatively quiet, unassuming male did not look like the others. In my haste at having used the technology to catch a student off task, I double clicked on his screen—which enlarged it on mine! The next thing I remember is an eruption of laughter from around the room...

In what felt like the longest twenty seconds of my life, I realised that I had forgotten to freeze the whiteboard, meaning this particular screen was now projected for the whole class to see. Unfortunately, the unassuming male student had visited a gaming website which caused a pop-up to appear. The pop-up was an advert for a dating website, featuring images of courting couples. The young man, whose screen I had just shown the entire class, went as red as a tomato and—despite my best efforts—I could not get the class to stop laughing. Quite frankly, I have no idea how I managed to not laugh myself.

At the end of the lesson, I apologised profusely to anyone that was offended by the images. Moreover, I proceeded to apologise to the young man once the class had been dismissed. Safe to say, the parent phone call I made at the end of the day was incredibly embarrassing for all.

Moral of the story … always check you have frozen the screen.

Maisie graduated from Sheffield University in 2014 and decided to train as a maths teacher the following year. Qualifying in June 2016, Maisie spent her first three years at one of the largest academies in Essex before getting her first head of department role.

Chapter 7

The Challenging Times

No two days in the world of education are ever the same, which is something we have certainly experienced during the global pandemic. It is so important for teachers to be flexible. We might have planned the most brilliant lesson and have a carefully crafted to-do list for the day ahead, but you can be sure that your microphone won't be working properly during your Zoom call, or your wi-fi is lagging, which interrupts the illustrative video clip you really wanted to show your class. Suddenly, it's the end of the day and you haven't managed half of what you'd planned to do that day. It happens to all of us. If I could go back in time and have a word with my early career teacher self, I'd make sure I realised that, while we are always striving for excellence, sometimes good has to be good enough!

In this chapter, teachers have shared their honest reflections and top tips as they remember times in the classroom where things did not quite go according to plan.

You Can't Pour From an Empty Cup: Prioritise Your Wellbeing

Sarah Mullin

2020 was an exceptionally challenging year in many ways, not least because of the challenges we faced during the global pandemic. 2021 has already presented education professionals with further challenges as we continue to educate the nation's children during these unprecedented times. We know that working in education can be tough, and so it is important that we are proactive about prioritising our wellbeing. The national lockdown in 2020 taught us that self-care is far from selfish; it is essential for us to survive and thrive in the jobs we love to do.

It's ok not to be ok

These really are unprecedented times that we find ourselves living in. The educational landscape is changing rapidly, and it feels as though the guidance is changing on a daily basis. Education professionals are committed to playing their part in the response to Covid-19, but it is only natural that we might feel anxious about our own health, and the health of our vulnerable loved ones. We may all be navigating these challenging times together, but each of us will be responding to the pandemic in different ways. Please know that your feelings are valid. Reach out and speak to someone you trust, and be assured that the Education Support UK helpline is available for free advice and support whenever you need it.

Look for the positives

Whilst every day may not be good, it is important to try and find the good in every single day—even if some days you have to look a little harder than others. Looking for the positive—finding the little things in life to be grateful for—helps us to focus on what's really important in life. It won't always be easy, and it may take some time to train your mind to flip the narrative, but positive thoughts breed positive thoughts.

Know your worth

Always remember your worth. Never judge yourself by someone else's standards and try not to let anyone else bring you down. Surround yourself with positive people who believe in you, support you, and challenge you to be the best version of yourself. Try to be an encourager for others too; the world has enough critics already.

Banish imposter syndrome

Imposter syndrome can strike at any time. It causes us to feel that we are not good enough, that we do not deserve the success we have achieved. Although we often internalise these feelings, it helps to know that many others experience the same emotions. So let's try to banish those bouts of imposter syndrome. You've worked hard to become an education professional, and you have a plethora of certificates, thank you cards, and praise emails to prove it. Please remember that you *are* good enough. If you feel like you're struggling, it really does help to talk to someone you trust for advice and reassurance.

Pursue excellence, not perfection

As education professionals, we often set ourselves impossibly high standards that are incredibly difficult to meet. Aim to work smarter: set yourselves high standards that challenge you, but are realistic and manageable. We do not live in a perfect world, so let us realise that mistakes will happen. We become stronger by working through errors and learning from them. The current health crisis has shown us the importance of being flexible and creative in the ways that we work; it is important for us to appreciate the value of reflecting on our goals and adjusting them for the ever-changing times we are currently in.

2020 was a challenging year for everyone, but we learned that we are far more resilient than we ever realised. Whilst we really do love to teach, we must remember that our health must come first.

Sarah Mullin BA (HONS), PGCE, PGCertED, PGDipED, MA, CTE, FCCT, CMgr FCMI, FInstLM, FRSA is a deputy headteacher and Doctor of Education student. She is the author of the number one best-selling book 'What They Didn't Teach Me on My PGCE' and she is the founder of #EduTeacherTips, the YouTube channel for teachers, by teachers. Sarah is on the board of the secondary education committee at the English Association and she is renowned for supporting Early Career Teachers (ECTs) and aspiring school leaders locally, nationally and internationally. She was recently named a 'Rising Star in Education and Academia' and has previously received the 'Contribution to Education of the Year' award.

Be What You Can't See

Yamina Bibi

Let me begin by telling you that I am a doubter. I doubt myself, my thoughts, my actions, my strengths. My internal voice can be a malicious one—telling me that I am not good enough and never will be. Perhaps it derives from years of allowing a fear of failure to envelop and engulf me; so much so, that I felt I had to aim for perfection just to be seen, heard and acknowledged. Perhaps it derives from the fact that, apart from my sisters, I did not know or see many Muslim women succeeding in wider professional life. I did not think I could succeed as many others did not seem to have either.

Yes, I had brilliant teachers, but I did not have any teachers who looked like me or who I felt understood my cultural or religious background. When I had my scarf pulled off at school or when someone spat on me on the bus home and made racist remarks, there were many witnesses—but no helpers. Therefore, I chose not to tell anyone; how could anyone help anyway? Would they understand? This was post-9/11, on the Isle of Dogs, after all, and I was a hijab-wearing teenager. Instead, I thought if I worked hard and achieved good grades, I could become a teacher and would be left to it.

I was wrong. Despite my qualifications, in my NQT year, I faced racism from students who called me a ninja and from some parents who seemed angry that I was teaching their child. I had students unashamedly tell me that their parents thought all Muslims were terrorists and that they thought Muslim women weren't allowed out of the house (I had to laugh). Despite this, I did not leave at the end of my NQT year. Why? Well, I felt a sense of responsibility to stay and educate those students—but also because I had some students who would speak to me about their own experiences of racism. It was then that it dawned on me that I had become the teacher that I needed as a teenager.

So, I used the texts on the schemes of learning to encourage students to discuss stereotypes and bias, probing them to explore alternative ideas. I also 'killed' them with kindness and tried to be a positive role model in my words and actions. When I eventually left the school, those same students (and some parents) showered me with kind words, cards and gifts.

Let's be honest, though: I did not achieve that overnight and probably would have given up had it not been for my mentor. Though I doubted myself as a new teacher, she never doubted me. She helped me understand my experiences and showed me what I could be. As a new teacher, it is incredibly important to surround yourself with people who challenge you, but also bring out the best in you because they want the best for you—whether that's your mentor, colleague or coach.

So now, as an experienced teacher, when my inner voice starts raging and telling me I am not good enough, I am able to mute that voice; my experiences have shaped me as a teacher and leader. I now tell myself I am gold dust—and that's how you should think of yourself too.

Yamina Bibi is an English teacher and lead practitioner in a school in East London. She is a coach and a network lead for WomenEd London.

Imposter Bear: Finding Your Voice

Cairon Wilkinson

I recently started an education blog. I spent hours creating it, making it have personality and, hopefully, be a relatable and useful place we can all share together. But I can't control how people view it; as soon as I click "PUBLISH", that's it—my baby is out there for the world to see and inevitably criticise.

"Who is this girl? How dare she think she has anything useful to say?"

The instant worry, anxiety and imposter syndrome that consume me makes me not want to click publish at all. I don't think what I have to say is worthwhile, even though I encourage other people to click publish. I've commented on multiple tweets—telling people I'd love to hear what they have to say—so why not me? This feeling is also what makes me not want to participate in discussions or put myself forward for things. It's what prevented me from applying for ITT earlier and it's even what made me hesitate in creating a #EduTwitter profile, which has somehow managed to grow to have a substantial following in just a number of weeks. Yet all I can ask myself is WHY? Why do they want to talk to me? Why would a university accept me into teacher training? Why me, when I'm no good?

Imposter Syndrome is something many people experience, no matter what their profession, gender, race or sexuality; it's basically the belief that our achievements and successes are not warranted. It's the belief that we haven't earned our place or we don't belong somewhere due to lack of experience, knowledge or some other factor. It convinces us that our achievements—whether they're degrees, published books, promotions or some other amazing thing—are still not good enough. That we're not worthy.

I've felt this a lot coming into the teacher world. I don't feel like I'm intelligent enough to be a teacher. I'm terrified to speak to some of the genius teachers I've come across on Twitter or to step into a classroom full of 30 teenagers, all looking at me for answers and being afraid to tell them "I don't know".

But here's the thing; no one has all the answers, and we're all still GOOD ENOUGH.

Whether you've been a teacher for 30 years or have yet to send your application, you are still a human who has lived through a multitude of experiences that are essential to teaching young people and each other about life.

So here I am, putting my thoughts out into the world in a pink format with bear filters and Bitmojis, because that's who I am. I want to be able to bring my personality and experiences with me into my future training and classroom. I realised I have so many valuable things to say and lessons to pass onto students and colleagues that have nothing to do with subject knowledge. And so do you.

Don't listen to that voice in your head; it's only hindering your success and progression. Run proudly towards that opportunity you've been unsure about. You're going to be brilliant.

Cairon Wilkinson is a PGCE student documenting her training journey through her blog "PGCE – Probably Gonna Cry Everyday" and her Twitter @MissTeacherBear26. She is currently training in the North East of England and is passionate about helping students and colleagues find their voice and value in this often-under-appreciated profession.

Never Say Never

Sara Lewis

I was always told that I should be a teacher, but after hearing horror stories of a work-life balance, I thought, "that's not for me". It was only when I ended up covering a teacher on long term sick leave as a Higher Level Teaching Assistant (HLTA) that I realised I actually enjoy being in the front of the classroom. However, the journey would not be easy to teacherhood. There were 3 hurdles in my way:

1. I had to re-study for GCSE Science (third time lucky),
2. I had to pass my maths skills test (maths being my weakest subject), and
3. I had a mortgage to pay, so taking a year out was not an option for me.

However, my teacher friend never gave up on me and kept pushing me. Before I knew it, there I was at the end of my PGCE and now I am at the end of my NQT year. No-one ever said it would be easy. The joke in my family is, "I never make it easy for myself!"

Finding the right school is so important when you're at the start of your teaching journey. It was incredibly important for me to find a school with a community feel and somewhere they truly cared and supported staff's CPD and wellbeing. Luckily, on my third job interview for an NQT job, I found that school.

Take any opportunity to talk to other teachers in the school. Many of them have some great ideas and strategies you can magpie into your classroom, and they are often willing to help in any way they can.

If you have a team of support staff, then count yourself to be incredibly lucky. Throughout my NQT year, I had the most amazing team you could wish for. We had moments where we laughed together and where we cried together. They add incredible value to the pupils we support and help them to succeed.

Never say that you can never be a teacher! Five years ago, that was me! Yet here I am.

Welcome to the best job in the world!

Sara Jayne Lewis, BA (Hons), PGCE, MCCP is an NQT SEND Teacher based in Bristol, UK. Sara is passionate about supporting and teaching SEND pupils. She has worked in SEN schools for 8 years and has extensive experience in supporting SEND pupils, specialising in supporting pupils with Down's syndrome.

Never Submit to Failure

Shamin Akhtar

After graduating from university (over 20 years ago), I went straight into supply teaching. I had no experience of a mentor or any NQT support. I had various schools that I worked in over the course of two years.

I worked in one particular school, which I loved. I got on with the children, staff and parents. I was mainly left on my own, which I liked.

One particular morning, the head and her deputy decided to observe me teach a maths lesson. I taught how I normally would teach. I thought it had gone reasonably well. Children were quieter than normal but responsive.

Lunchtime came and I was called into the office. I knew from the head's face, and her deputy's, that something was not right.

Her words still ring in my ear from time to time. "I'm disappointed in you!" She continued to say, "I thought you were good … better than this".

I felt that my world had collapsed. "What was she saying?" I asked myself. I could not listen anymore, so I ran out of the office and locked myself in the ladies' toilets.

The head came in after me and all I can remember is wailing, "I can't teach … I can't teach".

She eventually coaxed me out and apologised for sounding so harsh. She told me what I had to improve, and I went away to reflect. Now, there are two things I could have done. I could have taken her advice and thought, I disagree and I'm going to carry on, or I could have taken her advice and changed my practice. I did the latter.

With fire in my belly, I went away and planned that lesson again. Right down to each problem, question and response.

I taught it the next day and I had that glow in the pit of my stomach afterwards—the feeling you get when you know you have done something right. I called the head and told her what I had done and the outcomes. She was pleased and told me to continue.

You may be thinking that I was not ever called back: I was, and I continued to teach there until I had a permanent job.

The moral of this story is simply don't ever give up. Perseverance is key.

Connected to that, is a different sort of story. When I was teaching in a nursery, I had a range of parents and children that I came across. I noticed one parent who was well dressed, with perfect hair and makeup, who dropped off her daughter—who was also well dressed with perfect hair, and sometimes perfect nails.

One afternoon I had a small group of children around a table. We were talking about jobs and what parents do. This little girl piped up and said that her mum was a lack dancer. I asked her to explain that and she repeated the same words. She said it was a party that her mum goes to. I eventually realised that she meant that her mum was a lap dancer. (I did refer this to my Designated Safeguarding Lead (DSL).)

After graduating from university with a BEd, I decided to start supply teaching. I thought this would give me more experience with different year groups. I did the usual things; I researched supply agencies and spoke to friends on which was the best supply agency to work for. Then, I set about filling out forms and asking for references.

A few weeks later, I received a letter to say that I was unsuccessful in my application. I was surprised, and a little annoyed, so I rang the supply agency. I asked to speak to the head of the agency. She was a friendly-sounding woman and listened to my 'rant' about why my application had been rejected from the agency.

I explained that I had passed all my teaching practices and I had been a good trainee teacher. After I had finished, she commended me on my resilience and persistence. She said that she would employ me only after observing me teach on my first assignment and if I could provide her with another reference.

I was thrilled. So, you probably know how it ended. I was observed and they liked what they saw. I worked with that agency for two years and it was a steppingstone to a permanent job.

The lesson I learnt from this experience was to be persistent; don't accept a refusal and don't take no for an answer. **Never submit to failure.**

Shamin Akhtar is a Year 3 teacher at Birchfield Primary School.

Help! Being an NQT and the Dreaded Sex-Ed Talk

Jared Cawley

There comes a time, depending on your school, when upper key stage two will have their puberty talk, as part of the sex and relationship education curriculum. I remember back in the 90s when I received this as a Year 6 boy. For days before, excitement, giggles and euphoria spread across the playground. As children, we were erupting into fits of laugher about being able to say the word 'penis' in front of our teacher. When the day arrived, the legendary television was wheeled into the school hall, a very jumpy VHS tape was played, and—excuse the pun—it was a bit of a flop! I am sure the video tape was informative and contained all the relevant details, outlining the processes of physical changes to the body for when a child enters the adolescent stage. But honestly, the only thing I remember is my belly aching from laughing too hard and leaving the school hall more confused than before. As an NQT teacher, I did not want the students in my class to have a similar experience to that of my ten-year-old self.

I have never considered myself a prude, or a person who gets embarrassed when talking about puberty, sex or relationships. I am generally a confident, grown-up adult man who can function well under the professional pressures of being a teacher. Unfortunately, my PGCE did not prepare me for the dreaded sex education talk I was about to give to my Year 5 class of thirty boys. Beforehand, I had prepared well, practised delivering the lesson to a colleague, and had anticipated most of the common questions. I was ready and confident to talk about hair growing in different places and genitals growing larger and wider. Hmm ... maybe I am a prude; my cheeks are getting a little flush and I am feeling a little awkward as I write this.

As I began the lesson, students had the time and space to say all the colloquial names for genitals, share their prior knowledge, and to let out their roars of laughter from being nervous or feelings of embarrassment. When I started going through my slides, while trying not to be too serious, I found myself having an internal battle. I started to crumble. My mouth turned into cotton wool. I could feel particles of sweat forming on my brow, my hands became damp, and the pitch of my voice was pinging from baritone to falsetto. I was just as embarrassed and nervous as the children in my class. I paused, took a breath and composed myself. I remember my NQT mentor's advice of "fake it till you make it". And that is exactly what I did!

Thankfully, I had my colleague in the room for support and made it all the way to end. I had survived. My colleague shared with me that it went well. I was professional, sensitive and had created a comfortable, safe space for my class. What a relief!

Jared Cawley MCCT is a primary school teacher at The British School in The Netherlands. He is passionate about early career development and bridging the gap between research and practice in the classroom. Find him on Twitter @JaredCawley.

"Miss, How Do We Know the Stone Age Is Real?"

Mariya Begum

Haggarty *et al* (2011) states one of the greatest fears of an NQT is not being able to answer questions that children may have. Now, believe me when I say, I was absolutely petrified when this happened to me on my first day of teaching. This is how it went…

Child: "Miss Begum, if the Stone Age is a prehistoric era, how do we know if it is actually real?"

Miss Begum: "Well, it is archaeologists that do research over many years gathering evidence to suggest that there was a period of the Stone Age".

Child: "But Miss Begum, it is not actually confirmed because no one was there to witness it, and there are no papers from that time".

Now, I remember at university, my lecturer said if you cannot answer children's questions, tell them you will come back to them. So, guess what I did…

Miss Begum: "I will come back to that question of yours".

Once I passed that phase of having that fear, I knew I could accomplish anything. One of the greatest lessons you will learn as an NQT is that sometimes you do not have the answers to everything. Remember, you are learning as the children learn, and remember that no classroom is the same, no set of children are the same—everyone is unique, as we are told by the Early Years Statutory Framework. So why forget that?

Another unforgettable memory from my NQT year (I did have many) was the day after teacher training day. The training day was to train all of the staff members to become Level 3 first aiders. The very next day in the classroom, during out literacy lesson in which we were exploring setting descriptions, two children had a little incident; one consisted of a nosebleed and another was vigorously vomiting.

Now, I could handle the situation of a nosebleed and a child vomiting, but can you imagine these two incidents happening at the same time with no other staff member in sight? Everything was going through my mind—including me telling myself, "Mariya, you learnt the techniques and strategies on how to handle these situations just YESTERDAY!" So, once I remembered that, I pulled myself together, asked for some assistance from another staff member and everything turned out fine.

That's the beauty of your NQT year; you will experience things beyond your imagination, but every moment is unbelievable, priceless and special. Take every day as it comes, because not every one of your lessons will go according to plan—and reflect, reflect and reflect! One of my mentors once said that even experienced teachers get things wrong, so as an NQT you are bound to make mistakes—but it is important to always learn from it!

References

Haggarty, L., Postlethwaite, K., Diment, K. and Ellins, J., 2011. Improving the learning of newly qualified teachers in the induction year. *British educational research journal, 37*(6), pp.935-954.

Mariya Begum PGDip, BA Hons is a Newly Qualified Teacher (NQT) at a school in Birmingham. Mariya graduated in 2018 with a first-class bachelor honours degree in childhood studies, then continued her education, graduating with a Postgraduate Diploma in General Primary.

Be More Resilient and Less Self-critical

Samarra Chowdhury

Difficult. Challenging. Wonderful. Three simple adjectives to describe my second PGCE placement. There's a memory that has been etched in my mind; one that has taught me to be more resilient and less self-critical.

I popped out of my classroom to have a catch-up with my colleagues. I had forgotten to lock the door. When I returned, I didn't notice anything different or out of place. My Year 8s walked in and settled. As I took the register, I noticed a student missing. I asked the class if they had seen Student X but no one had. I marked them absent and informed the Year team of this.

Forty minutes into the lesson, I heard a sudden squeaking sound emanating from the back of the room, where a large, dilapidated cupboard stood. At this point, a few students shrieked aloud and some had stood up from their chairs. By now, a quiet panic had settled in and I was thinking the worst. Was it a big rat? Was it an intruder that had broken into the school? Whatever it was, I had to approach the cupboard and open it.

At this point, the teacher to whom the class belonged intervened. I could tell she sensed the fear on my face and had taken pity on me. As the teacher approached the cupboard, out jumped a student, screaming at the top of their lungs, "Ha-ha, I've been hiding in here since lunchtime!" It was, of course, Student X. By now, the class students were all very excitable and I needed to seize control. Luckily, I managed to do that with a little bit of silent reading.

I turned my attention back to Student X and then had a sudden realisation that, having left the classroom unlocked, I was responsible for this child locking themselves in the cupboard. I fought back tears as my confidence drained from me. I asked Student X to step out of the room. The lesson was coming to an end so I asked the class to pack up. I was still fighting back the tears, wondering how I let all this happen.

The class teacher, my mentor, and I sat with Student X. I personally dealt with the student, asking them why they had done such an act. I gave them a suitable sanction and dismissed them.

However, I was not so sorted. I felt awful. I felt like a failure. My mentor asked me if I had psychic powers, to which I replied no.

He said to me, "Well then, how were you supposed to know? You did all the right things. You flagged up on the register of his absence. You informed the Year team and asked your class if anyone had seen him. You dealt with him correctly. You kept the class calm and you were in total control the whole time".

Bizarrely enough, Student X had completed their class work whilst hiding in the cupboard, peeping through the keyhole!

The way I had dealt with that situation made me a better teacher. From every situation, you learn something new. It's important to reflect in order to improve but recognising when you do the right things is equally vital.

Samarra Chowdhury has been a secondary English teacher for 14 years. She is an examiner and is a mum of three girls, living in South London.

Chapter 8

Things Can Only Get Better

Whilst we strive to do the best we can, sometimes we make mistakes. Each and every one of us can recall an incident that has taken place at school that we never want to experience again! However, making mistakes is inevitable; we are human after all. It is how we grow, develop and learn from our mistakes that truly matters. It is on those days where we may feel a little deflated that we realise that we really are in the right job, because it is then that we know how much we care about our children and young people.

As teachers we give so much of ourselves to our children and our schools and so it is important for us to invest in our own learning. In this chapter, authors share their experiences in the classroom, explaining how they have grown personally and professionally during the challenging times they have encountered.

Finding Hope in the Helplessness of a National Lockdown

Sarah Mullin

During the national lockdown, we had the opportunity to experience a new way of life as we adapted to a whole new normal.As we navigated these uncertain times, we sought light in the darkness, clarity in the confusion, and hope in the helplessness.

Self-isolation and social distancing provided us with the time and space we needed to reflect on what is important in life, to appreciate what matters most and to look forward to new beginnings.

During the times of partial school closures, teachers set work for pupils to complete at home; this was important, of course, yet this unique period also provided the opportunity for children and young people to learn some valuable life lessons. Here are the things I hoped we might learn as we stayed safe at home during the national lockdown of 2020.

1. The importance of empathy

Our social media timelines are filled with the heartfelt memorials of loved ones who have lost their lives too soon. Friends and family members are pleading for prayers for our nearest and dearest. National Health Servicę (NHS) frontline workers are urging us to stay home and save lives. This time provides an opportunity for children to appreciate and understand the importance of empathy. As we paint rainbows of hope, donate parcels to our local food banks and clap for carers, we are recognising that our actions and behaviours have a life-changing impact on others.

2. The value of relationships

Whether we are baking together, playing family board games or helping one another with chores around the house, we are realising that there is nothing more important in life than family, friends and love. Unfortunately, we never truly appreciate the value of a moment until it becomes a distant memory. Thanks to technology, we can reach out and keep in touch with one another, but never again will we take for granted a sincere smile or a warm embrace; we will forever live in the moments where we are surrounded by our nearest and dearest.

3. To slow down and enjoy life

We are no longer dashing between dance classes, football matches and birthday parties; we are embracing a more relaxed pace of life. It is a time to focus on our blessings as we evaluate what truly makes us happy. We are taking pleasure in life's little joys: immersing ourselves in the beauty of a book and watching the clouds gently floating across the sky. Children are learning to be resilient and resourceful as they use their imagination to be creative in their surroundings, opening the door to new possibilities and opportunities.

4. The beauty of nature

Soft play centres, trampoline parks and video game arcades are closed. The little pleasures in life include a jog in the park and a walk down the street. The din of beeping horns no longer drowns out the sweet hum of tweeting birds and we are taking pleasure in noticing previously bare branches now blooming with cherry blossoms. Maybe this period will allow our children to realise that we are mere guests here on Mother Earth and we must do all we can to be responsible, respectful and courteous visitors. As we appreciate the awe and wonder of the beginning of spring, let us learn the importance of doing our part to be kind to nature.

5. To be kinder to ourselves

Life is precious, and during these unprecedented times children have the opportunity to reflect on the fragility of life. We are reminded that time waits for no one; we should do everything we can to live a joyful life devoid of sadness, negativity and regret. It is a time to seize new opportunities, pursue our dreams, let bygones be bygones and to be kinder to ourselves. We are learning to prioritise our health and wellbeing, investing in our personal growth and development.

Life is a continuous learning experience. As we stay safe at home during lockdown, let us hope that our children and young people learn to make every moment count. Let them appreciate the importance of living a life filled with love and experiences, and not material items. Let them learn the value of memories and not just the price of things.

Of all the things we can teach our children, we must teach them to be kind, thoughtful and compassionate people who will go into the world as confident, articulate and well-rounded adults. After all, some of the most important life lessons cannot be taught in the classroom.

Sarah Mullin BA (HONS), PGCE, PGCertED, PGDipED, MA, CTE, FCCT, CMgr FCMI, FInstLM, FRSA is a deputy headteacher and Doctor of Education student. She is the author of the number one best-selling book 'What They Didn't Teach Me on My PGCE' and she is the founder of #EduTeacherTips, the YouTube channel for teachers, by teachers. Sarah is on the board of the secondary education committee at the English Association and she is renowned for supporting Early Career Teachers (ECTs) and aspiring school leaders locally, nationally and internationally. She was recently named a 'Rising Star in Education and Academia' and has previously received the 'Contribution to Education of the Year' award.

It's Just a Work in Progress: Thoughts From an RQT

Emma Thorogood

As a geography teacher, you not only teach a subject but also "truly teach a person" (Chew-Hung Chang, 2015). I found this quote when I scrolled back through my Twitter page and I feel it encapsulates why I wanted to become a secondary school teacher. You can inspire students to have the same love for a subject, but teachers are also important in helping to shape students' teen years and mould their character to be the best version of themselves. Therefore, I find the phrase 'those who can't do, teach' inaccurate. Teachers *can* do—it's just a work in progress. No one can be expected to be perfect straight after teacher training. We are always learning as much as our students. Here are five key things that I've learnt since completing my PGCE two years ago:

Revisiting knowledge is crucial: Assessment *for* learning and assessment *of* learning were familiar concepts during my PGCE, but I now realise their importance more than ever. I embed recall/revision activities into every lesson.

Questioning is key: Seen as a 'fad' in the past, I use lollipop sticks with my GCSE classes. Colour coded by ability (the students don't know this!) to enable all to think, I ask the question before choosing an appropriate colour stick—remembering to bounce the question around the room afterwards to check understanding. This is also a useful form of differentiation.

There is no such thing as too much modelling: Ask your department to buy a visualiser for your classroom. It helps with pace in mixed-ability classes and will prevent you from going crazy when you realise no one knows how to draw a climate graph—not to mention the number of requests you will have to show students' work, which is excellent for praise and motivation. The latter especially for the quieter students who do not want to share their work aloud.

Differentiation doesn't have to be difficult: Students do not like to be seen as the odd one out. Save yourself from producing a rainforest-worth of worksheets and differentiate through the seating plan, modelling and questioning instead.

Make the outcome of your instructions clear: During my NQT year I told a student they needed to stay in their seat—they proceeded to stay glued to their chair and dragged themselves across the classroom. I was not expecting my directions to be taken that literally!

If you happen to be reading this as a teacher at the early stages of your career, like myself, remember that we play an incredibly important part in students' lives and although we may not always realise how much our students appreciate us, it is a given that they do.

So, keep working hard, and as Stephen Hawking once said, "Remember to look up at the stars and not down at your feet" (Hawking, 2010). One day you'll be able to look back and see just how far you've developed as a teacher and the positive impact you've had on future generations.

References

Chang, C.-H., 2015. Teaching climate change - a fad or a necessity? *International Research in Geographical and Environmental Education,* 24(3), pp. 181-183.

Hawking, S., 2010. *The Conversation: Stephen and Lucy Hawking (World News Tonight)* [Interview] (8 June 2010).

Emma Thorogood BSc (Hons), PGCE completed her PGCE at the University of Cambridge in 2018. She works as a geography teacher with responsibility for KS4 at a secondary school in outer London and marks for a major exam board during the summer. She tweets @lovetogeog

Teachers Teach, but They Never Stop Learning

Maha Mohsin

Your goal as you teach your students is that they are learning, but never forget that you are still learning yourself. Someone once told me that it takes five years to become a good teacher. Eleven years later I still remember that—it was, and still is, true. You need this time to develop your craft, to teach the whole spectrum of your subject to students of all ages and abilities. There will be times where you are overjoyed with the success (light bulb moments) and there will be lessons where you think "I've taught them nothing". My advice to you is simply to be patient. Navigate your journey with humility; acknowledge and be proud of your successes whilst being reflective and gentle on yourself.

Lesson #1: Always practice your practicals!

I learnt this early on in my teaching via my mentor who let me "fail" in my first lesson. I didn't check the gas tap; the practical didn't work, and the students became unruly (you can imagine the rest!). It was a hard pill to swallow, but it taught me the importance of being organised. I still discuss my practical methods now with my technician, especially if I have not done them for a while. Reading about Paterson's (2019) use of integrated instructions helped me to improve students' focus and understanding by reducing cognitive load.

Lesson #2: Choose your circle wisely

Those that you surround yourself with can affect you—I learnt that at my second school. I do not regret working there, but after having my own short breakdown it made me realise the importance of the company you keep. Look to connect with like-minded people that will support you; those that you can engage in professional conversation and feel inspired by. Moaning can be therapeutic, and everyone does it, but recognise if it becomes a regular occurrence and change something.

Lesson #3: Smash the ceilings

We are taught not to put ceilings on the potential of our students. This is also true for our own progression. As well as *supporting* NQTs, I *learnt* from them. I took on additional roles of responsibility within my own department, but I never felt that I was good enough to go further and lead my own team. It took a conversation with a close friend to shift my thinking. He gave me the encouragement I needed to believe that I had the potential to successfully lead and inspire others. Since completing my National Professional Qualification in Middle Leadership (NPQML) my own ceiling has been well and truly smashed and I have set my goals high. Taking the opportunities that challenge you can be highly rewarding but knowing when to ask for support is also important. It is not a weakness but a strength – to know your own personal limitations and find means to overcome them.

So, on your teaching journey, aim high; surround yourself with like-minded people and build your network. But never forgot the basics in your classroom. It almost cost me my eyebrows!

References

Paterson D.J (2019) 'Design and Evaluation of Integrated Instructions in Secondary-Level Chemistry Practical Work' *Journal of Chemical Education* 2019 *96* (11), 2510-2517

Maha Mohsin BSc. PGCE. NPQML has been teaching chemistry for over 11 years, across three different schools in the north of England. She is passionate about teaching and learning, an advocate of staff wellbeing, and seeks to support others in their own professional development while challenging her educational philosophy. She is an avid baker and has a love/hate relationship with running. She is currently head of science at Manor Croft Academy in Dewsbury, Yorkshire.

Never Ending Circles

Lorna Baldry

Circles are an ancient and effective method of communicating in communities. They have great application to any group of people coming together to communicate.

Sitting in a circle removes barriers—literally and figuratively. With no desks, laptops or other obstructions in front of us, we can really focus and engage in the conversation. Any power structure is flattened, particularly in a circle that uses a talking piece. The talking piece can be anything, but it's much better if it's interesting in texture and colour to engage and stimulate the senses. If you're holding the talking piece you can talk, and if you're not you should listen.

Of course, there is a lot more to it than this—and I really do recommend learning more as this communication technique can revolutionise engagement and learning. Anyone can hold a circle, and in community learning this was key to supporting learners.

My invitation to my teaching and support team was to begin and end each session in circle—as a minimum. The circle at the beginning helped to check in with everyone, share what they were bringing to the session in terms of thoughts and feelings and ensure there was clarity of activity and expectation. The one at the end was an opportunity to review learning and check understanding.

In some classes and outreach provisions, though, where there were younger learners in particular, some with emotional or behavioural difficulties or neurological differences, all parts of all sessions would be based in circle.

In a circle, everyone has a voice, everyone can see everyone else, we are all speaking to each other as equals and we're not psychologically or physically static.

There are many kinds of circles: for teaching and learning, for attendance, for check-in and check-out, for problem solving and for listening—among many other things.

Try using circles in your learning activities. Begin with something simple like a check-in circle. At the beginning of a week or a class, sit in a circle, introduce your learners to the circle talking-piece and what it means. If they already know each other, ask them how they are doing and if there is something they'd like to share with the group from their weekend. If they don't know each other, begin by asking them to introduce themselves and tell everyone who they are—then ask the other two questions. A check-in circle is about finding out more about each other and how we are, about acknowledging that what happens to us and what we think about it, affects how we feel, and that can affect our behaviours.

As a team, by which I mean learners/students/pupils, parents and staff working together, circles carried us through fun times, sad times and all sorts of difficult times. I wish I'd known about them when I began.

Lorna has 20 years' experience in education, beginning as a law teacher in further education (FE) in 1999. Initially managing law provision at an inner-city college, Lorna then progressed to managing all professional courses and became social engagement and community collaboration manager for the college and its community. Lorna worked across curriculum areas and levels of learning, with people aged 5 to 85. Lorna now runs Brightlink Learning.

Turning it Around

James Roden

For as long as I can remember, teachers in my life (and particularly those who made an impact on my life and my studies) tried to encourage me to go into teaching. I'm paraphrasing, but "you underestimate just how much your caring and supportive nature will see you right in a teaching career" is one of the comments made that stuck with me, and it was especially gratifying because it was said to me by probably the best teacher I still, to this date, have had the pleasure of working alongside. So, after many years of ignoring all the suggestions, I took the plunge and completed my PGCE in 2018.

Now, anybody who knows me well enough will know that my PGCE experience was not a positive one. In fact, it got to the point where I made an agreement with myself that if the first term of my NQT year was anything like my PGCE, I would leave the profession, becoming another one of those increasing numbers leaving the profession within the first few years. I did not want that for myself.

Thankfully, my NQT year was nothing like what I had experienced previously, and this is why my submission is called "Turning it Around." I went from scraping a pass to achieving "Good" and "Outstanding" lesson observations almost immediately. My pedagogy hadn't changed, so what was so different about the new environment that meant I was able to turn it around? Was it a supportive department? Was it a supportive whole school environment? Was it the students? Was it my determination to prove that I was a good or outstanding teacher? Arguably, the answer encompasses all those suggestions and probably even more.

This narrative highlights all the positive aspects of my NQT year, not just for you as a reader, but for me too. This allowed me to focus on the numerous positives that there are in the teaching profession—positives that can easily be lost when trying to escape a frightful prior experience or when you are so bogged down with data and marking that you can forget why you went into the profession in the first place.

If this narrative shows that there can be light at the end of the PGCE tunnel for one person, and that person sticks with the profession, it will be a job well done.

James Roden is a Secondary English Teacher.

From Single Islands to a Community

Nicola Mansfield Niemi

I was called to a behaviour incident one June where staff were unable to safely calm a very distressed child in the classroom. I knew as soon as the behaviour call came in who it would be—and there were well established routines in place for this child. I went running along with my head to the area and on the way said, "I've got this class next year, haven't I?" His response confirmed it.

I inherited this little boy, along with the rest of that class where he was not the only challenging individual; however, he was certainly the most volatile, and I have honestly never spent time in a class like it. They were 30 little satellites that rotated around each other, their interactions as a whole class were minimal and there was a lack of any cohesion between them. Behaviour expectations and rules were consistently adhered to and it was eventually accepted that my views on behaviour were not going to change. Everyone still just seemed a little sad, and as a teacher, parent and human this just broke my heart.

I chose very early on to let the children know me personally; I opened up to them and let them see me as a human and not just someone who was always on standby for the next incident. I shared stories of my life with them and let them into my thoughts and opinions. I used books and stories that I loved to create shared experiences in the class; admittedly, it took a long time before they responded in kind. Gradually, behaviour settled. I believe this to be primarily as a result of consistency and expectation—but also relationships. We knew they could do better; we knew they were capable of amazing things—and we made sure to tell them at every opportunity. Every adult who came into contact with this class did this; we raised the expectation on 'that' class, and they raised their own.

They slowly began to support each other outside of their friendship groups when answering questions and were proud of each other when things went right. We made our classroom be their space, a sanctuary, in school.

My proudest moment came when another member of staff came in to speak to me during a lesson—a noisy lesson filled with group work and discussion—and they commented just how different it was without a particular child there, the child with volatile behaviour. Of course, he was right in the middle of the melee, being challenged by a member of his group about his answers, responding reasonably and respectfully; he'd just found his place.

Nicola is an assistant headteacher in a two-form entry school in Milton Keynes. She is a passionate advocate of reading for pleasure and believes reading to be at the heart of drawing people together in shared experiences.

Chocolate: An Essential Tool in Teaching

Natalie Sinclair

I sometimes think cocoa runs in my veins: I have a notoriously sweet tooth and, being a Birmingham girl, Cadbury World was a semi-permanent fixture growing up. However, it wasn't until I began teaching that I realised just how powerful those little pieces of sugary goodness could be. Please find an essential, but not exhaustive list of chocolate's uses within the secondary education sector.

Ultimate Reward: Never underestimate the power chocolate can have on pupil engagement. Mention the prize is chocolate and the stakes are upped. Do not, however, ever promise chocolate and fail to deliver. A barrage of disdainful looks will follow; a sugar-hungry teen takes time to get over that kind of betrayal.

Apology Symbol: We all have bad days. They're normal. They happen. There are days when our colleagues have to put up with a lot from us, when we've perhaps been a little short, a little scatterbrained or seriously lacking in energy. Nothing quite says "I'm sorry" like chocolate.

Drama Fixer: My form are well aware that there is an emergency stash of chocolate under my desk. One morning, one of my form pupils asked if she could have two of the smaller chocolates. When I asked why, she said she needed to stick them to the front of an apology card she'd made for a friend after a silly fallout. When I saw them later on in the day, both girls were beaming! Problem solved.

Distraction Tool: Need to distract staff from the realisation that it's twilight and they're here for another two hours? Chocolate. Need to encourage them to buy into a new strategy? Chocolate! Sugar sweetens any bitter pill.

Pain Fixer: The magic paper towel whimpers in significance by the time high school rolls around! I once had a Year 10 boy come to me after being head-butted in PE. Despite checking him over and giving him the all clear, he still looked dejected. I offered him some chocolate. Suddenly there was a glowing grin. I'm adamant it should be part of the First Aid Kit.

Bad Days: I made a reference to this earlier but bad days are normal. They're normal for us as adults and they're normal for our pupils. When our pupils are sad, they need a pick me up just as much as we do. Chocolate can be an effective distraction from the trials and tribulations of teen life.

Chocolate will not solve every single problem you face as a teacher—but it will definitely help to offer a sweetener to life in education.

Natalie Sinclair is a lead practitioner of English and a hands-on mentor to trainee teachers in Sandwell. Natalie places huge value on the importance of establishing and fostering good relationships with staff and students alike.

Four-Letter Words

Jon Zeb

After two decades in education, seventeen of those years in pastoral management and senior leadership, I have seen a number of educational 'fads' hailed as key to 'transforming education'. Does anyone else remember being told to do star-jumps with the students as part of every starter and plenary to get their brains working before sitting down to study the Tudors? This decree was soon shelved. My NQT mentor, a retiring head of year, shared the pearl of wisdom that "educational strategies are like buses, another will be along in a bit".

My pastoral approach until this point was based upon other 'pearls' he shared, including the famous "don't smile until Christmas" and "when you shout in the face of the student, make sure you have coffee breath as it makes it more uncomfortable for them". I am ashamed to say I followed his advice in the early stages of my tenure as a pastoral leader. Fortunately, I soon found an approach considerably more effective than 'coffee breath screaming'. It involves 'four-letter words' … no, not those ones … although, as a pastoral leader, I have had many used towards me by students, parents and, as SLT, sometimes staff!

I believe our classroom interactions with those we serve should be driven by a series of 'four-letter words'. Be a ***font*** of enthusiasm for your subject and role, showing the students you are excited to be sharing your knowledge and experience with them. ***Hear*** them; listen to what they have to say and find out what motivates them. Be ***fair*** in your interactions and attention, ensuring students are afforded the chance to make the right choice. Every lesson is a new opportunity for them and us. Be ***kind*** and generous in spirit, welcoming them to your classroom and sharing what inspires you. Show ***care*** and ***love*** for your subject and the privilege of working with your young people but, more importantly, towards them. Unfortunately, some of the young people you serve may not receive this from their homes. You saying "Good Morning Imogen and Ava" may be the first time that they have heard their name said positively since walking out of the school gates yesterday afternoon. Our approach to the students should be the same as what we expect from our leaders: to be known, valued and supported.

The final four-letter word is ***hero***. My *hero* role-model is my mum, Irene, who attended school in Sheffield during World War 2, dodging bombs and leaving with no qualifications. As a single parent, she worked hard all her life for my two brothers, sister and me, always putting us first. She instilled the value of education in us and finally, in her 50s, got the opportunity to become a 'mature student', receiving her BA (Hons) on her 60th birthday. Attending her graduation as a teenager filled me with such pride after seeing her juggle two jobs, kids and home study. I was so lucky to have such a *hero* at home. But many of those sat before us in the classroom don't have this luxury.

So, I ask you, how will you be the *hero* they need?

Jon Zeb (PGCE, PGCert, NPQH, FCCT, CMgr FCMI, FInstLM, CT(Hist)), is father to Imogen-Poppy (4), Ava-Rose (2), husband to Claire, teacher of business studies at NEW College Pontefract, and currently studying towards his MBA and MA (Open). Inspired by the curator of this book, he hopes to progress to studying towards an Ed.D next year.

A Realistic Recipe for Teaching

Azadi Mir

Colourful stationery symmetrically aligned upon a bright-pink table, positioned closely to a pretend mug of coffee (usually some cola), the seven-year-old me was ready to take on the world as a teacher...

This was always my dream, and soon it became the norm for me to re-enact scenarios and behaviours I observed at school from my former teachers. I was a shy pupil at school, but even so, I was determined to create this reality. I was ecstatic to secure a job during my final placement, a perfect opportunity to learn from experienced individuals! It wasn't long before I began to picture my own classroom, bright colours, organised trays and beautiful resources set to inspire the imaginations of the children I taught. My summer holidays were spent learning how to use a laminator (surely teacher training needs a module purely dedicated to this?). I lost count of the endless amounts of times the photocopier refused to enlarge my resources, and how many times I wondered how on earth—being as short as I was—would I reach the high walls without breaking a limb? No amount of teacher training prepares you for this!

September 2016, my first day as an NQT, I was bursting with excitement. Feeling absolutely humbled to work around such caring colleagues, the well-wishes flooded in for my first day. On a side note, the cute travel mug gifted from my partner teacher ensured I had enough caffeine in me to get through the day! It takes a moment or two and then it hits you—for me this was whilst I was on break-time duty. My own class ... 30 little humans in my care, looking up to me to learn the ways of the world. Their future was in my hands and I was motivated to work really hard for them.

I learnt very early on in my teaching career that communication was key … talk, talk and TALK! Considering how much time you spend at school, the job becomes an integral aspect of your life. There are so many wonderful colleagues and parents; all happy to support and help. I found, as an NQT, I took risks in my lesson observations; I always felt I was the one individual who loved to think outside the box.

Those risks and focus on communication paid off for me. Post-NQT, I volunteered to take on a Teaching and Leadership Responsibility (TLR) for Religious Education (RE) across three school sites. This made me want to work even harder and, in my third year of teaching, I was promoted to phase leader, which is the post I currently hold. I am so grateful that the shy and timid pupil I once was is now a confident teacher who is sharing her resources, advice and tips with others.

Regardless of the laminating or photocopying fiascos, I urge you to believe in yourself. With the right concoction of care, a whimsical whisk of determination, a sprinkle of love and a dusting of enthusiasm … YOU CAN DO IT!

Azadi Mir is a teacher with 5 years experience in teaching across Key Stages 1 and 2. She has been a Phase Leader for 3 of these years and hopes that you, too, can perfect your recipe for teaching during your everyday practice!

The Art of Developing Your Teacher Persona

Mia Bano

The thrilling moment of stepping into my classroom for the very first time is a memory imprinted upon my mind. I can say with certainty that I'll never forget being taken aback by how effortlessly that moment evoked a number of emotions within me. I felt honoured that I'd now be contributing to a profession which endeavored to keep the passion for learning burning brightly in the hearts of our future generations. But more so, it was the prospect of transforming lives that captivated me the most. You see, coming from an area of high deprivation, I knew that the children in my community would not have shared similar life experiences to those residing in more privileged areas. I understood that this role that I was serving would be one that transcended beyond these colourful surroundings.

Whilst voyaging through my journey as a teacher, I naturally encountered waves of individuals who offered well-meaning words of advice in relation to my teacher persona. *Don't be too kind or smile at your kids because they'll walk all over you. Watch out for the one with a reputation.* It all sounds familiar, doesn't it? There is a possibility that this was something you may have been recommended too. It didn't take long for me to soon learn that, had I accepted that guidance and refused to be driven by my own moral compass, I would have potentially been deprived of all those beautiful moments that defined me as the teacher I am today. Had I refused to smile, I may have missed that precious moment where one of my children, who had been seeking refuge, felt welcomed.

We didn't share the same language, but that reassuring smile developed trust and was enough for him to know that he was going to be okay—he was safe. It was enthralling watching this shy, timid child blossom into a cheery, confident individual who brightened up the classroom with his intellectual curiosity. Had I already formed a preconceived opinion of that child with a 'reputation' prior to meeting her, I know that I'd have done her a great disservice. Like the other children entrusted within my care, she was highly perceptive and reflected the climate I created, and she simply needed to understand that I'm human too. Through sharing my experiences, my expectations and just how much I believed in her, she was thriving. One can simply not underestimate the power showing kindness holds.

The art of developing your teacher persona is a craft in itself. It will take time to master and refine. You all have something unique to offer your children, so don't be afraid to inspire them.

Mia Bano, a class teacher, has taken the role of arts lead at Arden Primary School, Birmingham. She shares an absolute love for the creative arts and has promoted the subject through the delivering of the Arts Award programme.

Spinning Plates

Andy Lewis

Teaching is brilliantly chaotic. You expect the unexpected, and it will often be joyous and hilarious on reflection, but stressful and difficult at the time. This doesn't change. It happened to me from day one, when I realised that seagulls would peck at the skylight above my desk in my newly adopted classroom, and it certainly happens now despite many more years in the classroom.

In 2015, I attended a conference called Northern Rocks and went to a session by David Cameron. I have no recollection of what the session was about, but something asked stayed with me—despite being 10 years into being a teacher—which I wish someone had asked me a lot earlier.

"How do we sort our IKEA from our Wedgewood?"

Working in schools is all about plate spinning. We run up and down; we spin that one, readjust another, and catch yet another just before it falls. Spend some time on YouTube watching plate spinners and, however good they are, there is an element of random chaos.

The difficulty as teachers is that we are not just plate spinners in school; we have to keep it up out of school too. I have to balance being a husband, a dad, a son, a brother, a friend … we don't finish the day at 3.30pm very often (although we should try to when we can), and our weekends are not always a time to kickback and forget our work. We also take on other responsibilities: I'm an author and a school governor. I love playing hockey and running keeps me sane and happy.

I'm no different to anyone else; I furiously move from one plate to another, trying to keep them all spinning—just like we all do.

But then one drops.

Did I see that coming? Was it an accident? Or the one I know I should drop?

We do so much in schools—so much more than simply deliver lessons. Every teacher takes on more and more.

I've come to realise that we need to create the time to stop and ask what is the most effective? What has the biggest impact on the students? As important as it is to ask "What more do we need to do?", we need to ask, "What do we need to stop doing?" After all, schools can be notorious for being places where we do things simply because we always have.

The world record for plate spinning is 108 plates. Most teachers have 108 things in and out of their day by break time, at the latest. The longest plate spin is 2 hours and 14 mins. Every plate falls at some point.

If I am honest, I see other teachers—particularly on social media—who produce better lesson resources than me, read more educational books than me, and attend more CPD than me. Especially on a weekend.

I've made my peace with that. We all have different plates to spin.

At every stage of your career, and possibly your life, you need to consider which ones can, and perhaps should, drop. Make sure they are the right ones. You want to be dropping the IKEA, not the Wedgewood. Thank you David.

Andy Lewis is a deputy headteacher at a Catholic comprehensive school in East London. He is an author, blogger and tweets regularly at @ andylewis_re.

All Work and No Play

James Birchenough

For much of my first two years as a Year 3 teacher, I experienced what many teachers face daily: feeling overwhelmed and exhausted from too much work to fit into reasonable working hours! I would wake up at 6am, scramble to get the early bus to get into school when it opened at 7, and then leave at 5.30pm when the cleaner kicked us out, carrying a huge gym-bag full of books to mark and my laptop too. When I got home to my one-room bedsit, I'd get my marking out, put a ready meal in the microwave, and keep working until around 9pm—at which point I'd be too exhausted to do anything fun!

And most days this cycle continued; I became increasingly isolated from my friends and increasingly worn out. There were some fantastic memories from working at this school—I'm so grateful I was given the opportunity to begin my teaching career there—but the workload was unsustainable. After those 2 years, I changed jobs and was fortunate enough to become headteacher at a secondary alternative provision.

If your current situation is like mine was, I want you to know that it can change! You'll build habits, find shortcuts, and get things done quicker. I picked up a lot of tips and tricks which helped me back then—which have also helped me in my current role—and, for the last couple of years, I've been leaving work at 4pm and taking nothing home during evenings and weekends. Some of that is down to the culture of the organisation our school is part of, called Transforming Lives for Good (TLG), and some is down to the habits I have cultivated myself. I was no longer willing to compromise my wellbeing or my family's wellbeing, so I became more assertive in limit-setting, which has enabled me to still be there now and to be thriving in my role.

I also want you to know that, in the meantime, there are so many others in your position—you're not alone in this! Keep going, take it one step at a time, and one day you might find a better balance. If you don't, you can always change jobs. But if you do find a balance, and you can continue in teaching, you might even end up becoming a school leader who places staff wellbeing right at the heart of their school's culture—thus making a massive impact on the wellbeing of lots of teachers *and* the young people they serve.

James has been a headteacher at TLG since 2016. In April 2020, he founded Wellbeing for Educators and Leaders in Learning (WELL), which helps individual teachers improve their work/life balance and helps senior leaders create a school culture conducive to staff wellbeing. He has also written "Leaving Work at Work".

Teaching Makes You Braver

Natalie Sinclair

We're all very lucky to do the job that we do. We influence the lives of young people in both significant and minute ways—influences that last a lifetime—but I am often struck by just how powerful the influence of our pupils is on us.

In the academic year of 2017/18, I'd found my teaching groove and knew my teaching style. I had connected to the amazing Twitter education community (#EduTwitter) and, motivated by the amazing resources shared online, had begun actively trying these out in my own classroom, mainly with my Year 11s. They were that rare class that feels like a complete family; we'd started in the same year and I had taught most of them in some capacity since those first tentative days. They were always open and honest—sometimes brutally so—and I felt able to trial and test new ideas with them, safe in the knowledge that they'd be forthcoming with their feedback.

Both that year 11 class and I had found the love for whole-class feedback (WCF). They openly commented on how they felt that they got a lot from it, knew where they stood and, crucially, knew clearly how to improve. One of my more aloof boys interrupted in the middle of one of these feedback sessions to say "Miss, can you please tell other teachers to do this? This is actually useful—more than loads of dead red pen". I laughed it off and attempted to wrangle the class back but he'd opened a can of worms. Many others began to chime in with their views on marking and feedback.

It's important to say at this point that I'd been asked numerous times by our teaching and learning (T&L) lead to share my practice in our weekly T&L briefings. But as a natural introvert and a teacher who had only completed 5 years in teaching, one unqualified and one as a Schools Direct (SD) trainee, I felt like a fraud. How could I tell people who'd been teaching for years longer than I had how to give feedback?

The pupils continued to reiterate their views every time we completed WCF until I was eventually worn down. I decided I'd agree to share my experience of WCF.

Despite frequently standing in front of pupils for five hours a day, a room of 200 colleagues is a different matter. Amidst my racing heart and churning stomach, I somehow managed to explain the process to my colleagues with positive and enthusiastic reactions.

I can safely say I never would have done that without the encouragement of my pupils, some of whom had wished me luck beforehand.

Two academic years later, I am thankful for their encouragement; it definitely made me feel braver. That inspired me to complete my lead practitioner qualification and become an avid sharer, if still a reluctant speaker.

Aside: there's also nothing like a classroom of kids to make your anxiety about a raging wasp at the height of summer disappear! A quick way of becoming braver.

Natalie is a lead practitioner of English and a hands-on mentor to trainee teachers in Sandwell. Natalie places huge value on the importance of establishing and fostering good relationships with staff and students alike.

Chapter 9

Being Employed as a Teacher

Working in education means working towards goals such as statutory examinations and end-of-unit assessments. Sometimes we are so focussed on those end results that we forget to celebrate the little wins that happen every single day in our schools. It is important that we enjoy the careers we have worked so hard to achieve. We must enjoy the now! Yes, it is a job. Yes, it is challenging. But there's always a reason to celebrate—so we need to try and find the positive every single day!

In this chapter, authors share their stories about the highs and lows of working in education. From the joys of making memories on a field trip, to embarrassing tales when supervising children in boarding school accommodation, you will hear about the weird and wonderful events that happen outside of the classroom. Contributors also share their advice about dealing with anxiety, the importance of self-care, applying for jobs, attending interviews and making difficult decisions when they felt that a particular workplace just wasn't right for them.

Lessons Outside the Classroom

Fiona Ruck

I live for fieldwork. As a geography teacher, having the opportunity to take my pupils out, and put their learning into context, satisfies my soul. Context and cultural capital are crucial in providing our children with effective learning experiences. Trips are a chance to develop their knowledge, progress their understanding and ignite their passion. And sometimes it is just refreshing to be out of school! But don't be fooled into thinking field trips are holidays. Here are my top tips for preparing to take your learning outside of the classroom.

Pack your sense of humour

Every year, without fail, on our Year 8 river studies coach trip to Shropshire, I hear the same question: "How can that sheep stand on that massive steep mountain side without falling over?" Over the years, I have developed a pretty impressive poker face when I tell them that it is easy; sheep have one set of legs longer than the other to enable them to do just this. And every year they accept it and I have a little giggle to myself. Obviously, they are quick to correct me when we arrive and are greeted by sheep who do not, in fact, have wonky legs.

Do your research

Do not go along on a history trip to Berlin, on an excursion to the Brandenburg Gate, with a group of GCSE pupils and ask one of said pupils to take a picture of you in front of the Brandenburg gate—a gate that is actually a beautifully ornate, oversized, domestic garden gate. You will not live it down. Ever.

Choose carefully which member of staff you share a room with

Secret snorers are the worst. Especially when the room you have been given has a double bed for you to share—and you've only been at the school for your six weeks teaching placement. It is also probably best not to mention said snoring; you might find that the member of staff then informs you that you actually woke her that night by sitting bolt upright, wide eyed, shouting to the troll that was hiding under the bed.

Read the guidebook

Even on fancy field trips abroad when you have a tour guide, it would have been good to know—before the coach trip to the Blue Lagoon with a bunch of sixth-form students—about the non-negotiable rule for naked showering before entering. Eek!

Do not be fooled into thinking you will get a full night's sleep

Never assume that the children or teenagers that you take away will give you more sleep than your toddlers at home. Big mistake. Huge. Sitting on the stairs until all of the over-excited, giggle-ridden, sugar-high children are asleep is the norm. If you're super unlucky (yep, I was) you will encounter a sickness bug amongst all twelve of the girls when you are the only female member of staff; emptying buckets of vomit, rubbing backs, fetching water, relentless changing of bedding and disinfecting rooms was not what I had planned!

Yet, as you can see, field trips have given me wonderful memories and fantastic learning experiences. Make the most of every opportunity you are lucky enough to be presented with. But always be prepared!

Fiona Ruck is second in geography at a secondary school in Birmingham.

Tales From the Boarding House

Ceri Stokes

Sometimes you need top tips for outside the classroom. This could be for school trips, residential visits, or, if you are lucky enough, boarding school life. It can be a hard balance. You know you cannot be the same person in the classroom that you are in the boarding house—you are their guardian after all, and will be the person that they will turn to in tough times or when they are feeling poorly.

Students often struggle with this differentiation. A good example—one that still freaks me out now thinking about it—was a night when I was on duty watching Embarrassing Bodies with my sixth-formers. I cannot (or chose not to) normally watch it with them, often finding jobs to do—like refilling the cereal boxes or sorting out lost property—but this episode was about breast cancer and how to check for lumps. I thought I was safe, and it was an important topic.

The PSHE head of department would have been proud of me … until the girls decided that they needed to practice and compare. It quickly became a situation that I was not comfortable to stay in—falling over the cushions as I thought I heard the duty phone ringing. While it was lovely that the girls felt comfortable and safe in my presence, as a teacher every alarm bell was ringing and the school code of conduct was flashing before my eyes.

It can be so hard to get the balance right, but talking the situation through with other boarding staff has to help. You may want to let your designated safeguarding lead know about out-of-the-ordinary situations that you have found yourself in. Another example that comes to mind and still fills me with dread, was when an overseas boarder was feeling unwell and couldn't get out of bed. I took her temperature and suggested that perhaps sleeping in a 'onesie' by the radiator and having three duvets on might be why she was feeling so hot. I tried suggesting she take a layer off—which she didn't understand—so I was standing in the room, miming my suggestion, when suddenly I heard a voice from the child's laptop speaking in Mandarin. The child's mum had been watching me the whole time, unbeknownst to me.

Talking not only shows that safeguarding yourself and the pupils is on your radar, but it can also help your team work together. I found that if I shared with the team and asked for their opinion or support, we worked better as a team, especially when I was the Housemistress. When I first started, I presumed that being a leader meant that you would get it right all the time, and you didn't need help. Now, I realise this couldn't be further from the truth.

Ceri Stokes is the designated safeguarding lead at an independent boarding school. She talks a lot about the need for good PSHE, including helping with mental health, e-safety and healthy relationships. She ran a boarding house for 13 years and was house tutor for 4 years before that.

Teaching the Ones Who Are Listening

Dr Branwen Bingle

I was working as a long-term supply teacher in a secondary school, a job that became available in the January term because four other supply teachers said they wouldn't come back at various points during the autumn term. After my first week, I understood why: knowing that a staff member was due to be off on long-term sick leave, the head of department carefully selected all the classes that were seen as "challenging" and put them on the timetable for the cover teacher to cope with.

I was there for two terms.

Over that time, some of the students did their best to break me. It was the only time in my career that I left a classroom crying, mostly in frustration at the behaviour and lack of engagement. But each day I got up, I got dressed and I went to work. And little by little, the students stopped trying to make me leave.

One memorable lesson with my rowdy Year 8 class started with the usual ignoring of my pleas. "Ok class, we're ready to start. Class? Could you please turn this way and listen? We have a lot to get through today..."

Out of the corner of my eye, I saw them. The tiny group, ready and waiting expectantly, like they always were: they knew their peers, knew what I was trying to do for them, and were helping me the best way they knew how.

I decided enough was enough. I signalled to them to move their desks together and pulled up my chair. We started our lesson, each of them eagerly contributing, all ignoring the general chatter from their classmates.

Suddenly, a voice cut through my teaching: "Oi! That's not fair! You're only teaching the ones who are listening!"

"Yep," I responded. "Pull up a chair." She did. Then so did her friend. Soon it was enough of the class that the chatter had died, and the others reluctantly started paying attention. The lesson continued to the end. "Good work, everyone. See you tomorrow," I said.

I can't pretend it was perfect after that, but it was definitely better. The class worked out that I wasn't going to give up on them and leave, but equally, I wasn't going to battle with them on their terms. We made it to the end of the year together and I was proud of the way they turned around; no longer just another challenging class but a group of willing participants in their own learning—well, most of the time!

It was one of the most difficult, but rewarding, jobs I ever had. I got a permanent job in another school over the summer, but remember those two terms as if they were a lifetime. I have only one regret: I never told that quiet group of young people how much I owed them for their silent awareness, interest and respect that day. I hope they knew.

Dr Branwen Bingle, Head of Primary ITE at Newman University, SFHEA, co-author of 'Lessons in Teaching Grammar in Primary Schools', 'Lessons in Teaching Reading Comprehension in Primary Schools' and other writings about Initial Teacher Education, English Literature and Diversity.

Take Care of Yourself

Bretta Townend-Jowitt

Teaching is an amazing profession that provides achievements and exhaustion in equal measures. We face family, friends, acquaintances and the media who believe we work 9.00am to 3.00pm, term time only; this will probably leave you feeling frustrated or angry that they don't understand, and your reaction may be to battle their opinions or to choose to ignore them. It is only when you are—or have been—in the profession that you truly understand the magnitude of the role.

We frequently try to do everything yesterday; we have a never-ending job list and we always strive to better our teaching (thinking we are never good enough) and the learning of our pupils/students. Along with the addition of having children and families, we constantly worry about supporting children with educational needs or those suffering trauma, all while dealing with the day-to-day business in school and all it throws at us, as well as anything and everything we need to do outside school to maintain family life. However, a word of warning: it isn't entirely possible. Many teachers try to save rest and relaxation time until the weekend—or worse still, school holidays—which leads to exhaustion and, even worse, could lead to total burnout. Being good is good enough.

Why do we do it? Quite a loaded question: some would blame school culture, toxic leadership, and/or constant new initiatives. What can we do? Well, there are many schools that do not have a toxic culture, who take workload seriously, advocate part-time and flexible working and ensure they have staff wellbeing at their heart; find one of these schools to work in. Find one that aligns with your values and principles, and that has senior leaders who care and model wellbeing themselves. Ultimately, your wellbeing rests with you and the actions you are willing to take to ensure it remains at a good level.

Wellbeing is used to describe our health, both physically and mentally. Having good wellbeing means we have the ability to cope and 'bounce back'. So, how can we take care of ourselves as teachers?

Here is a list of tips you might want to try; it isn't an exhaustive list—nor is it in any particular order—but it might get you started:

- Ensure you keep at least one day each weekend free of schoolwork;
- Don't have your school email on your phone; decide when you will answer mails and have a time to stop checking;
- Take time out of the busy school day to catch up with colleagues; for example, five minutes at break time, 20 minutes at lunchtime, 10 minutes for coffee at the end of the school day;
- Connect with family and friends regularly;
- Exercise regularly;
- Surround yourself with colleagues who help and support;
- Get a mentor or coach;
- Eat and drink healthily; and
- Ask for help if, and when, you need it.

Remember, wellbeing is for everyday and for everyone, so support and take care of each other to help ensure we have a positive culture in EVERY school.

Bretta Townend-Jowitt BA(Hons), PGCE, MCCT is the headteacher of Kingham Primary School, Oxfordshire. She is a member of The Advisory Board for Teacher toolkit and the Learner Engagement Strategy Group for Oxfordshire County Council. She is an advocate for the grassroots organisation Maternity Teacher, Paternity Teacher Project #MTPT. Bretta is passionate about staff wellbeing—she holds a Gold Award from Teach Well Alliance—and coaching; she is a coach for Women Leading in Education.

Ruminations on the Self-Doubting School Teacher

Isobelle Mason

Sometimes my brain feels like a broken pessimistic record, stuck on a hypnotic loop of concerns about my class and their learning that I'm supposed to have already dealt with. I'd call it mind-numbing, if it wasn't exactly the opposite. I'd be a lot smarter to term it anxiety; I recognize the monster I have battled with for years, though it seems to have grown three heads since I stepped into the classroom.

And I know, at least consciously, I'm not alone in this. At a very basic level, anxiety is an emotion that we all feel at some point. In Britain, 1 in 4 people will experience a mental health problem during their lives (Mind Mental Health Charity, 2017).

When anxiety strikes, it tries to make you think you are alone. You're trapped inside your own head with the certainty that you're ruining your lessons, your co-workers think you're annoying and desperate, your mentor thinks you're needy and stress-inducing and your students think you bring nothing new to the lessons that is interesting and important—you're wasting their time and you're wasting your own time, and you're screwing up and you can't fix this…

I remember the first time at school I made myself sick from anxiety. It was fifteen minutes before a particularly difficult class—one that I grew to love eventually—that made my palms sweat and my mouth gnaw at my fingernails and my voice stutter. My mind was crippled by these achingly harsh thoughts that they hated me, that I didn't deserve to stand in front of them and teach them, and that I didn't even know what I was talking about. I remember laying their books out, my heart racing, my mind filled with thoughts that I didn't deserve to be anyone's teacher and that I was going to ruin this golden opportunity for myself—and I promptly whizzed around and hurled straight into the bin. Grim, right?

As far as classes go, it was fine. The scenarios that had played out in my head in a hypnotic repetition hadn't happened; no one had screamed at me for being a rubbish teacher. In fact, as far as I could tell, not one student could sense my shaking hands as I wrote on the white board or the crack in my voice as I questioned them about Lennie and George's friendship. Anxiety can be a contagion—it spreads like wildfire, permeating every thought and reflection about yourself and your ability, if you let it.

It was that class, with that furious manifestation of self-doubt—where that petty monster worked to convince me that the way I teach Steinbeck's intentions is a dire choice between life and death—that helped me realise I had gripped onto this anxious mindset as a way of surviving and navigating my classroom. If I could clutch and grip and hold on at work, I could fix this. That realisation made the decision for me to speak to a leader at the school.

That conversation was hard—but illuminating and needed. From then, I decided to reframe my self-doubt and anxiety. It became a sign that I cared about my teaching and my classes, that I was on the right path, that I could grow, and that the outcome matters to me. It made me realize I wasn't alone. You aren't either.

Trust that you deserve the euphoric things teaching has to offer. That euphoric state of mind has more power than you realise.

If you are struggling, please reach out for help. Book an appointment with your GP, or visit: www.samaritans.org/ or www.mind.org.uk/.

References

Mind Mental Health Charity (2017) *Mental Health Facts and Statistics,* Available at: *https://www.mind.org.uk/information-support/types-of-mental-health-problems/statistics-and-facts-about-mental-health/how-common-are-mental-health-problems/* (Accessed: 20th May 2020).

Isobelle is an NQT at a school in south London. Raised in New Zealand, she received her Bachelor of Arts in History from King's College London in 2019.

100 Words of Teacher Wisdom

Nicola Owen

Smile. Be kind. Listen. Watch. Learn. Sleep. Eat. Drink water. Exercise. Plan. Think. Enjoy. Laugh. Giggle. Hug. Mark. Report. Rest. Read. Write. Party. Be with your friends. Go on visits. Tidy. Organise. Label. Journal. Be thankful. Be spontaneous. Ask. Be brave. Be honest. Cry if you need to. Support. Befriend. Join a union. Challenge. Find balance. Invest in your children. Build connections. Have hobbies outside of work. Spend time with family. Find bargains. Collect rubbish. Run a bath. Relax. Unwind. Always pour from the overflow—keep your cup filled with positive wellbeing.

Nicola Owen is a mental health and wellbeing educator. She is a qualified teacher and is the Director of Zennic Wellbeing Ltd.

Newly Qualified ... What Comes Now?

Emily McCabe

I am a Year 4 NQT trying to figure out the ups, downs and ways through early-career teaching. So far, since beginning my NQT year, I have navigated OFSTED the week before Christmas, school improvement visits and much more—not to mention a global pandemic. And I'm loving every minute.

In July 2019, I qualified as a teacher after completing a three-year degree with qualified teacher status (QTS). As much as it might be a cliché, it was all I had ever wanted to do, and now I felt ready. Ready to step into the wonderful world of primary schools and share all the fantastic things I had learned for the past three years. And why wouldn't I be? I had had more than the required 120 days across four placements and five year groups. I'd been to all (okay ... most of!) my lectures and submitted all the assignments. I was ready.

Or so I thought. As fate would have it, the one thing I hadn't managed to do was find a job! I had many interviews over the last few months of my degree and got very close at times to that coveted position, but always just lost out. By the end of the academic year, it was clear I wouldn't have a teaching post for September. Luckily, after a few weeks on supply, I managed to secure a post teaching Year 4 in a two-form primary school. I was so excited and couldn't wait to get started.

The first few weeks were challenging, as I had expected. I worked hard to implement the things I had picked up during my training and I designed my classroom to be as calm and relevant as I possibly could. But things just didn't seem to be improving in my eyes. I recall one particular playtime. I was trying to get my class in one straight, silent line and, for whatever reason that day, they just wouldn't cooperate. Just then, one of the Year 5 teachers came out to collect his class. With one look, his whole class stood to attention and headed inside. I was in despair: why didn't my class do that?

Later on, I was chatting with my NQT mentor. She looked at me and asked, "How long have you been teaching, Emily?" I thought about it for a moment, but before I could reply she continued, "You've been teaching for four weeks. 'Mr S' has been teaching longer than you've been alive." This really stuck with me, and has done ever since.

Sometimes I think it is easy to get caught up in the utter whirlwind that is your NQT year—I know I still do. I remind myself of the conversation with my mentor almost every week—that almost every teacher in the school is more experienced than I am. It's a huge learning curve but, at the end of the day, it's one I am really enjoying. It's nice to get together with the other NQTs in my school to share stories! Just like with the children we teach, everyone learns at a different speed. I've learned not to compare myself with others and to believe in what I am doing—and I truly believe my teaching has improved since.

Emily McCabe BA (Hons) is a Year 4 teacher and history coordinator based in the North East of England.

Applying to Be a Teacher

Caitlin Hadfield

I applied to a primary SCITT course that consisted of a full application day with multiple stages. The first half of the day consisted of going into a school to demonstrate my classroom capabilities and to read a story to a class of children. Then there was a lunch break with the tutors of the course, which was followed by the second half of the day held at the teacher training centre. This consisted of a group discussion, a presentation, an interview, and a written task.

I got placed in a lovely school for the first half of the day, and while there I got chatting to some of the primary school teachers about their routes into teaching. One teacher told me how she'd been teaching for a few years and that she originally did the same course that I was applying for. She told me that she was the only one at her application day and she had to just do everything on her own with the teaching staff. I joked that it must have been an awkward experience doing it on her own and having to sit and have dinner with all the staff; we had a laugh about the situation and I remember saying "Imagine if I was on my own today". Not even five minutes after that, the headteacher came into the room and said to me, "Oh, just to let you know, you're the only one doing this application day today". After laughing about her situation, I just looked at the teacher who I'd been talking to and thought 'just my luck'. The dinner was a tad uncomfortable, surrounded by all the staff I didn't know while I nibbled on some granola; the group discussion ended up being a question and answer session, which I didn't really fit in with—but hey, the granola was nice. Oh, and I got the place.

Caitlin Hadfield is an aspiring primary school teacher who is currently completing her teacher training.

Finding the Right School for You

Andy Taylor

Firstly, arrange to spend a morning in the school and walk around with a notebook. Jot down displays that appear in every classroom, the behaviour management strategies that you see, reward charts and systems. Identify what is consistent in every classroom. That should guide you in what the key expectations are for how you present your classroom. There may be consistent systems that are presented differently; this will show you where you can add personality and reflect your ethos. This is also a great way of magpie-ing great practices that you want to incorporate.

Look in students' books. Are there targets present? Presentation policies clearly being implemented? How does the marking system look in practice? All these things will help you to know what expectations you will need to have of the children and the frequency and style of marking you will be expected to adopt.

Secondly, ask, ask, ask—ask everything! Schools make huge assumptions about what you know or will absorb by osmosis. They don't always know what you don't know. If you've been given key policies and things seem unclear, ask. There may be a simple explanation as to what something means (policies can be tricky to interpret at times, particularly if you weren't there at its inception). Chances are, all the exercise books you need will have been ordered for you. If it is not obvious what something is for, double check with someone. We once went a half-term with an NQT having created their own spelling grids for children instead of using a spelling book that the children had. This was our fault, not theirs; an assumption was made and if schools know what you don't know, they will support you with it.

Someone far wiser than me once said that each school has its own secret language. The acronyms they use, the location of the glue sticks, and why things happen a certain way. It takes time to learn these things; of course, there will come that time when you fully understand them and you will be explaining them to someone else—then you know you are fully part of the school. Utilise the strengths of others around you—don't feel threatened by an experienced Teaching Assistant (TA). Relax and know you've got someone in the room that can help if you need it and draw on their knowledge of the children, the parents and the school to make your life easier. (They will also, hopefully, bring you a drink on those days you don't make it down to the staffroom at break time.) The best person to befriend on day one is the school secretary. They know everything that happens in the school and will be your first line of defense for parents—and they usually keep the glue sticks! Next is to befriend the school cook, if you have one, for obvious reasons.

Mr T has been an NQT mentor for 11 years and has mentored more than 16 NQTs during that time. @MrTs_N

The Offside Rule Got Me on Side

Ginny Bootman

When I first qualified, it was back in 1993 when there were more qualified teachers wanting jobs than there were teaching posts. It really was a trying time. I used to get the Times Educational Supplement every Thursday morning as I got on my bus to go to my lectures at university. That bus journey filled me with hopes of the jobs I would apply for—and, in my dream world, get. Of course, I risked my dreams being shattered given there seemed to be no jobs available for me.

Fast forward to the applications having been sent off and then the waiting, waiting, waiting. I had handwritten each application, having had to wait for the application form to arrive by post. Remember this was way before the internet, or even mobile phones!

Often, I didn't even get an acknowledgement that I had even applied for the job. One day, I felt a bit miffed at this lack of general politeness—so I rang the school up. Their reply was that they had received over 300 applications for the post I had applied for. This being the case, they decided to get the staff together and, over a cuppa, asked if there was anything not specified on the job description they would like for the soon-to-be-appointed member of staff. Apparently, someone piped up: "Someone who could play the piano would be great". And so, with that, all applications not piano-playing ready were swiftly dispatched to the circular filing cabinet. Harsh, I hear you cry. Guess what I did next … went and had piano lessons!

Eventually, I got my first teaching position as a PE coordinator. All very exciting until I met the previous PE coordinator, who had been moved onto being maths coordinator. The first time I met him, I realised he was not going to bow out of PE coordination gracefully. "So, tell me the offside rule then", he piped up with a glint in his eye. Guess what I did next...I became a qualified football referee! He got his own back though. At the end of my first year of teaching, a member of staff asked me what I thought of the maths scheme of work for the school. To which I replied, "What maths scheme?" With a glint in his eye, the former PE coordinator piped up, "Did I forget to tell you about the maths scheme?"

Ginny has been teaching longer than she hasn't. She has been a Headteacher, Senior Manager and class teacher teaching all ages in the primary age range. She is currently SENCO of 2 primary schools in Northamptonshire. She lives by the mantra #followtheempathyroad. You can find her on twitter @sencogirl and at www.ginnybootman.com

What Is It Like to Teach in the School You Attended as a Student?

Helen Pipe

Walking down the main corridor towards the hall for our final Year 11 assembly before our GCSE examinations commenced the following week—my tie with the short side showing and talking with friends—I never would have dreamed that just over five years later I would not be sitting on the plastic chairs facing the front, but would instead be standing against the window looking at the tutor group I was allocated to cover that day.

In September 2007, my mother went to ask her employer if she could have the day off in November to attend her daughter's university graduation ceremony. The headteacher honoured this request and asked what her daughter was doing now that she had finished university: "Nothing at the moment, she's not sure if she would like to be a teacher".

On Monday, the 1st of October, I started as cover supervisor covering my first lesson, set 1 Year 9 English, back in the same classroom I had my English lessons five years previously. Time has flown, and now thirteen years later I am still working at the school I attended as a student—except that I am now head of geography, KS4 geography trust lead and mentor.

From that first week covering classes, I knew I had found my passion: I wanted to be a teacher and was delighted to be able to secure a school-direct salaried position to gain my qualification. Currently my classroom door states my journey—and it is the same classroom I was taught maths in Year 7, left-hand side, third row back, on the end (the same room where I learnt that glasses were probably a good idea)—and I love when I teach a new class and they say "You came here?". Sharing my experiences creates a connection; pupils know I have a genuine care and affection for them and will bend over backwards to ensure they have everything they need to be successful. I feel the same nerves, every year in August when my classes receive their exam results, as I felt when receiving mine.

This year I became a Year 7 tutor for the first time. During my tutor group's transition week last July, I shared my first-hand experiences of tackling the stairs after having been asked on my first day why I was so slow going to the top floor: "Was it because I lived in a bungalow?" Little did the 6-foot-tall Year 10 boy know that yes, I did live in a bungalow! I continued to share, and the Year 7 students visibly relaxed, not only knowing their nerves would cease but also that their form tutor enjoyed secondary school—in fact, she had returned and stayed.

I am now a person who strives for challenge and have embraced every opportunity that has been offered; as I write this, my National Professional Qualification for Middle Leadership (NPQML) project has been submitted and awaits grading. I have been fortunate to be successful in progressing my career and, as my teaching role has evolved over time, so too has the school. It is not the same school I attended as an 11-year-old; it has overcome challenges, broken down barriers and is accomplishing great things—and I am proud to have been a part of that, as a student and a teacher.

Perhaps, in the future, I will seek to establish myself somewhere new, but for now I can say, with a huge smile to my classes, "I have been here longer than you have been alive!"

Helen Pipe is the head of geography in a secondary academy and leads the development of KS4 geography across a trust in Warwickshire. She is an experienced newly qualified and early career teacher mentor and is passionate about delivering CPD relating to giving high quality feedback to pupils.

Age is Just a Number

Katie Ridgway

"Hey you! Students cannot take their lunches out of the dining hall; you will have to eat here." The embarrassment, as I realised that the assistant headteacher was actually talking to me, was excruciating—and made worse when other students turned to see which of them had tried to break this cardinal rule.

This was the first day of my PGCE … and I had already been mistaken for a pupil!

Twenty-one years and 7 months old, 5' 3", blonde and still somewhat baby faced—I could understand why the assistant head might think I was a sixth-former at the college where, today, I had started my first placement. I was only 3 years older than some of the students I would be teaching.

Sure, I tried to appear mature: I purchased suit trousers and blouses after all! But it seemed that being taken seriously in this profession was going to take a little more than a new wardrobe.

For the first four years of my career, I was the youngest in all of the 3 departments I worked in, and it took me those years to demonstrate that I was more independent, resilient and ambitious than I might have looked. My challenge was to find a way to translate this feeling of inexperience—and subsequent 'imposter syndrome'—into confidence.

"There has to be something else in this world that I know how to do", I thought desperately as I drove home in the dark after another day of being berated and scolded for yet again 'not being good enough'. It was my NQT year and I had misguidedly taken a job in a school that did not nurture its trainees—its potentially excellent teachers and future leaders. I found myself on those 45-minute drives home, after exhausting days of uploading full lesson plans for every lesson to be scrutinised by SLT and countless 'support plan' meetings, asking myself the same question. I had considered leaving the profession entirely, but if I was going to begin my journey towards leadership, I instead needed to make a change within the confines of being a teacher. Teaching is what I had always wanted to do—I was not going to give up—and with all the hard work I had done, I had come too far to throw it away. I changed my environment and moved to another school by the end of my NQT year.

In subsequent years, I have learned these lasting messages:

4. Be confident. Trust yourself. Don't doubt yourself. Come up with some positive affirmations related to your strengths as a young leader. "I have recent and, therefore, up-to-date training" or "I have lots of passion and enthusiasm" were two of mine.
5. Do not let anyone decide your path or your goals for you—only you know when you are ready to take the steps you desire.
6. You do not need to fundamentally change yourself to be a successful, young leader.
7. Create a community of support: reach out and network using tools such as Twitter, attending conferences and training to meet other likeminded people in your position, or who have been in your position, at some point in their careers.

References

Clance, P. and Imes, S. (1978) Psychotherapy Theory, Research and Practice, vol. 15, #3, Fall 1978

Kate Ridgway is a Lead Practitioner and a Teach First North East Lead Mentor. She is an AQA English Literature examiner, an oracy pioneer and a WomenEd North East Regional Network Lead. Kate is also a ConnectEd subject advocate.

Find the School That's Right for You

Natalie Davis

The job flashed up on the screen and I knew it would be interesting; there's usually a valid reason for why only experienced teachers should apply. I called the school and within minutes was speaking to the headteacher of a very large comprehensive. They'd done it in maths, he explained; could I come in next week?

A few months later I found myself in front of classes of disadvantaged pupils. Concerned about an imminent OFSTED, the SLT had chosen to spend their allocated Pupil Premium (PP) money by employing a subject teacher who would take them out of their usual sets and teach them all together, but in slightly smaller classes. The thing is, I couldn't be further from the ideal candidate for this position. My three previous schools had been big-name independent boarding schools. I'd come from a place of black-tie English Society dinners, marking 6-page Milton essays and playing croquet on the front lawn.

In anxious preparation for my new role, I read several books. I was determined not to let these pupils down. I worked hard early on at forming good working relationships with them and I found myself really enjoying it. Some moments were difficult; some downright dangerous. I dealt with violence, poor behaviour, aggression and, worst of all, many pupils had very low self-esteem. Was I even teaching before this?

I realised very quickly that my life had been in a glass bubble and it felt refreshing to be out of it. But there were significant doubts. Was it really fair to put all the PP kids into one room together? Didn't this create the sort of atmosphere most schools wanted to avoid? And, more concerningly, did it ironically hold back brighter PP pupils who had been taken out of their usual set to join this group?

As the weeks went on, this experiment began to feel like a punishment for some of the pupils—more aimed at satisfying OFSTED inspectors than actually improving pupils' education. I was fortunate to have incredible support from the English department, with kind faces offering cups of tea—some of whom were unable to conceal their delight at having some of the most challenging pupils removed from their classes. The Head of Department (HOD) was exceptionally well-organised and supportive, which I'll always be thankful for.

Eventually though, after a term, the wheels fell off. There were no explosions of bad behaviour to tip me over the edge—even though an actual firework was let off once outside our block! Nor did the challenges of what I was doing ever get me down. (One of the promises I made to myself was that I would never cry in the toilets.) The problem was that I just didn't believe in it anymore. Surely the whole point of a comprehensive is to take pupils, regardless of background, and help them to be the best they can be? In these new, special PP sets, pupils were now categorised by their background and it felt uncomfortable and undemocratic. I left.

Natalie Davis is an educator from rural Worcestershire with a specific interest in outdoor education and using IT in English lessons. Natalie holds a postgraduate degree in Shakespeare Studies and has formerly worked The Globe Theatre, London. She has worked as an international teacher trainer for Cambridge Assessment and is an examiner for GCSE and A-Level English Literature.

Not Just a Teacher

Lucy Flower

"I'd like to step down from my leadership role and become ... just a teacher".

When I started my maternity leave, heavily pregnant, heavily emotional and heavily naive, I was someone who blindly prioritised the next steps of my career above almost everything else. I regularly claimed I felt stressed, but sailed through, buoyed by my confidence and my seemingly unending capability in getting everything done briskly, efficiently, and perfectly. So, after the birth of my beautiful daughter—to my utter shame and devastation—struggling with my new identity, with the lack of using my brain, and with post-natal depression—I couldn't wait to return to the place where I was always a winner—where I knew what I was doing.

My return brought the utter shock of realising I was no longer effortlessly perfect. Simple organisational tasks took me hours longer than they used to—and I would always find afterwards that I had missed something crucial. Everyday decisions that needed to be made on the spot became days of agonising over every detail, until the problem that needed a decision was long past and no longer relevant. Fellow leaders who were my ultimate confidantes had new cliques, and new roles.

More and more I began to feel as though I was an inconvenience. Far from being overjoyed at returning to be a 'winner', I felt lonely, isolated and utterly useless. Already painfully aware that I was letting my colleagues down, I didn't share my feelings—unconsciously believing that if I acted like that once joyful and confident leader, it would all somehow come flooding back, in time.

The day came when I'd made a mistake too far—when I couldn't even start my to-do list out of paralysing fear of incorrect action. When the time arrived that I could barely get dressed through anxiety of making the wrong decision, I finally said the words at the start of this piece to my headteacher.

For a long time afterwards, the sting of shameful failure consumed me. Without the next rung on the ladder to ruthlessly aim for—without the reward of achieving the next goal—who was I, and where was I going? I grieved for the loss of my life as the 'winner'.

Slowly, gradually, I rebuilt. My prevailing emphasis on my career became secondary to living—to being a parent, a partner, a person. I felt elation at rediscovering my love of the classroom. I re-experienced the joy of learning new things. I unearthed the values that brought fire to my core. My excitement and wonder grew as I realised that, far from being a failure, I now had endless possibilities before me.

In time, I am sure I will return to the career path that leads back to leadership. But right now?

I am a teacher ... but I am not *just* a teacher.

Lucy Flower is a school leader and mother. She is proud to be a regional representative for WomenEd and the Maternity Teacher Paternity Teacher (MTPT) Project. She tweets @MrsLFlower.

Chapter 10

Top Teacher Tips

Never before would we have ever imagined a time in our careers where we would be teaching behind facemasks, educating through a computer screen and taking regular lateral flow tests in order to educate children and young people. It has been a challenging time, but we have persevered. Showing resilience, innovation and creativity, we've adapted our practice to respond to the ever-changing educational landscape.

Our children and young people are truly blessed to have teachers who are continually striving to provide the best possible learning experience for their children. When times are challenging, as they have been this year, it is really important to reflect on your motivations for entering the profession. Teaching is one of the most important jobs there is – the profession that creates all of the other professions. You will be shaping the hearts and minds of children for the rest of their lives. You will be helping them to maximise their learning potential. You'll be giving children and young people the very best start in life. Please never forget the impact you will have on a child's life. It is so important to periodically reflect on your 'why'.

In this chapter, authors share top tips that they have learned throughout their time in the classroom.

Some Words of Experience

Jan Marnell

I've been teaching since 2003. My passions are English and geography in the primary setting. I'm currently a Year 5 teacher in Birmingham and love it. There are so many stories to laugh about—and cry about too!—as well as so many tips to offer you. But for student teachers, I'd advise:

Make time for at least one hot drink, loo break and lunch break during the day. Look after number one: you! Meal prep in advance; making enough to take for lunch the following day will save precious time in the morning (especially if you're juggling your own kids).

Organise a tea making rota for your team. A brew brings people together!

Have a few copies of your class list that you can use if the register fails or when you're collating letters. It's organised and saves time.

Buy a diary that has a place to record marks in.

Group children by ability for maths, reading and writing and friendship groups for topic lessons. Mix this up every term. It nurtures relationships and friendships in class.

Ask questions of your team—and don't be afraid to ask again if you're unsure; I still do this after 17 years of teaching!

Admit to mistakes. We all make them.

Actively mark as you're walking around class, and try to incorporate your schools marking policy. Saves time at the end of the school day.

Go home at a reasonable time at least twice a week, especially when it's sunny!

When gathering books in, ask children to leave them open on the page they'd like you to mark. Collect these up with highest ability first, at the bottom of the pile, then middle ability, then lower and SEN. This saves so much time. Also ask your Teaching Assistant (TA) to mark the books of the groups they've been working with. An informal chat about the group will give you something to talk about and build professional relationships.

Have a stash of stickers and rewards. Praise the good, gently discourage the unsavoury—and sprinkle smiley faces and stars everywhere!

Jan Marnell is a mum to two amazing boys, a primary teacher of 18 years, a phase leader and a lover of all things English and geography based.

In the End, It All Comes Down to Engagement

Barbara Anna Zielonka

Have you ever thought about what characterises teachers who are agents of change? In my teaching career, I have had the chance to meet outstanding educators during conferences, seminars and workshops. These educators have a great impact on their students every single day, and they often impact their colleagues and communities as well. If I were to choose only one word that all these educators have in common, it would be engagement. Teaching that involves the intellectual, social, physical and emotional engagement of students is one of the most important tasks we, as teachers, strive to achieve in our classrooms all over the world.

Intellectual engagement is often defined as an ability to build connections between classroom content and everyday life, as well as personal commitment to exploration, investigation, problem solving and inquiry over a sustained time period. Teachers who focus on authentic and active learning, connections-based learning and inquiry-based learning engage their students so that they can boost their creativity and problem-solving skills in a school setting, as well as in their future workplaces. Students who are engaged intellectually are not afraid to connect with peers and experts who are outside of their own classrooms and can easily break out of their comfort zone to learn about new and complex global issues.

The ability to build interactions and positive relationships between students and their peers and between staff and students is the essence of social engagement. It contributes to students' success in school and also makes the transition to higher education or workplaces much smoother. Students who are socially engaged in both online and offline environments care for their own communities and become responsible citizens. They are also much more likely to take risks and set high expectations for themselves.

The third type of engagement that is worth mentioning here is physical engagement. Teachers who are agents of change know that physical engagement provides multiple health and educational benefits to their students. Hypertension, obesity, diabetes and a lack of concentration among students are just some of the problems schools face in the 21st century. Even though we all know about the long-term consequences of these problems, not all of us do something that could prevent these problems from happening.

Finally, there is the emotional engagement, which is often perceived as students' involvement in and enthusiasm for school. Teachers who are aware of its importance use strategies such as positive feedback, praise and recognition. Research has also shown that students who are emotionally engaged have better memory recall in the long term.

Teachers who are changemakers address each level of engagement in their classrooms on a regular basis. They know that the creation of a perfect learning environment is not a magic trick and that it requires a constant focus on these four levels of engagement.

Barbara Anna Zielonka is a full-time high school English teacher, global educator, educational technologist, teacher trainer, writer, project manager, judge in international competitions, lifelong learner, catalyst for change and reader. In March 2018, Barbara was named one of the top 10 finalists of the one million dollar Global Teacher Prize.

Creating a Positive Environment for Learners to Succeed

Lisa Vann

After many years of teaching, there is a particular class that stands out—perhaps as it fell as my last lesson of the week! The group had a diverse range of complex needs: cognitive, language, linguistic, emotional, and medical. They often arrived after a full day of challenges and events that had the potential to impact on their attitude to learning. There was also, typically, a stream of detentions for them following my lesson.

A classroom is a complex environment, and many factors are at play to ensure a positive learning atmosphere. In this short narrative, I aim to highlight some of the key points which helped me with this class.

Calm arrival to classroom

When students arrived to my classroom, I would greet them at the door. This helped to set the tone for entering the classroom with the mindset to study. Where students were in distress from events earlier in the day, I took time to talk with them. Sometimes the issue causing the problem could be resolved by conversation, but sometimes it had to be agreed that the student might need to take further steps after the class. The key message was that, where possible, these issues should be left at the classroom door so that the focus was on learning.

Positive relationships

Having positive relationships with students and ensuring they know that you care, helps students to settle in the classroom and feel safe enough to tackle the challenges they face with learning.

Greeting students at the door meant that an activity was needed for students to complete as they arrived to the classroom. This would typically be a retrieval activity to bring students back to our subject. It may be a task to introduce new vocabulary or be an image that students could begin to ask questions about.

Clarity

Lessons followed a clear structure to support learning and give reassurance. Students knew the learning path that they would take through the lesson. Remember to take account of the personalities of individuals when planning group work. Some students find this very difficult so students should be encouraged to make their own choices about what would work best for them.

Understand your curriculum and key learning focus

I would focus on depth of knowledge of key topics to support understanding and give greater time to focus on written tasks. Time was given to draft work with teacher feedback and discussion. Scaffolding was provided, including key vocabulary, so that students understood what was expected. This helped students to see that their first attempt was not their only attempt.

Create an environment where students *want* to succeed

In this class students met or exceeded their targets. This was clearly something to be proud of. A bigger achievement, however, was that students *wanted* to exceed. Key strategies here were use of oracy to clarify understanding, risk taking, drafting and modelling. Students were challenged and understood the high expectations that were placed upon them—and had the support to help them.

Clarity and consistency

Students value clarity from their teacher. They respect consistency of praise and sanction. They appreciate a sense of humour and a teacher who takes time to show they care. Consequently, this helped the students to focus and supported their self-esteem as they succeeded in their learning.

Lisa Vann is an associate headteacher at Transform Multi-Academy Trust, with a focus on Early Career Teacher development.

From Trainee to NQT

Amy Unsworth

When completing my training year, I was so close to quitting. There, I have finally said it. I became almost obsessed with being the 'perfect teacher' and being portrayed as this by my pupils. The thing is, I was far from perfect, and knowing this made me question and rethink everything I did. The amount of times I lay awake at night taunting myself over saying 'innit' instead of 'isn't it' again was unreal. I have come from a less-than-working-class background, in a deprived area where no one had ever corrected my speech, including my school, college and university. But suddenly, every little mistake—when I am supposed to be a professional—haunted me and made me cringe. I wish someone would have sat me down and said:

1. It is okay to make mistakes—just make sure you correct them and reflect on them.

2. Trainee = inexperience. Fact. Learn to accept that you are at the start of something great and greatness takes time and effort. Think of yourself like whisky; for it to be at its greatest, it takes years to develop under the correct conditions.

3. Perfection is a myth. Strive for greatness and to be better. In teaching, we are never a finished article; we need to be able to not just acknowledge that, but to accept it.

Then I moved to placement B in my training year, where—thankfully— I was taught how to build professional relationships with pupils and how to speak to them authoritatively. I realised it was more than okay to be myself, to talk as 'myself' rather than regurgitate an experienced teacher's language and style of communication. In this placement, I built solid relationships with a Year 8 class. They listened to me, they completed the work, but most importantly—they respected me.

I can proudly say that building relationships is now my strongest ability and is something I am praised on regularly. The journey to creating relationships is tough. Here are my two top tips to creating a great relationship with challenging classes:

1. On your first-ever lesson with a class, set your expectations and let them know what kind of teacher you are. You need to make sure they know what you expect and do not change it—no matter what. Will pupils rebel? Absolutely. Hold your ground. It takes around 6-9 weeks to build a solid relationship with a challenging class. If you say there will be a consequence for 'x' and 'y', make sure you give it.

2. Be human—and let them see that. With difficult classes you need to show them that you are not a robot; you are simply a person like them. Make those mistakes, and hey—even guide them to correct you! Acting 'perfect' with these classes will put a barrier between you and them.

Amy Unsworth is an English teacher at The Co-Op Academy Walkden. Amy completed her degree at Liverpool Hope University in 2018 and then completed a SCITT course in 2019. Amy has a passion for building relationships in her classroom and behaviour management.

Headteacher Comment: Could do Better (Report Writing)

Emma Kuyateh

I dedicate this piece to the colleague who showed me how to use the 'find and replace' function in Word—I am forever in your debt.

In May of 2005, I was on the home straight of my first year of teaching in Year 3 as a Newly Qualified Teacher. Yet one final rite of passage awaited me: report writing.

Nobody ever teaches you how to write a report; you generally rely on a kind colleague to share their wisdom (or a selection of last year's offerings). That colleague was my very experienced Year-group partner who had a heart of gold—and at any point could tell you how many weeks she had left until she retired. She slipped me a red foolscap card folder containing a full set of printed comment banks for report writing—I was winning at life!

Equally, no one ever tells you just how long it takes to write a full set of reports. The answer to this, of course, is forever and a day. I should've known this when my uber-organised mentor causally dropped it into conversation that she liked to start hers in the Easter holidays. There were rumours that my colleague, a Recently Qualified Teacher in the Year 4 class, had worked right down to the wire the previous year—and the head and deputy had ordered pizza and made him stay at school on the night of the deadline until he had finished them all! This year, he was leaving it fashionably late, yet again, and was powering through, with less than a week to go, on copious amounts of Pro-Plus.

Sadly, I can't look back at the reports I wrote as a Newly Qualified Teacher as they were stored on a floppy disk (cue bewildered looks from younger colleagues). I still remember the click, click, click sound the computer made saving your work while working on the archaic PC in the corner of the 'Yellow Room'—a room that was just that—where teachers could go for the newly created Planning Preparation and Assessment (PPA) time. Laptops weren't a thing back then.

Believe me, you have never experienced horror like seeing the message 'The disk in drive A is not formatted, do you want to format it now?' appear on inserting your floppy disk in anticipation of retrieving your reports. No, no and NO! This basically meant you'd lost the lot because, despite the repeated advice from your superiors to back them up, you hadn't. There was no 'Cloud' on which to store your reports or work collaboratively in real time on One Drive. We were given a flash drive each the year after.

Once my reports were finished, I printed them out and placed them in another foolscap card folder and left them in the headteacher's pigeon hole. There was no emailing or uploading them. A couple of days later, the same card folder reappeared in my pigeon hole; my reports had been 'marked' and the verdict was 'could do better'. The head had indicated which reports needed attention by marking them with a pink post-it. Back then, that was most of mine … so much for my proof-reading abilities! I dutifully went to do my corrections, mainly of pronoun confusion.

I have come to realise that in 16 years, apart from technology, the yearly ritual of report writing is very much the same. Reports still take me absolutely ages to write.

The final stage of the process every year is writing my general comment. The general comment is by far my favourite part of the report to write—and I believe this is the part that most parents value the most. Those little Year 3 children that I wrote reports for 16 years ago are now in their early 20s. I can still remember the names and exact positions those children sat in the classroom, and when I conjure up the image of each individual in my memory, I can also recall the types of things I would have written on their general comments—all as individual as each of them. I hope, if any of those pupils have kept their report, they will look back fondly on the time we spent together.

Emma Kuyateh has been a primary school teacher for 16 years in Kirklees, West Yorkshire. She has taught all year groups from Nursery to Year 6, is a practising SENCo and leads the Early Years Foundation Stage.

The Power of Relationships: Blood, Sweat and Tears

Megan Owen

"*Just to say a heartfelt thank you for all your patience, encouragement and support… Thank you also for putting up with demanding parents! We hope the results he achieves reflects the commitment you have shown*".

On first glance, this may seem like a far-from-humble brag. However, this message represents so much more than a student concluding their studies. It demonstrates the power of relationships, and the blood, sweat and tears (metaphorical and real) that we often need to invest to help the young people we teach recognise their potential.

When I joined the school where this story is from, taking on the role of Head of Food Technology, Jake (as he'll be known here) was in Year 10. Well known throughout the school for his behaviour and questionable decisions, Jake quickly adopted the role of 'class clown'. After a few lessons, I contacted home to raise my concerns. Initial conversations were difficult, with an element of defensiveness: was I meeting Jake's learning needs? Jake continued to be defiant and disengaged, but I persevered. I refused to shoehorn Jake into the naughty boy corner. I saw his potential, particularly in practical lessons. I praised his efforts, however small, and I was firm, but always fair, when his behaviour fell short of expectations. A few months in, something clicked; whilst working on his first coursework task, Jake came into his own. Back then, GCSE Catering students were tasked with producing an afternoon tea with four different components, all made from scratch. Jake's impressive spread made it onto the front cover of the school newsletter, and a copy made its way home to his mum—now framed and on display in their kitchen—serving as a reminder to Jake, and anyone else who may have doubted him, that he CAN do it.

With a newfound growth mindset, and a part-time job in a fish and chip shop, Jake finished his Year 11 catering class with a grade B—his best subject, alongside PE. Whilst his change in mindset and attitude may not have been across every subject, Jake, on the whole, worked his socks off for this outcome. Scoring one of the highest grades in the cohort for his coursework, Jake recognised his culinary talents and he was proud of them. His family and I were unitedly proud of him too.

This story serves as a reminder that it is important to see past the bravado of our most challenging students and learn what is underneath. Every student has their strengths, and it is our responsibility to help them recognise what they are. Below, I suggest how this can be achieved:

Build relationships. Dedicate time to learning who your students truly are – what they like and dislike, what makes them laugh. Get to know THEM.

Be consistent. This is important in terms of expectations, praise, sanctions, tone—in as many areas as possible. It helps students—and parents—get to know you, as well as where they stand.

Lead by example. Model to students that the expectations you have of them are the same as you have of yourself. Roll up your sleeves and show them that you won't ask them to do something you are not willing to do yourself.

Celebrate the 'wins', however small they are. Contact home, contact their tutor, contact their head of year. Break the cycle of negative conversation that often overwhelms students like Jake. Their gratitude, whilst perhaps hidden, should not be underestimated.

Seek opportunities to highlight students' strengths. For example, in a previous school, I organised a teacher versus student cook-off challenge, with the student team comprised of 'disengaged' boys from Year 9 whom I saw potential in. These opportunities can encourage colleagues to see students in a different light whilst helping students to make the switch from fixed to growth mindset.

Stick to your values. I have been told on more than one occasion that I have done 'enough', that it would be wiser to focus on students X, Y and Z who are more willing and/or easier to move up a grade. This is wrong. I want my students to achieve good grades, of course, but my greater duty is to make a difference to as many lives as possible, in whatever way that may be. Giving up on someone doesn't sit right with me, and this sort of narrative needs to change to avoid contradicting our purpose as teachers and nurturing self-fulfilling prophecies rather than talents and potential.

I was unexpectedly reunited with Jake at the Year 13 prom; he was someone's guest having left Sixth Form part way through Year 12. I'll never forget the smile on his face and his wide-armed embrace, beer in hand, keen to tell me about what he was up to and how he was doing. He's currently a roofer as opposed to a chef, but I'll continue to hold out for my invite to the launch of his own menu at some swanky restaurant. I know I'll be near the top of his list.

Megan Owen BA PGCE MA is a secondary school design and technology teacher. With a passion for pastoral care, she is currently head of year at a mixed comprehensive school in Wiltshire. Having completed a Masters in Education: Leading Innovation and Change, Megan aspires to become a senior leader, with a determination and passion to help transform the educational landscape for the better.

Know Your Learner

Sneh Wadhwaney

What does it mean to know your learner? When I say this, I don't just mean the learner as a student in your class. I don't limit it to knowing their academic strengths and next steps. Neither do I mean the stuff we write in reports or share in parent-teacher conferences. I mean the learner as a person. It is crucial to know the social-cultural-linguistic-historical background of the child. It is important to know the interests and passions of the child. This knowledge helps the teacher to make learning connections with the child's previous knowledge and experiences.

I always recall an incident that took place in my class in India a few years ago. As part of transition practices from one year group to another, we get information about the child in detail from the previous teacher. However, not satisfied in one particular case as there appeared to be gaps in information and the story seemed incomplete, I requested a meeting with the parents with the focus on asking them some questions to help get to know their daughter better.

The meeting was so revealing and helped me build that positive relationship with the family. It made the parents feel that I genuinely cared, was keen to learn and understand their child. It basically set the tone for positivity and happiness for that year as I got a head start into knowing this child better and learned about the multiple stories and experiences that made her who she is.

She grew up on a farm and had never been to school before, as is practice in that country. I got to know the different languages she was exposed to at home. I found out more about her interests and what made her eyes twinkle! The gaps were not due to a deficit or a special educational need; they were simply a result of her previous experiences—or lack thereof. The child needed interventions and booster sessions, and once those were put in place, she began to thrive and grow in confidence.

The reason I share this is because it is crucial to know the multiple stories that make up a child. Your interest in learning more about the child not only establishes strong relationships but also enables you to support the child better with clarity and knowledge. Where possible, involve the student in activities and self-reflection opportunities that enable you to gather a well-rounded picture of the child. Caring can make a huge impact.

I end with a quote from the movie *The Blind Side*: "Coach, you need to get to know your players."

Sneh Wadhwaney works at The British School in New Delhi, India.

Choose Your Tasks Carefully

Claire Lotriet

"What did you do over the weekend?"

It's a well-meaning question to ask your class, but one that can also feel like a lot of pressure to the child who hasn't been anywhere and, perhaps, never really gets to go anywhere. Instead, try asking children to share any news they might have. Somehow, there's less pressure to come up with something fantastical; I've had everything from "My cat had kittens!" to "It was my nan's birthday" to "My sister moved away and I really miss her."

"News" can be anything from the wonderful, to the ordinary to the difficult stuff.

Claire Lotriet is an acting co-headteacher and WomenEd network leader. She is also an author and Tedx speaker.

Your Classroom Toolkit: Tips and Tricks to Make Your Life Easier

Emma Platt

I've been a teacher for 20 years—gosh, that's a long time! I remember my first day as a student teacher, a keen 22 year old. Oh, the nerves! What if no one likes me, what if I forget what I'm teaching, what if ... what if...

Be aware, the days, weeks and months will fly by! Wear comfy shoes! Don't go around with your poor toes in heels all day; there's nothing worse than hobbling around all day in uncomfortable shoes. Stock your desk drawer with an assortment of items you might not expect to be so useful: deodorant, Lemsip, make-up wipes, nail varnish remover, mints, a toothbrush/paste, and especially tissues for the pupil who is full of a cold and doesn't stop sniffing all lesson! Coffee, milk and chocolates for the staff room are a must—that's a real ice breaker. Get to know people; it can be hard to be the first one to say "hi", but you have to put yourself out there.

Set your classroom up from the get-go. Be organised. Preparation is key. Have spares of things in your teaching tool kit—pens, pencils, rulers, rubbers—but be prepared for them to go 'missing' too. You will never find the lid to the final glue stick in your set!

Plan, plan, plan: plan your time, plan your marking, plan what you are wearing the next day and have it out ready the night before to save you time.

Communication and honesty are key. It's okay to say you're finding things hard. Celebrate the 'wow' moments—there will be lots. Keep on top of things and make sure you build in time for yourself. You must look after yourself. This is important.

Be prepared for the embarrassing questions—children are curious and they want to know about you. Over the years, I have been asked so many questions, including awkward ones like, "When did you lose your virginity?" or "Miss, have you ever smoked weed?!"—and let's not get into the look on pupils' faces when I told them I was pregnant. I remember very well one of the most embarrassing moments in my career. A pupil very confidently said, "Miss, are you cold?" My reply of "No, I'm fine, but thanks for asking" was met by a class of muffled laughter and smirks. Get it? Needless to say, I wore a padded bra from then on—and have done ever since! It's the little things you don't even think about that pupils will pick up on!

It goes without saying that the children and their learning is the most important thing. Be their positive role model. When you're having a rubbish day, you must remember to smile. To some of them, you are the reason they get up in a day: you are the one constant in their lives, you are the one who cares, you are the one they talk to, you are the one that makes a difference to them. This is such an important thing to remember.

Have a 'Positivity Box'; mine is filled with all the cards of thanks from pupils, the lovely messages, the lovely bits and pieces of positivity I've received over the years. On a dark, snowy break time when you're having a bad day and close to tears, put the kettle on, eat some chocolate, open this box and read all the positive messages people have said about you: you make a difference, you matter, you're doing a great job—remember that!

Finally, I leave you with a crazy game of 'Are you even'.

Are you even a teacher if:

- You haven't broken wind in class and listened to the pupils blame each other.
- You haven't talked about the wrong pupil at Parents' Evening because you can't remember their name.

- You haven't come into school feeling a bit hung over, and it takes a Year 11 pupil to inform you that, not only are you wearing odd shoes, but they are different colours and have different sized heels!
- You haven't confiscated beer on a ski trip and drank it yourself.
- You haven't bumped into a pupil in a nightclub and informed the bouncer that the girl is 15 years old.
- You haven't changed your privacy settings on your Facebook and the pupils find your profile.
- You haven't had a pupil try to clone your Facebook account—and your husband's too!
- You haven't typed the name 'Jade' into Google in front of the whole class on your Interactive Whiteboard and watch in horror as 'Jade' the Porn star is there in all her glory.
- You haven't tried to buy a bra in a shop, only to hear a pupil with his mum shout, 'It looks better in black Miss!'
- You haven't had a pupil faint when delivering the 'period' lesson to Year 7 girls.
- You haven't had to put a condom on a cucumber during a sex education lesson.
- You haven't lost a pupil on a school trip.
- You haven't had every pupil in your class hold up a poster reminding you it's your duty day, because you always forget.
- You haven't been pooed on by a bird during a break or lunch duty.
- You haven't had a wasp (or bee) in your classroom during an observation.
- You haven't had to change classrooms ahead of an Ofsted inspection observation because of a water leak, only to then change classrooms again *during* said observation with the inspector in the room.
- You haven't received a letter from a pupil apologising for his awful behaviour and stating how much he enjoyed his English lessons with you ... from jail!
- You haven't received a love letter from a 15-year-old pupil declaring their undying love for you.

- You haven't googled something a pupil asked you about because you didn't know the answer.
- You haven't had to protect an injured seagull from a swarm of children circling it in the playground!
- You haven't had to break up a crowd of pupils pushing each other into a bees' nest in the school ground!
- You haven't asked a question at the very end of a staff CPD workshop, only to get the death stare from everyone in the room!
- You haven't taught a lesson where the pupils learnt absolutely nothing!
- You haven't bumped into a parent of a pupil at the most inconvenient time.
- You haven't bumped into a pupil whilst drunk on a Saturday night.
- You haven't experienced the carnage the wind, a wasp, torrential rain, or snow will bring to your lesson!
- You haven't had to ski after a pupil who is skiing down the wrong ski slope on the annual ski trip.
- You haven't fallen off the chair lift on a ski trip.
- You haven't had a phantom whistler who whistles EVERY lesson and you don't know who it is!
- You haven't taken part in the school pantomime as one of the ugly sisters in Cinderella.
- You haven't said, 'FFS' in your mind during a lesson.
- You haven't had a pupil tell you that your lesson is shit and they fu**ing hate you.
- You haven't had a parent complain about you every week.
- You haven't dropped a plate in the school canteen to a rapture of applause and shouts from the pupils.
- You haven't missed the memo for own clothes day.
- You haven't eaten the sweets/chocolate you confiscated from a pupil.
- You haven't taught completely the wrong lesson and not realised.
- You haven't messed up the fire alarm drill.
- You haven't made a pupil cry.

- You haven't left a set of exercise books unmarked for weeks on your desk and the headteacher does a cover lesson in your classroom.
- Your line manager hasn't sent you an email asking 'for a chat'.
- A parent hasn't called you a 'twa*'.

Emma Platt BA [Hons] English Literature, MSc in Education, Leadership & Management, NPQSL, assistant headteacher for Teaching and Learning, has been an English teacher for 20 years and an assistant headteacher for 7. She works at a secondary school in Manchester. She is on Twitter as @TeachingMrsP.

Positivity

Ussamah Asad

The moment you first step inside a classroom, it is time to be positive. Remember children are a reflection of the teacher; if the teacher is positive whilst teaching then children are positive in their learning.

Positivity can be achieved through praising children and acknowledging their hard work and effort. This will encourage children to work harder, whilst also motivating their peers to do the same. Another way in which you can increase positivity in the classroom is through the environment, such as creating colourful displays that are all about the children and make them feel at home. All of these ideas can bring positivity into the classroom.

Ussamah Asadhas recently completed a PGDipEd from the University of Birmingham.

The Organisational Queen: A Practical Guide

Abigail Mynett

During an NQT interview, the following question was posed to me: 'What personal attributes make you a good teacher?' It took me a split second to reply: "Organisation".

I had written it down again and again on my interview question checklist (five pages long) as the answer to so many questions regarding my skill set. Organisation meant that I had used the Marie-Kondo system in my house to the extent that on a weekend, my entire work-week's wardrobe was cleaned, ironed and placed together for easy access. Organisation meant that I had bought a large travel style rucksack with individual pockets so that I could carry around glue sticks, notebooks, folders, hole punchers and a partridge in a pear tree. This is because secondary students are moving from classroom to classroom on an hourly basis. Organisation meant that I had an online system for back up, a spare USB flash-drive and an external hard drive because I had accidentally lost a week's lesson plan due to a faulty USB. In short, I was a good cub scout and 'be prepared' was my motto.

I'm in front of a classroom and introducing myself to a Year 8 bottom set using my usual mimic to help them learn my name. This is my second placement in my PGCE year and I'm working in Rotherham. "It's Ms Mynett, like where do you catch a fish? You catch a fish in My-nett." I get a few titters, and some rolled eyes as the students try to decide what they can get away with in my lesson and who is going to try it first. I don't mind, as anything is better than being called 'Ms Minute' with the corresponding time jokes that I'd experience. This class has behavioural issues and the energy is high; the lessons need to be heavily differentiated with a myriad of different tasks in order to keep the students engaged. The topic we are studying this half-term is Romeo and Juliet, with a focus on the themes of love, patriarchy and honour. The lesson plans take a lot of time; students are used to shouting out in class and discipline needs to be strictly adhered to in order to get the students back on track. A student asks me for sticky tape as her glasses have broken, and she knows that I have a bag filled to the brim with stationery, books and tissues. I have what she needs, and the class swiftly moves on.

As someone going into their PGCE year, I knew that organisation was going to be important. There are the copious amounts of paperwork for the teaching standards, the pro forma detailing exactly what will be in your lesson (even though your PowerPoint is pretty self-explanatory) and, not to forget, the hours you will spend cutting and pasting and wishing you had a guillotine. However, all thoughts that your previous levels of organisation were going to be satisfactory should go right out of the window. Start with a large backpack, a good notebook and a teacher diary, and everything else you will pick up along the way.

Abigail Mynett is a full-time PGCE student with the Sheffield SCITT. She is currently writing her PhD in literature at the University of Sheffield where she focuses on the reception history of early Holocaust memoirs. She has a literary master's degree from the University of Leiden and a bachelor's degree in Arts and Culture from the University of Maastricht.

How to Have the Best Day

Sarah Kralj

With the hundreds of interactions that you have within the classroom, you need to wear a metaphorical suit of armour, a smile and maintain a sense of humour. Every morning before getting out of bed, take five minutes to put on your armour; focus yourself and plan your day. Close your eyes, smile and focus on feeling grateful for the people in your life and the privilege of teaching and shaping young minds. Mentally, recall three things that went really well recently and celebrate how well you handled the situation.

In order to grow, we have to reflect upon areas for development. So, next think of an incident that you wish you had handled better. It might be an altercation with a pupil, parent or colleague. Replay what happened mentally and identify exactly what upset you about the incident. Was it the other person's behaviour or attitude, or your own response? Try to put yourself in their position and think about what might be going on in their life to have caused them to behave or react in that way. Then take a deep breath and let it go. In your mind's eye, watch the incident fade away. Accept that most people are doing their best and that we can only really control our personal response to an event.

Now, polish your armour by taking another deep breath, and resolve to make today even better than yesterday so that each and every day you, and those under your care, continue to grow into amazing human beings. Set your intention for the day, such as 'Today will be a great day in Year X …we will learn … and we will be the best version of ourselves.'

Plan to be happy and to bring positivity into the lives of those around you by mentally visualising how much you will smile, laugh at the crazy moments in your classroom and enjoy your interactions with your class and colleagues. Think about positive outcomes, particularly involving any trickier characters. Mentally rehearse likely conversations and ensure that you focus upon potential flashpoints, such as personality clashes, transitions between lessons or moving around the classroom or school. You're now armed and ready with a plethora of positivity that is infectious. You can now get out of bed with a smile on your face, ready to laugh at yourself and life!

Spending time visualising your lessons with the best possible outcomes will help both you and your students to have the best possible day.

Sarah has been a teacher for twenty years and has taught across the primary age range, predominantly in Year 6. She has been a leading maths teacher and a leading SENCO.

Say Thank You

Rosie Georgiou

Say thank you—and say it often. Thanking your teacher colleagues might seem obvious because you work closely with them every day. However, it's important to remember that there are several other teams supporting you behind the scenes: the cleaners who tidy your classroom at the beginning and end of each day, the canteen staff who make your lunches, the site staff who rush in to replace a broken bulb at the speed of light, the IT staff who will run in to fix an overheating projector, and the excellent reprographics team who will photocopy your resources for you at the last minute! Then there are the admin staff, cover supervisors, behaviour support team … the list goes on. Thank them for looking after you. A school couldn't function without these every-day heroes!

Rosie Georgiou is a deputy leader of English.

Making Connections

Matthew Jones

My first, and probably most important teaching and learning tip, is get to know the young people in your classroom. Good teaching and learning pedagogy is built on solid relationships with pupils; they love to learn from an adult that they see is invested in them and fundamentally cares about them.

My next big tip is to get yourself on social media! It can be Twitter, a Facebook forum group or even a teacher-based Instagram; there is a wealth of experience, knowledge and support waiting out there if you go looking in the right places for it!

Matthew Jones is a teacher of Religious Education at a school in North West England.

Life Experiences Are an Advantage

Naomi Jones

I am coming to the end of my PGCE—and what a year it has been! I have loved it, but even without the impact of the Covid-19 coronavirus, it has been a massive rollercoaster of ups and downs. When I think about my journey to becoming a teacher, it started way before that. I am a lot older than most of the people on my PGCE course, and before I started I thought I was going to be at a disadvantage to them. But I soon realised that had I started my PGCE when I was in my early 20s, I would have not been as committed or conscientious. That is not to say that people shouldn't do it then, but I know that would not have been the best time for me. I am older and wiser, and my life experiences are an advantage.

When someone asks me why I want to be a teacher, my answer is always the same: I want to make a difference. I know that for some children I can be the one constant in their life when they may not have that at home. I have worked with children for the last 20 years and I have loved it; it is not an easy job, but for me it is the most rewarding one in the world.

When I was at school, I was not seen as academic—even by my family. My brother and sister were much more academic than me and as a teenager, for various reasons, I found it so hard to believe in myself. I will never forget my first teacher, Miss Aileen. She was the most wonderful teacher; in fact, no other teacher has ever come close! I think what was special about her was the way she genuinely cared for the children in her class. I had other teachers along the way that had true belief in me—including my psychology tutor at college who said I should go to university when I never believed it was a possibility—but she was the one that encouraged me to start my journey over 20 years ago.

When I was on my teaching practices, the most important thing to me was to build relationships with the children—which I did successfully. I wanted them to know that I respected them and that they were important. I wanted them to know that I believed in them and that they should believe in themselves. I wanted them to know just how powerful they are. I can't wait to have my own class and really start my teaching journey.

Miss Jones is a mature PGCE student studying at Liverpool Hope University. She has a teenage son and tweets at @MissJonesLH

Afterword

Teaching: The Best Job in the World

Sarah Mullin

As you will have read in this book, many teachers feel that teaching is a vocation: we feel called to give children and young people the very best start in life. We have chosen to be a part of one of the most important jobs there is: the profession that creates all of the other professions. It is teachers who have taught our doctors, nurses, receptionists and engineers. Our hospitality staff, retail staff and entertainers have all learned from teachers like you.

The multifarious role of a teacher

The role of a teacher is incredibly diverse. We are the child's parent figure during the day, providing stability, consistency, routines and love. We are the child's support, helping them to build happy memories as they grow and learn. We are the child's coach, encouraging them and cheering them on when times are tough. We are the child's mentor, offering guidance, advice and support when it is needed.

The transformational power of education

As teachers, we truly believe in the transformational power of education. We are in the privileged position where we can equip our learners with the knowledge, understanding and skills they need to survive and thrive as global citizens.

Teachers shape the hearts and minds of children for the rest of their lives, helping them to realise their aspirations.

Positive role models

As teachers, we are role models—inspiring and encouraging children and young people to strive for excellence so that they can become the best versions of themselves. We encourage learners to take risks and to learn from their mistakes so that they can achieve the high expectations we have for them.

Relationships, with pupils and other staff

Teachers are committed to building positive relationships with children and parents or carers so that we can collaborate and work together more effectively as we share knowledge and facilitate learning.

We also work with a strong team of staff: caretakers, admin staff, teaching assistants, cooks, lunchtime supervisors, cleaners, finance team, librarians and all those who ensure that we can do our jobs to the best of our ability.

Love to teach

Teaching is a wonderful profession with limitless opportunities, but it does not come without its challenges. In recent times, teachers have demonstrated resilience, resourcefulness and readiness as they have educated the nation's children and young people in creative ways during a pandemic.

Despite the challenging times, the unexpected moments, and those cringe worthy incidents we wish we could forget, the truth is that there is no other job in the world we would rather do. It is the inspirational moments that happen in classrooms across the country every single day which make our jobs feel so worthwhile. It is the teacher tales which have us crying with laughter that nourish our souls. It is those heart-warming, inspirational stories which make us feel that we have truly made a difference to the lives of others.

The positive influence of a wonderful teacher can never be erased. And here, in this book, our stories will be our legacy.

About the Curator

Sarah Mullin, BA (HONS), PGCE, PGCertEd, PGDipEd, MA, CTE, MTLA, FInstLM, CMgr, FCMI, FCCT, FRSA

Sarah Mullin is the deputy headteacher of an all-through school in the West Midlands. She is renowned for raising standards and school improvement. Sarah has supported teachers and school leaders across the UK for over fifteen years, and she delivers CPD to educators globally. She is a Chartered Teacher of English, a Chartered Manager, and a Founding Fellow of the Chartered College of Teaching, along with being a Fellow of numerous other organisations, including the Chartered Management Institute, the Institute of Leadership and Management and the Royal Society of Arts.

Sarah is the best-selling author of *What They Didn't Teach Me on My PGCE*, and she regularly contributes to educational journals, books, blogs and podcasts. Sarah attends the All Party Parliamentary Group for the teaching profession at the Houses of Parliament, and she is on the Board of the Secondary Education Committee at the English Association.

Sarah was named a 'Rising Star' in Education and Academia in 2020 and she received the 'Contribution to Education of the Year' award in 2019. She has previously been a shortlisted finalist in the categories of 'Headteacher of the Year', 'Teacher of the Year', a 'Woman Who Achieves through Networking', and in 2019 she was shortlisted as a finalist from over 28,000 nominees as a 'Positive Role Model (Gender)' by the ITV National Diversity Awards.

Sarah is passionate about promoting equality, equity and diversity in education; she is currently in the final phase of her Doctorate in Education, where she is researching the under-representation of women headteachers in secondary schools in England. She has coached many aspiring women leaders through the DfE Women Leading in Education programme, and she has delivered presentations about educational leadership at global conferences and events including WomenEd, BELMAS and IPDA.

As a skilled practitioner who is committed to driving social change, Sarah has helped thousands of children to maximise their learning potential, enabling them to achieve academic and pastoral success, which has increased their future life choices. Out of all her accolades, Sarah credits becoming a mother to her three children as her proudest achievement in life.

Books in the Series

by Sarah Mullin

What They Didn't Teach Me on My PGCE

Teacher training programmes are incredibly valuable, yet there is a limit to what can be taught in a short amount of time. Teachers are always learning and always growing as professionals. *What They Didn't Teach Me on My PGCE* captures the voices of over 200 educators who share their heartfelt advice, top tips, honest reflections, disastrous experiences and laugh-out-loud anecdotes about early-career teaching. This book is not an instruction manual, as all teaching is complex and situational; rather, we invite you to 'dip in and out' of each chapter as you navigate the recurring themes, patterns and paradoxes. We hope you will be inspired, uplifted, amused and engaged as you reflect on these experiences, compare them with your own, and celebrate being a member of the teaching profession.

"A must read for teachers everywhere; a wonderful reminder of the joys (and lows) of being part of our wonderful profession." —*Professor Dame Alison Peacock DBE, DL, DLitt, CEO of The Chartered College of Teaching*

"Teaching is fundamentally a humane profession. Teachers tend to be attracted to it not only because they love learning, but also because they love people and the relationships learning involves. This book captures the magic of this, as well as being full of practical (and hilarious) anecdotes and advice. It gives a sense of the journey as well as the inevitable ups and downs (and sometimes cul de sacs) this involves. I thoroughly recommend it to teachers at every point in their career." —*Professor Samantha Twiselton, OBE Director of the Sheffield Institute of Education, Chair of the DfE ITT Content Group*

"This book stands as a testament to the perpetual enriching of a teaching career, the constant learning, adaptation and improvisation required of really good teachers. The stories within this book, stories of experience, learning, professional expansion and deep devotion to children, mark it out from the current crop of prescriptive and reduction texts that haunt staffrooms. It is a joy to read." —*Professor Damien Page Dean of the Carnegie School of Education, Leeds Beckett University*

"In this collection Sarah Mullin has admirably demonstrated that to be a teacher is to be, first and foremost, an educator. In bringing together the accounts of teachers 'in action', the power of narrative to help us make sense of our day-to-day interactions and the world of teaching is made vivid, and perhaps only in the way that a good story can." —*Professor Dave Trotman, Newman University, Birmingham*

What They Didn't Teach Me in Teaching College

Updated with some additional content reflecting the experiences of teachers educating children and young people in innovative ways during a global pandemic, *What They Didn't Teach Me in Teaching College* contains a plethora of advice, practical tips, reflective accounts, and laugh-out-loud anecdotes about early career teaching. With narratives from over 200 educators, we hope you will be inspired, uplifted, amused and engaged as you reflect on these experiences, compare them with your own, and celebrate being a member of the teaching profession.

"*What They Didn't Teach Me in Teaching College* is a treasure trove of authentic life stories that highlight the journey into teaching, offering insights into real experiences for potential students and future educators. It is a 'must read' for all, elucidating the reality of teaching in accessible and often hilarious ways. Keep it on your bookshelf to remind you that all will be okay in the end. This is the new best friend of Initial Teacher Education students, Newly Qualified Teachers and long-term educators alike!" —*Miriam Colum, Lecturer in Education, Marino Institute of Education, Associated College of Trinity College Dublin*

"I'm a great believer in serendipity—those unexpected moments from which so much can be learned—and this book is full of them! The entire book celebrates the community of teachers—a deep well of professionalism and expertise, ideas and advice, humour and joy." —*Professor Tony Gallagher, Queen's University Belfast*

"A powerful toolset of voices, narratives, and strategies for current teachers and students alike." —*Dr. Jennifer Cassidy, Departmental Lecturer, University of Oxford*

Printed in Great Britain
by Amazon

69471162R00193